SEEKERS OF TRUTH

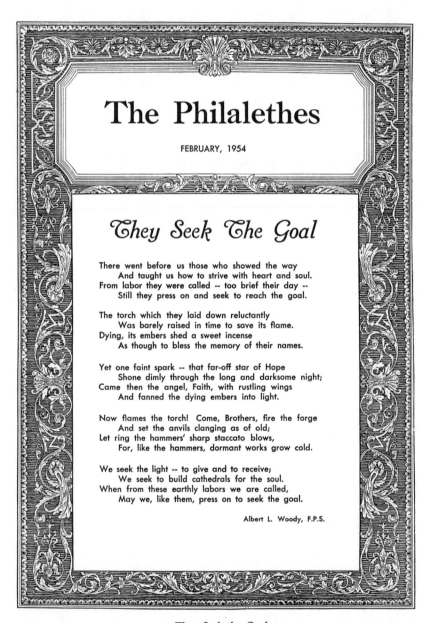

The Philalethes

FEBRUARY, 1954

They Seek The Goal

There went before us those who showed the way
    And taught us how to strive with heart and soul.
From labor they were called -- too brief their day --
    Still they press on and seek to reach the goal.

The torch which they laid down reluctantly
    Was barely raised in time to save its flame.
Dying, its embers shed a sweet incense
    As though to bless the memory of their names.

Yet one faint spark -- that far-off star of Hope
    Shone dimly through the long and darksome night;
Came then the angel, Faith, with rustling wings
    And fanned the dying embers into light.

Now flames the torch! Come, Brothers, fire the forge
    And set the anvils clanging as of old;
Let ring the hammers' sharp staccato blows,
    For, like the hammers, dormant works grow cold.

We seek the light -- to give and to receive;
    We seek to build cathedrals for the soul.
When from these earthly labors we are called,
    May we, like them, press on to seek the goal.

Albert L. Woody, F.P.S.

They Seek the Goal

SEEKERS OF TRUTH: THE STORY OF THE PHILALETHES SOCIETY 1928–1988

BY

ALLEN E. ROBERTS

Buy the **truth,** and sell *it* not; *also* wisdom, and instruction, and understanding.

Proverbs 23:23

ANCHOR COMMUNICATIONS
Highland Springs, Virginia

Printed in the United States of America

ISBN No. 0935633-06-5

FOREWORD FROM MISSOURI LODGE OF RESEARCH

The Missouri Lodge of Research is proud to offer *Seekers of Truth* in keeping with the Lodge's reason for existence—to aid and encourage Masonic research and present the results of that research to the Craft for their edification. As Right Worshipful Brother McLeod (who is a Fellow of The Philalethes Society) said in his Foreword: "Education is important," and the Society has always attempted to share that knowledge.

The history of The Philalethes Society has awaited a Masonic scholar such as Allen E. Roberts to seek out the facts and assemble them in a readable fashion. Your Lodge Editorial Board feels that he has done this in an admirable manner.

A history of the Society is special to Missouri Freemasons because it reveals the part played by Missourians in it. One of the six Founders and first Executive Secretary was George H. Imbrie of Kansas City. Other state connections mentioned include John Black Vrooman, Ray V. Denslow, Harry S. Truman, and Lawton E. Meyer of St. Louis was appointed Secretary in 1952.

C. W. Ohrvall, Editor
The Missouri Lodge of Research

BOOKS BY ALLEN E. ROBERTS

House Undivided: The Story of Freemasonry and the Civil War
Freemasonry in Highland Springs
A Daughter of the Grand Lodge of Virginia
Sword and Trowel
Masonry Under Two Flags
Key To Freemasonry's Growth
How To Conduct a Successful Leadership Seminar
Freemasonry's Servant
Fifty Golden Years
Brotherhood in Action!
The Craft and Its Symbols
G. Washington: Master Mason
Frontier Cornerstone
Shedding Light on Leadership
A Chronicle of Virginia Research Lodge
Freemasonry in American History
Who Is Who In Freemasonry (2 editions)
Brother Truman
La Francmasoneria Y Sus Simbolos (Spanish version of
　　The Craft and Its Symbols)
The Diamond Years
The Search for Leadership

MOTION PICTURES WRITTEN, PRODUCED AND DIRECTED

The Pilot
Growing the Leader
Breaking Barriers to Communication
Planning Unlocks the Door
People Make the Difference
Virtue Will Triumph
The Brotherhood of Man . . .
Challenge!
Precious Heritage
Lonely World
"Fraternally Yours"
Living Stones. . .
　　The Saga of the Holy Royal Arch of Freemasonry

FOREWORD

What is the most important thing that we as Freemasons do? Is it reciting the ritual and conferring degrees? Many lodges must think so, because that's all they ever do; they make the Craft into some sort of primitive life-form, whose sole function is to propagate itself. Well, then does our main function lie in charity? A recent book leaves that impression, and shows that every day American Freemasonry spends $835,000.00 for benevolent purposes. Still, we never think of ourselves as a service club, and good works have always been incidental to our other activities.

All right, we say that Masonry is a beautiful system of morality, so can that be our main activity? No, that's not possible either. Important as morality is, Masonry is not out to reform the world; it's not in the rehabilitation business. It just takes a man who is already good and tries to make him a little bit better. What is left? Is Masonry's main objective, after all, educational? The answer must be a resounding yes. Not just the sort of thing we generally call Masonic education. If you are active in lodge, you learn all sorts of useful things, things that carry over into the outside world. You learn to appreciate the proper use of language and to understand the lessons of the past, you learn how to present a motion, how to preside at a meeting, how to preserve order, how to deal tactfully with your fellow man, how to teach through symbolism, how to use your memory, but above all how to speak in public.

Of course you can get your Masonic education from other bodies besides the constituent lodge. We think of the various study groups, and the research lodges, and the grand lodges, and the constituent orders, and the publishers of so many magazines and books, and The Masonic Service Association. But of them all, the most successful in America (whether you measure success by staying power, membership, quality of publications, breadth of interests, popular appeal, or prestige) is The Philalethes Society, "an international society for Freemasons who seek more Light and Freemasons who have Light to impart."

All right, if education is so important, who is the most effective educator in the Masonic world today? Some of us have written books, and we know they're good. But look at them; they don't attract many readers, because they are either designed for a single grand lodge, or else they deal with some particular narrow topic. One man stands above the herd, one man sees what American Masons need, and then goes ahead and gives it to them. A few examples will establish the point. The business world has long known about man-management and leadership-training. Who brought these techniques into

Masonry? Allen Earl Roberts, that's who! Isn't it time we had a good clear up-to-date book on Masonic symbolism, a book that can be safely put into the hands of a brand new member? Yes, it is, and in fact Allen Roberts gave it to us fourteen years ago! Many groups of people, politicians and film-makers and authors and architects and lawyers, have their own biographical dictionaries, to tell who is working in the field, why he is important, and how we can get in touch with him. Shouldn't there be one for Masons too? Yes, there should, and Al Roberts produced it. The War Between the States probably did more to shape the face of modern America than any other event in history. Has anyone ever written about the part played in it by Masons, and the effect of the War on Freemasonry? Not until Brother Roberts did it! And as well he has told us about *G. Washington: Master Mason,* and about *Brother Truman,* and about *Freemasonry in American History*—books that should be familiar to every American Mason. And he has done so much more besides!

Al does not pretend to be a "scholar"; in fact he's rather proud that he is not. His particular strengths lie in sifting through vast amounts of material, recognizing what is important, and then relating it to the real world around us. He writes with clarity, in down-to-earth straightforward American English.

Does this paragon have no faults? Well, yes. In addition to being bright and hard-working, Al Roberts is outspoken, and he is thin-skinned. This has brought him problems, sometimes in unexpected quarters. Sad to say, not all those who attain high rank in the Craft are concerned with the quest for truth. And so, not for the first time, or the last, a Masonic educator has run into difficulties with Masonic politicians. But happily these troubles lie behind him, and earlier this year Al was honoured with the George Washington Distinguished Service Medal of the Grand Lodge of Virginia. He still feels a sense of affinity with other clear-sighted men who have crossed swords with those of exalted rank and restricted vision, and that is one reason why he finds the founders of The Philalethes Society so congenial.

The Philalethes Society, a great educational institution, is fortunate to have persuaded its Executive Secretary, a great educator, to write the history of the first sixty years. Once again Allen Roberts has skilfully integrated the story with the events of world history. He says that he was "hooked" once he started to investigate. I have seen the text as it came out, and I too am hooked. Read on, and you will be hooked.

Wallace McLeod
Toronto

April 1988

PREFACE

Research has been an important part of Freemasonry since the operative days of the Craft. The *Regius Poem* or *Manuscript* or *Halliwell Manuscript*, written about A.D. 1390 is an example. There have been many Research Lodges chartered, especially during this century. There have been, however, few research *societies* organized throughout the long existence of Freemasonry. Only one has been able to stand the test of time.

This one is The Philalethes Society, an international association of Freemasons who seek light and those who have light to impart. It has been shedding light and truth since 1928. For its first eighteen years its officers and small, but enthusiastic membership, had to find space in those few Masonic publications that would accept articles from the Society's writers. One of these was the *Square and Compass* of Colorado.

A year after the Society was formed by dedicated Masonic writers, researchers and historians, the "Great Depression" struck. For the following twelve years Freemasonry in general suffered. Lodges and Grand Lodges were forced to devise intricate methods to hold their membership together. Consequently the growth of The Philalethes Society was marginal. Not having its own publication didn't help.

When the all-out war in Europe started, the depression was somewhat eased. After the Congress, by a slim margin, permitted President Franklin D. Roosevelt, a New York Freemason, to build up the Armed Forces of the United States, the economy improved. After the Japanese attack on Pearl Harbor, Hawaii, the depression ended, and the United States was again at war.

With the war came shortages of every type of material. Paper was no exception. Plans of the officers of The Philalethes Society to publish its own journal had to be postponed. As it always does in times of adversity, Freemasonry grew, but the Philalethes wasn't a beneficiary. Except for a few Masonic scholars, nobody knew it existed.

This began to change in March 1946. That's when the first edition of *The Philalethes*, The Philalethes Society's own Masonic journal, made its appearance. It continued with one slight interruption throughout the history of the Society.

From its beginning the Society's writers have expressed their own views. It was because of censorship by well-meaning Masonic leaders that the Society was born. Therefore, the leadership of the Philalethes has never practiced censorship. The leaders believed every side of every subject should be explored. Only in this manner can the truth be determined, and it is TRUTH Freemasons should be seeking.

Because the officers and writers for *The Philalethes* presented various sides of many issues, this history has been made possible. It is from the pages of the magazine that we can follow world events as they pertain to Freemasonry and the Society. The caliber of the writers and the policies of the Executive Boards (or Committees) of the Society have contributed to the realization of the remarkable history of Freemasonry. Much of this experience can be found nowhere else.

The history of The Philalethes Society is in fact the history of Freemasonry. During the Society's sixty years of existence its Fellows and Members have passed along their knowledge of the Craft through the pages of *The Philalethes*. Much of what they wrote should be preserved for the ages. Consequently the Executive Board asked me to include these records in the pages of this book.

This I have done, but have supplemented what the pages of *The Philalethes* contain with information gathered by later research. Wallace E. McLeod and Jerry Marsengill have checked behind me and offered valuable historical and grammatical suggestions. I can truthfully say that this is a much better book because of them. However, any errors in fact and composition are mine alone.

I thought I wanted to write this history, but once I started I was "hooked!" The material found in our magazine since 1946 was amazing. My problem became mammoth. What to leave out was a predicament I've found difficult to solve. So, I've followed the advice of Carl H. Claudy who suggested the pages of *The Philalethes* "cut down the evangelical, the religious, the inspirational, and give us more *fact* stories, history and intelligent interpretation of symbols."

Forty years ago I had to make a decision about footnotes and other scholarly notations. Months of discussion with scholars and teachers I respected set the stage for my writing then and for the future. There would be no footnotes, except for *rare* occasions. What would normally go into footnotes would be included in the text. While I hope scholars have read, and will read, what I write, the majority, like me, read for enjoyment and information. There are no footnotes in this book. The documentation is included in the text. Candidates for high academic degrees must use them; Ph.D.s expect to find them, and many use them exhaustively.

It has been a joy to live with those great historians and writers of yesteryear and today. I hope you will find I have done justice to their memory. Above all, though, I hope you will find you will be inspired to work with the extraordinary Fellows and Members of The Philalethes Society of this era.

Allen E. Roberts
Highland Springs, Virginia
    April 1, 1988

ACKNOWLEDGMENTS

Without question, the first acknowledgment for this history must go to the founders who saw the necessity for a Research Society. They were George H. Imbrie, Robert I. Clegg, Cyrus Field Willard, Alfred H. Moorhouse, Henry F. Evans and William C. Rapp. They later became the first Fellows of the Society. They should also be commended for the appropriate selection of the name—**Lovers of Truth.**

Next must come the dedicated Editors of the Society's journal, *The Philalethes*. The countless hours they spent poring over the words sent for possible publication have been amazing. It's even more amazing when we consider they received no coin of the realm for their labor; just "Masters' Wages." Without their dedication, knowledge of and devotion to Freemasonry, this book would be mighty thin.

Without writers an editor cannot wield his blue (or red) pencil and there would be nothing to edit. The hundreds of writers, many of them excellent, deserve the plaudits of all Freemasons everywhere. From the beginning The Philalethes Society has been an open forum and the pages of its magazine have presented all points of view. Often the officers and readers didn't agree with the writer, but seldom was he criticized for his statements. Freemasonry in general was the beneficiary of the differing viewpoints expressed. To all who have written for *The Philalethes*, we owe our gratitude.

Others have helped in numerous ways to make this book a reality. Wallace McLeod spent many precious hours checking every word of the manuscripts. Jerry Marsengill also took time from his busy schedule and checked the historical content for accuracy. The discussions we three had won't be recorded here!

As always, Keith Arrington of the Iowa Masonic Library came through with needed information. The reference personnel at the Richmond Public Library and the Virginia State Library graciously helped when called on. Priscilla Ridgeway of Mystery Writers of America pointed me in the right direction to learn about Lee Wells. Fred Kleyn concluded my search in San Diego.

Dottie, my ever faithful wife, continued doing the chores I should do so I could do what I've been doing at the computer for many years. I must continue to insist that it's she who deserves any credit for what I may accomplish, not me. When I state this publicly, those who know whole-heartedly agree. And I really don't wince when they shout—AMEN!

To all who helped make this book a reality, my heartfelt appreciation.

Allen E. Roberts

Contents

Appendixes

Illustrations

1. BIRTH
(1928–1945)

*P*etty tyranny gave birth to The Philalethes Society.

Some Masonic leaders, "dressed in a little brief authority," had attempted to inhibit the spread of truth. They had attacked, in many cases successfully, the publishing of the written word. They had endeavored to warp the minds of the greatest intellectuals in Freemasonry.

It was because of this tyranny that six men were brought together who had long been interested in researching and preserving the history of Freemasonry. Much that they had discovered and recorded had been condemned by some of the Masonic leaders of the day. These writers and editors had destroyed many of the favorite myths of some of their overly-enthusiastic predecessors. This hadn't endeared them to many of those who held Masonic authority at the time.

These men were witnesses to what was happening to the young Masonic Service Association. It had been formed in 1918 because the federal government refused to let Freemasonry help American servicemen. This service organization was being rapidly smothered by falsehoods so that most Grand Lodges boycotted it. The truth would eventually win out, but there were difficult years ahead.

The founders of The Philalethes Society were determined to relate the true story of Freemasonry. They had learned, however, that isolated individuals could be suppressed and persecuted by those who held authority for a short time. By banding together they believed the tyrants would consider "the prospect of being held up to the scorn of the whole Masonic world." It was easy to crucify an individual, but a group, or society, was a completely different question.

Who were these men who met on October 1, 1928? What qualifications did they have that made them anxious to write and print the truth about Freemasonry? What made them different from those who would condemn them?

George H. Imbrie of Kansas City, Missouri, was one of the foremost researchers of his period. He would become the first Executive Secretary of The Philalethes Society. Robert I. Clegg of Chicago, Illinois, was an Englishman who became a United States citizen in 1891. He was a professional editor of technical publications, and wrote extensively for Masonic periodicals. He was best known, Masonically, for his complete revisions of *Mackey's Encyclopedia of Freemasonry.* He became the second President of the Society.

1

Cyrus Field Willard, the first and fourth President of the Society, and its second Executive Secretary, was another fine researcher. Alfred H. Moorhouse of Boston, Massachusetts, was editor of *The New England Masonic Craftsman,* and would become the third President. Henry F. Evans of Denver, Colorado, edited the *Square and Compass,* which would publish many of the masterpieces of the Fellows of the Society. William C. Rapp of Chicago was editor of the Chicago *Masonic Chronicler.* He would serve the Society as Vice President.

No verbatim recording was made of that first meeting, but the published objectives speak volumes. The new Society was formed "to create a bond of union for isolated Masonic writers and also to protect editors of Masonic publications from *undeserved aggression*" from the tyrants of the day.

As originally organized, the Society "was composed of prominent Masonic writers and editors in all parts of the world." It had, and still has, "no special creed or dogma, and the members express their individual opinions only." It had, and has, "the purpose of binding together those who are anxious to help make Masonic journalism and literature more efficient, and to encourage Masonic writers in their quest for **truth** and **light.**"

The emblem chosen was distinctive. Its motto placed at the bottom proclaimed: **There is no religion higher than Truth.** This would create a misunderstanding among narrow-minded religious elements, and would later be dropped.

It was made clear that "the Society does not seek members, they being chosen by the nomination of a Masonic writer, who is already a member." The Executive Committee approved or rejected the nominee. This would be the criterion for more than fifty years, and was the reason the membership remained small. Eventually the wisdom of the members prevailed; it was determined the Society should be opened to all Master Masons "who seek light or have light to impart."

The name chosen has been discussed by scholars since the inception of the Society. In 1987, Wallace E. McLeod, FPS, a Professor of Classics said: "Maybe as the Society's tame Greek I should write a note on this. 'Philalethes' is a real Greek word, not a made-up modern coinage; it's in the big lexicon, and is used in philosophical jargon, by Aristotle, and those boys. It is an adjective, singular form, and means 'loving truth'; or, since in Greek you can use any adjective as a noun, 'one who loves truth'; 'a lover of truth.' "

In the February 1988 issue of *The Philalethes,* McLeod added to his earlier thesis. "Our dictionaries have over 100,000 words of Greek origin, many of them invented in modern times by scientists or other pretentious people who needed a new word for something they were talking about," he wrote. About the word "Philalethes," he said, "it is not of modern coinage . . . ,

2

but is found in ancient authors. Perhaps the first man to use it is the philosopher Aristotle (who lived 384–322 B.C.); he says somewhere in *Ethics,* 'The lover of truth (*philalethes*), who tells the truth in things where it doesn't matter, will also tell the truth in things where it does make a difference. He will avoid falsehood because he thinks it is shameful.'

"From the time of the Reformation on, the word was often used as a penname by people who wanted to 'tell it like it is,' but didn't want to use their own names. . . . The best known and most prolific was the seventeenth century poet and alchemist Thomas Vaughan (1622–1666), who published nearly all his works under the pseudonym, 'Eugenius Philalethes,' 'The noble-born lover of truth.' Actually, he has at least three indirect Masonic connections. In the first place, he was a particular friend of the scientist and military engineer, Sir Robert Moray (1600?–1673), who was admitted a member of the Lodge in Edinburgh on 20 May 1641—one of the earliest 'gentlemen Masons' known to us." Vaughan also published a book about the Rosicrucian brotherhood; moreover, Diana Vaughan, Leo Taxil's fictitious informant, was supposedly a descendant of Thomas Vaughan.

McLeod, like others, has no idea where and how the founders of The Philalethes Society got the name, but he concludes: "In any event, the name is suitable, and should always remind us of the Society's aims. *Fiat Lux,* 'Let there be light,' is its motto; let there be light, to help us see what we're talking about, to illumine the shadowy by ways of our minds, to dispel the darkness of ignorance and falsehood. Here we are all lovers of truth, committed to uncovering it, and devoted to making it known. 'Great is truth,' said Thomas Brooks in 1662, 'and shall prevail.' To that, we can all say 'Amen.' "

Actually, the mystery of where the name came from was cleared up by Willard in 1937 in an article printed in the *Square and Compass*, but not "discovered" until 1988. "In 1928, when The Philalethes Society was organized and George Imbrie, the editor of the Masonic magazine, *Masonic Light,* then published in Kansas, Missouri, asked me for a name for the new society," wrote Willard, "I suggested the name of The Philalethes Society, as I had just finished reading *Souvenirs* (Memories) by the Baron de Gleichen, in which he told of the Philalethes Lodge in Paris. It had invited Cagliostro to appear before it at one of its meetings and he declined to do so, unless they would destroy all their records which he declared worthless." The "records" were untrue stories about Cagliostro published by the Jesuits and were the basis for the lies that are still found concerning him. Cagliostro had been convicted by the church in Rome in 1791 for the crime of being a Freemason.

Writing about the Society in 1933, Willard told more about the organizational meeting. "Those who have been members of the Fraternity for a number of years have known men who were little more than 'good fellows'," he said. "But because they were appointed to some minor position by a friend who was a Master, they continued to 'go up the line' until eventually they landed in the Master's chair. And after serving in the office for a year, they had signally failed 'to set the Craft to work and give them instructions whereby they might pursue their labors.'

"It was the realizing sense of this that prompted the formation of an association to bring together in one body the writers who felt that the great mass of Freemasons in the United States should have more information on the fundamentals of Freemasonry."

Soon after the formation of The Philalethes Society became known, requests for membership were received from several foreign countries. From the beginning it has been an international association of Freemasons.

A year after the formation, the Executive Secretary, George Imbrie, died. Willard asked Clegg to take over as President so he could assume the office of Secretary. This was done. Then Clegg too died on December 3, 1931, and Moorhouse was elevated to the Presidency. The ranks of the leaders were being depleted. Then, too, the "great depression" was taking its toll, and would continue to do so until the start of World War II.

The National Masonic Research Society of Iowa ceased working at this time, also. That Society had performed an excellent job in Masonically educating Master Masons. But, as too often occurs, some of the active workers, particularly George L. Schoonover, "the father of The Masonic Service Association," were disliked by the leadership of the day. With the loss of that Society's superb publication *The Builder*, Freemasonry lost its only historical and educational voice. Another organization was needed to fill the void.

R. J. Meekren, the last editor of *The Builder*, said his magazine was financially successful; but "its funds were used to support other things." He told John Black Vrooman: "There seems to be no reason why The Philalethes Society should not replace the N.M.R.S., it not being burdened by an elaborate constitution that never operated."

The Masonic Service Association employed several of the men who had made the National Masonic Research Society a success. Among them were Dr. Joseph Fort Newton, W. E. Atchison and Jacob Hugo Tatsch. It published *The Master Mason*, which, under Newton's editorship, was acclaimed by its readers, with the exception of an influential few. It also established a "book Department" which published several outstanding volumes. Events a short way down the road caused the Association's work to be discarded. The full story is told in *Freemasonry's Servant*.

Before Clegg died, he and Willard, along with the other officers of The Philalethes Society, determined the working members should be rewarded with the title of "Fellow." It was decided to limit the number to 40 at any one time, the number selected by the French Academy and the Royal Society of England. (See list of "Fellows of The Philalethes Society" in Appendix C.)

Willard observed: "It did not take long to select and elect 40 Fellows from noted Masonic writers in Europe and America. Rudyard Kipling, who had done more than any other writer to spread true Masonic principles, was elected the 40th Fellow." Although the date these first Fellows were selected isn't clear, from information printed in the *Square and Compass* of Colorado in 1932 it would appear the year was 1931.

The Society had no publication of its own in the early days. It actually couldn't afford one. As a result, the early records are fragmentary, but Henry Evans, the editor of the *Square and Compass* of Denver, Colorado, was most hospitable. He opened the pages of his journal to the members of The Philalethes Society. Quite regularly his magazine included articles written by Fellows and members of the Society. These were printed under the Society's crest. The Secretary was given space for a regular column to report on the activities of the members, or for his comments on the state of the world. Because of Evans's generosity, a goodly portion of the early history of the Society is known.

Ten more Fellows were chosen between then and 1937, Among them was Carl H. Claudy of the District of Columbia, Executive Secretary of The Masonic Service Association, and John Black Vrooman. Claudy saved the MSA from extinction; Vrooman had been, and would continue to be, the cord that kept The Philalethes Society together for almost fifty years.

Two other outstanding Freemasons, for some unknown reason, were not chosen as Fellows. One of these was Edgar A. Guest of Detroit, Michigan, an American poet who had become world-famous. He would be elected to the Society of Blue Friars in 1954. About Freemasonry he said: "Masonry has greatly enriched my life. It has given me friendships that I cherish dearly. It has, I think, whispered subconsciously to me in the silent hours, words of caution and encouragement. I like going back to my lodge. I have found it refreshing and good to step aside out of the path of my busy life and sit again with the Masons who have carried on in my absence." Many of his poems were, and would continue to be, Masonic in nature.

The other prominent Masonic writer and editor not chosen was Joseph Fort Newton, an outstanding Christian minister, who had been, and would continue to be, loved and respected by Master Masons in every clime. His books on Freemasonry will live as long as freedom exists. He began writing for Freemasonry in 1914 and continued until his death. As has been noted, he was an editor of Masonic magazines without peer. His ministry was treasured on two continents. His love for the Craft was never more evident than when he fought for the survival of The Masonic Service Association. During a particularly stormy session he calmed the combatants by saying: "Freema-

The Philalethes

AN INTERNATIONAL RESEARCH SOCIETY

CYRUS FIELD WILLARD, F. P. S., International President, San Diego, Cal.

GEO. H. IMBRIE, F. P. S., International Secretary, Kansas City, Mo.

(Address communications to Geo. H. Imbrie, 930 Baltimore Avenue, Kansas City, Mo.)

TRUTH

ALL ARTICLES appearing in this column, devoted to the Philalethes Society, express the ideas and opinions of individuals only, and in no way are pretended to be, nor are they the opinions of the Society. The Philalethes is a

---

THE ROSETTA STONE

By GEORGE H. IMBRIE, P. M., F. P. S.

corners, about the size of the page of a newspaper, and has written thereon a decree of the priests of Memphis, in which are recorded the good deeds of Ptolemy Aplphanes (205-182 B.C.). It proclaims that divine honors shall be paid him. and further orders that

Every Freemason in the world is under a sentence of death by the Roman papists! Inability to enforce the edict prevents its consummation.

---

the lodge, King Emanuel, then the Italian ruler, being at the time Grand Master of Italy. The record of this incident will be found in Mackey's *National Freemason*, June 1874 (page 520).

WITH ROUGH ASHLAR AND TRACING BOARD

"READING₀ MAKETH A FULL MAN"—Bacon

A page devoted to Masonic Study and Improvement, under the auspices of the Bureau of Information of the International Philalethes Society, a group of Masonic writers and students throughout the civilized world.

TRUTH

The Philalethes Society

An International Body of Masonic Writers

Its Fellowship is limited to 40, like the French Academy, but the Correspondence Circle is unlimited in number. All articles appearing in Masonic Magazines, devoted to the Philalethes Society, express the ideas and opinions of individuals only, and in no way are intended to be, nor are they the opinions of the Society. The Philalethes is a society formed solely by independent thinkers and has no creeds nor dogmas. Its purpose is to bring together the Masonic writers of the world who seek the Truth in Masonry.

Truth

OFFICERS

Alfred H. Moorhouse
President
Boston, Mass.

Henry F. Evans
First Vice President
Denver, Colo.

William C. Rapp
Second Vice President
Chicago, Ill.

Ernest E. Murray
Treasurer
Billings, Mont.

Cyrus Field Willard
Secretary
621 West Ivy St.
San Diego, Calif.

Further Information Can Be Secured from the Secretary

The Winter of Liberty

Address by R. W. AND REV. JOSEPH FORT NEWTON, Chaplain of THE MASONIC SERVICE ASSOCIATION OF THE UNITED STATES, before the Seventeenth Annual Meeting of that organization, February 21, 1936, Washington, D. C.

SOME time ago, through the kindness of a very dear friend, I read a sermon that was preached 140 years ago. Not many sermons last that long, though they may seem to do

The Philalethes Society

An International Body of Masonic Writers

Its Fellowship is limited to 40, like the French Academy, but the Correspondence Circle is unlimited in number. All articles appearing in Masonic Magazines, devoted to the Philalethes Society, express the ideas and opinions of individuals only, and in no way are intended to be, nor are they the opinions of the Society. The Philalethes is a society formed solely by independent thinkers and has no creeds nor dogmas. Its purpose is to bring together the Masonic writers of the world who seek the Truth in Masonry.

Truth

OFFICERS

Cyrus Field Willard
President
San Diego, Calif.

Henry F. Evans
First Vice President
Denver, Colo.

William C. Rapp
Second Vice President
Chicago, Ill.

Silas H. Shepherd
Secretary-Treasurer
San Diego, Calif.

Further Information Can Be Secured from the Secretary

Cyrus Field Willard, Litt. D.

President of the Philalethes Society.

IT is with a feeling of deep personal grief that the Secretary has to announce the transition from his labors on earth to his entrance into the Celestial Lodge above of Brother Cyrus

7

sonry's simplicity, its dignity, and its spirituality sustain me in all that I try to do, and permit me to forget the incredible pettiness of mind that we sometimes encounter, sustaining and enabling me to join hands with my Brethren everywhere, to do something, if it be only a little, before the end of the day, to make a gentler, kinder, and wiser world in which to live."

The "Great Depression" which followed the stock market crash of 1929 played havoc with Freemasonry, as it did with all organizations. Stories are abundant throughout the land of how lodges and Brethren helped one another and the less fortunate. It was hardly the period for starting and building a new organization.

But the new organization had made something of an impact in the Masonic world. The French magazine, *L'Acacia*, said in 1932:

> This Society merits our attention from its nature and from its works, and also because our Brother Cyrus F. Willard is its Secretary-General.
>
> It is constituted under the form of an Academy and is composed of 40 members only, chosen from the Masonic writers of all countries and from among the editors of reviews dedicated to questions concerning our Order.
>
> The Philalethes Society has as its president the Very Illustrious Brother Alfred H. Moorhouse, who published the *Masonic Craftsman* at Boston, Mass. He was elected several months ago as the result of the regrettable demise of the Very Illustrious Brother Robert I. Clegg, who passed to the Eternal Orient on December 3, 1931. He was a very distinguished Masonic writer whose death has been a cause of mourning for us all.
>
> The purpose is to encourage Masonic study, to develop intellectual relations between the Masons of all countries and to contribute thus to the moral unity of our institution, in spite of the divergencies that may exist in certain details of the art in accordance with the rites in different countries. But the original feature which distinguishes The Philalethes Society from other international groups lies in its having taken the form of an "academy" (like the French Academy) which gives to it a special place as well as a special role.

Blame for the depression was centered on President Herbert Hoover, and this caused his defeat in 1932 by Franklin D. Roosevelt, a member of Holland Lodge No. 8 of New York City. Many reasons for the depression have been proposed. The principal reason appeared to be "protectionism" laws adopted by politicians. The lessons of the twenties were not learned; the same factors are at work in the political arena today.

Regardless of the reasons for the calamity, no person living through the years preceding World War II could ever forget the horror. Habits were formed that would endure forever. Many of them would haunt Freemasonry throughout the rest of the century.

Joseph Fort Newton

The government, professions, businesses, and organizations were crippled. All types of schemes were adopted to try to combat the dire effects of unemployment. Few were successful. It wasn't until shortly before the United States was forced into the war then raging in Europe that the depression ended.

In the meantime the Society continued to operate on a meager scale. A "Bureau of Masonic Information" was set up and operated by Vrooman. Willard and other writers sent articles for publication under the name of the Society to other magazines. These appeared along with the emblem of the Society and many included the caption "With Rough Ashlar and Tracing Board." They covered every conceivable Masonic topic.

From the pages of the *Square and Compass* we learn that Willard was convinced The Philalethes Society had much to offer Freemasons. He wanted its members and Fellows to share the Society with all their Brethren. Then, he said, "they can go forth to give light to their Masonic Brethren, a light which shall finally illumine the whole world."

Willard, a strong-willed man, in 1932 called the depression "an euphemistic term for the bankers' panic," and although it had created economic havoc it had caused less than four percent of the members to quit The Philalethes Society. He also noted that Moorhouse's editorials in the *Masonic Craftsman*

9

were being translated into French and were being published in Paris and Geneva.

Early in 1933 Willard temporarily lost his eyesight. Ernest F. Murray of Billings, Montana, was appointed Willard's assistant, but resigned a short time later. Most of the correspondence was in French and he couldn't translate it. John Black Vrooman, "who not only reads but writes it also," was handed the job.

When his sight returned late in 1933, Willard told his readers: "At this time the world needs the truths embodied in Freemasonry more than ever before. How few realize that Freemasonry has within it a philosophy which tends to make its followers stronger and more self-reliant. We are in a position now to give out the facts and that is what the people want. We now have completed the preliminary work of organizing and have our forty Fellows and some thirty or more corresponding members in as many different countries."

Later Willard added: "We, as Masonic writers, are intensely interested in this matter [gathering facts and spreading truth], since we must realize that Freemasonry is the only great organization that seeks to develop the individual. It has an individualistic economic philosophy which caused the Socialistic Labor Party of Great Britain to forbid its members from becoming Freemasons and learning to think for themselves."

The President of the Society, George Moorhouse, appointed a committee to study what services the Philalethes should offer the Craft. The membership of this committee reads like a "Who's Who" in Freemasonry: Silas H. Shepherd of Wisconsin, Chairman; John Black Vrooman of Kansas, Secretary; Carl H. Claudy of the District of Columbia; Arthur C. Parker of New York; Charles C. Hunt of Iowa; Reynold E. Blight of California; and Robert J. Meekren of Quebec, Canada.

As early as 1934 Willard warned all who would listen about the situation in Europe. "It seems advisable now to sound a note of warning to the three million Freemasons in this country to be on their guard for the same unrelenting enemy that has worked against Freemasonry in Italy. It will do the same in the United States if it has the power, and will follow the same campaign of slander and falsehood that is now being pursued in Holland, Belgium, France, Switzerland and Spain. All the dictators must abolish Freemasonry because its members are free men, free in thought and conscience, and cannot accept the idea of a despotic state.

"[However], Freemasonry all over the world is standing firm against all attacks. Mussolini in Italy, Hitler in Germany and Dollfuss in Austria, all dictators, were part, or are part and parcel of the Roman ecclesiastical tyranny." He said a Catholic political party had been "in the German Reichstag for years before Hitler came into power." One German Grand Lodge had gone into exile in Jerusalem; the other Grand Lodges had been dissolved. Russian Freemasonry was in exile in Switzerland.

Again in 1935 Willard continued his warnings: "American Freemasons should remember that much of the talk in the profane [non-Masonic] press derogatory to Freemasonry is but the echo of the clerical and Fascist press who wish to suppress Freemasonry because Freemasons are free men who think for themselves. Masons in the United States have no idea of the bitter campaign that is being carried on in Europe from Sicily to the Baltic and from the confines of Russia to Holland. Freemasonry in Europe now is really a secret society as of old. The signs of recognition are still of value, as in the days of the traveling operative masons."

Writing for The Philalethes Society in the *Square and Compass* later in 1935 Willard had learned more: "The cowardly manner in which the German Masons have accepted the dictatorship of Hitler on Masonic matters is in strong contrast with the spirit that activated Masons in years gone by, when they would rather die than renounce Masonry. . . . The Symbolic Grand Lodge of Germany . . . forestalled any action from Hitler by 'putting itself to sleep,' as is the term in Europe for the cessation of all work. . . . All the German former Grand Lodges renounced all relations with all foreign Grand Lodges. . . . All of the three old Prussian Grand Lodges, as well as the National Mother Grand Lodge, have sent in their submission to Hitler.

"The Grand Lodge of the Three Globes has changed its name and now calls itself 'the National Christian Order of Frederick the Great.' It has expressly stated that it has no connection with foreign countries and would work for the grandeur, unity and liberty of Germany. The Grand Lodge of Hamburg has done the same." But all wasn't lost. Willard said four new lodges had been organized in Madrid, Spain, and the Swiss Grand Lodge Alpina was taking steps to combat the lies spread by the Hitler regime.

But not all German Freemasons submitted to the wiles of Adolf Hitler and his regime. Some of the more dedicated Master Masons went underground. For identification they wore a little flower called a "blue forget-me-not." This later became a national Masonic symbol in Germany. In the United States an organization that honored Masonic writers and teachers was formed to commemorate their dedication to the principles of Freemasonry. It was named "The Masonic Brotherhood of the Blue Forget-Me-Not."

The precarious financial condition of The Philalethes Society was revealed in an article Willard wrote in June 1935. "In the beginning," he said, "Robert I. Clegg, our former much beloved President and the Secretary, paid all the expenses of the Society. The latter and the Assistant Secretary, Brother Vrooman, after Brother Clegg's death, have met all the outlays for postage and printing. As things are now beginning to look brighter all along the line, some financial system is necessary that will meet the ordinary expenses of the Society. The Secretary would be pleased to hear from the Fellows and Members on the subject." He suggested the dues be raised from three dollars to five dollars a year.

The depression, according to Willard, caused a three and one-half percent loss in the Masonic lodges in the country, "whereas some organizations opposed to Masonry have suffered a tremendous reduction in membership."

Rudyard Kipling, FPS, died on January 16, 1936, and the Society mourned his passing.

In 1936 Willard found William Moseley Brown of Virginia. "Brother Brown not only speaks and reads Spanish, French and German, but also reads Italian, Portuguese, Dutch and Greek, and his linguistic ability will be of great help to The Philalethes Society, to which he has pledged his earnest co-operation." Brown kept his promise right up to the time of his death.

The Society was in its ninth year in 1937 when Willard asked how many would be interested in contributing fifty cents to a dollar a month so the Philalethes could publish its own paper. "It has been the idea ever since the Society was started," he wrote, "that some day we would issue some organ of our own. [This would enable] our members and Fellows to express themselves more freely than in a magazine privately owned, depending on advertisers who are immediately made a target when anything is published that does not suit some people." He noted that Arthur Edgar Waite of England had been elected a Fellow, along with another Englishman, Albert F. Calvert.

In 1939 Charles H. Johnson of New York, Walter A. Quincke of California, Herbert I. Callon of England, and Clarence Brain of Oklahoma were elected Fellows. This brought the membership to 39 Fellows and 39 members. Then "all hell broke loose."

The one-time paper hanger and former corporal in the German army ordered his troops into Poland. He hadn't been satisfied with the gift of Czechoslovakia which the gullible allies gave him so there would be "peace in our time." He hadn't been content to control Germany and its neighbors. Nor was it enough for him to find little or no resistance in his torture and murder of Jews, Freemasons, and all who opposed his schemes. He had found his opponents more interested in material comforts than liberty. He took advantage of this weakness. Another country with dictatorial powers would do the same a few years later.

Freemasonry having ceased to exist in Germany, except for a few dedicated members who went underground, Masonic literature from Europe became unavailable. Correspondence dried up.

When Winston Churchill, the Freemason, was called to be Prime Minister in England, replacing an ineffective predecessor, he called on the United States for assistance. He found some help, but only because another Mason

12

named Franklin D. Roosevelt was willing to flirt with impeachment. Roosevelt assisted Great Britain while the isolationist Congress insisted the United States remain strictly neutral. The Congress had learned little about dictatorships—it never would.

It wasn't until the sneak attack by the Japanese on Pearl Harbor, Hawaii, on December 7, 1941 that the Congress and people of the United States awakened to the danger of having inadequate armed forces. It was almost too late. The United States declared war on the Japanese Empire; Germany and Italy declared war on the United States!

The Japanese quickly gained control of the Pacific and many of the islands, including the Philippines. Some of what happened was related by Antonio Gonzales, the Grand Secretary and a member of The Philalethes Society. In 1946 he would be elected a Fellow.

During the meeting of the Grand Lodge of the Philippines in 1941 the members adopted a resolution of support for the allies. The support was short-lived; the Japanese took over Manila and put Freemasonry on trial. The records, books, and files of the Grand Lodge were sealed. The Grand Master was imprisoned in the Santo Tomas concentration camp. The Deputy Grand Master, Jose P. Guido, was imprisoned at Fort Santiago. Gonzales joined him there, where he was questioned repeatedly about Masonry and Masons. He refused to tell the Japanese officials anything. He remained a prisoner in his own home throughout the war.

Although the "Great Depression" and the growth of Nazism had deterred the growth of The Philalethes Society, its few members continued their crusade for Masonic education. Articles by its writers appeared continually in the leading journals. Its officers and members met informally as often as possible. Money was scarce, so national meetings were out of the question. Correspondence among them was constant. The greatest benefit was the moral support afforded the few Masonic researchers. No longer were they isolated and threatened.

The events of the '30s and '40s did hinder the development of The Philalethes Society. They were devastating. Yet the Society clung to life and worked for the cause of Freemasonry. This continued throughout the "great war," but with rationing of paper and other essential items, growth was virtually impossible.

2. FREEDOM
(1945-1947)

*T*he war ended in Europe and President Harry S. Truman, a Past Grand Master of Masons in Missouri, permitted a Masonic fact finding commission to travel overseas. The mission was proposed by Carl H. Claudy, Fellow of The Philalethes Society, and Executive Secretary of The Masonic Service Association. This Association, under the leadership of Claudy, had put Freemasonry into action throughout the war.

The Commission also included Ray V. Denslow, another Fellow of The Philalethes Society. Its report to the President and The Masonic Service Association pointed out the difficulties the Freemasons had encountered during the Hitler years. This record was made available to the Masonic press throughout the country. It depicted in all its horror the calamity that had been suffered by the Freemasons of Europe. It was evident it would take years for the organization to regain its former strength. Years later it would be learned that although Freemasonry had suffered, the devastation wasn't as horrible as at first suspected.

Freemasonry in the United States grew in numbers throughout World War II. Once again it had shown that the Craft prospers during times of adversity. Lodges, particularly those close to Armed Forces camps, had actually become "degree mills." The growth was alarming. In later years the decrease in membership would be even more alarming to the Masonic leadership.

With the unconditional surrender of the Empire of Japan in September 1945 economic conditions in the United States began to improve. Rationing of essential wartime materials was gradually eased. Among these items was paper.

This paved the way for an historic day for The Philalethes Society. In March 1946 Volume I, No. 1 of *The Philalethes* was published. The Society finally had its own magazine. The cover carried a poem by Edgar A. Guest: "The Temple, What Makes It of Worth." This first issue listed the following officers: Walter A. Quincke, President; William C. Rapp, First Vice President; John Black Vrooman, Second Vice President; Silas H. Shepherd, Secretary.

Among the articles was "Our Masonic Heritage" by Quincke. In it he wrote: "Being optimistic, I am confident that when the history of the 20th century has been written, it will be possible to speak of it as the *spiritual* age marked by social revolutions which should result in a more 'neighborly' organization in which we shall learn that the interests of individuals are best promoted only when they exercise their talents for the general good of humanity."

Shepherd wrote "Notes On Indian Masonry." He covered two Indians who were Freemasons, George Copway and Joseph Brant. Leo Fischer, FPS, editor of *The Cabletow* and *The Far Eastern Freemason* of the Philippines, wrote about "Masonic Martyrs in the Philippine Islands." He included an item from a newspaper about a Past Grand Master: "Jose Abad Santos of the Philippines Supreme Court refused to renounce his allegiance to the United States and was killed by a Jap firing squad by order of Lt. Gen. Masaharu Homma. Santo's son said that he heard the volley, and that afterward a Jap interpreter who witness the execution said: 'Your father died a glorious death.' " Fischer noted others who were murdered. He was proud to say that "work of rebuilding the Temple of Masonry in the Islands" was moving ahead.

"Just Between Us" was the title of an editorial by Walter A. Quincke. "*The Philalethes* magazine is designed to meet the requirements of Freemasons who are interested in learning more of the Fraternity to which they belong," he wrote. He noted that most Masonic magazines "cater to local interests and contain little of permanent value." The Society would have an extensive Masonic education program. From time to time, as funds permitted, books would be made available to the members. Masonic books would be reviewed. Writers for *The Philalethes* "must be given full liberty of choice of subject and treatment, the majority of them will be original and fall under the heads of 'practical' and 'philosophical.'

"No copyright will be obtained on any of our issues and the Masonic Press is, therefore, privileged to reprint any of our articles providing credit as to its source is given." No advertising was to be accepted. The magazine would be supported entirely by dues from members of the Society and subscriptions.

Remarkably, this policy has not changed in the past forty-two years. *The Philalethes* continues to endeavor to carry articles of lasting value. Its writers are not censored. No advertising is accepted. The magazine is still not copyrighted, so others are free to reprint its work. Bonus books have been made available to the members occasionally.

The second issue of *The Philalethes* was published in May 1946. Elbert Bede of Oregon, a future President of the Society, wrote an article entitled "Grand Lodge Is Not a Separate Entity." Silas H. Shepherd, the Executive Secretary, wrote "What Was the Early Ritual?" On the back page the President placed "Silas H. Shepherd, F.P.S., Passes On." He had died on March 20, 1946. Silver Gate Lodge No. 296 of San Diego, California, conducted his funeral on the 23rd. He was 72.

15

"It is with a feeling of deep personal sorrow that I have to announce the sudden passing from his labors on earth to his entrance into the 'Grand Lodge Above' of our beloved Brother Silas H. Shepherd, who so conscientiously filled the office of Secretary and had made himself an integral part of the life of our Society," wrote Quincke. "Few men could possibly be missed as Silas will be!" Allister J. McKowen was appointed Secretary.

Robert O. Jasperson, a Past Grand Master, said that Shepherd had been a gangling, red-headed and freckled youth who enjoyed laughing. They had enjoyed their youthful days together, then Silas moved to Chicago. Years later they met and Jasperson learned that Silas had become a Mason and loved books. He gave the credit to Freemasonry for what he had become. "From the greatness of his heart," wrote Jasperson, "he felt keenly for the underdog, the forgotten man, the under-privileged, and ascribed much of their plight to the injustice of the system under which we live, and in his kindly way would argue long and well in support of his theories." He later added: "The brilliance of his mind was not always at once manifest; but no one could know him long and not recognize in him a rare spirit. Indeed, to know Silas Shepherd was to love him."

The Society was fortunate in having Leo Fischer as one of its writers. He could read and speak several languages. From him the readers of the July 1946 edition of *The Philalethes* learned something of "Masonry in Foreign Lands." From Finland came some of the first truths about the Soviet Union and how its leadership was as evil as the Nazis had been, if not more so.

"The Masons of Finland have been made special victims of Ludendorf's anti-Masonic campaign," reports Fischer from a letter received from Dr. Valter V. Granberg. "The Russians now endeavor to break the Finns physically by imposing unbearable economic burdens on them. However, with the aid of Sweden and America, he believed the Finns will manage to live through the eight years of war payments to Russia. He reported that one-half of 'the products of our forests' must go to Russia, 'and one-fourth is used for rebuilding our destroyed homes.'

"The Grand Lodge of France, on the initiative and with the assistance of the American Brethren, gave an entertainment for the children" on December 23, 1945. It appeared Freemasonry in France was bouncing back quickly. Freemasonry in Switzerland had operated throughout the conflict, and it supported the activities of The Philalethes Society. It was learned that the Grand Master of Masons in the Netherlands "was murdered by the Nazis in the infamous Buchenwald concentration camp." His Grand Lodge held a Lodge of Sorrow for him in Amsterdam on December 20, 1945.

Hungarian Freemasons had many difficulties. In March 1919 the Craft had been outlawed by a dictatorship which, under the pretext of Masonry being the cause of the war, confiscated all Masonic property. Masonry was accused of being treasonable, anticlerical, and in association with Jewish revolutionaries. With the close of World War II the government permitted Masons to again meet. They refused. They wouldn't accept the governmental compromise until Masons were publicly cleared of the slanderous charges.

In November 1945 *The Cabletow* of the Grand Lodge of the Philippines published its first edition since December 1941. It reported Freemasonry was climbing from the ruins and devastations of war.

The January 1947 edition of *The Philalethes* carried an account by M. Jattefaux. Deputy Grand Master of the Grand Orient of France. It was translated by Leo Fischer.

On May 14, 1944, M. Jattefaux of France arrived at the Buchenwald concentration camp. He quickly learned there were a number of Freemasons there who had been meeting in secret. Each Sunday a small group would meet in an enclosure where new arrivals were held in quarantine. Shortly after his arrival a Past Master of a French lodge died. They held a Masonic memorial service for him. It should be noted these Freemasons ran the risk of being hanged, or worse, if they were discovered.

The number of Freemasons in Buchenwald increased to about 100 in October. They determined it was time to organize the system. Jattefaux was put in charge, assisted by six other elected officers. He, being classified as a nurse, was able to move about the camp without arousing suspicion. The Masonic officers met daily, and each was assigned the supervision of the various "blocks" in the camp. They sought out "foreign" Masons so all of them could learn more about Freemasonry in general.

"The cultural work received our special attention," said Jattefaux. Food and other supplies were scarce, particularly after the Allies had landed in France. Morale was low. "By occupying their minds and giving them intellectual nourishment," he continued, "we would prevent them from thinking too much about their hunger and would relieve their anxiety concerning the events which to us appear to progress with sometimes disheartening slowness."

The manner in which information was disseminated is interesting. "The committee would choose a subject, work at it, and prepare a questionnaire, which would be transmitted to each committee member orally in the blocks under his supervision and would be the subject for study. Each block would then have a resume of its conclusions ready for the committee member concerned who, on his next visit, would pick it up and take it to the committee. The latter would then communicate the result to all concerned by the same method."

The article closed with just pride. "Today, a year after the Camp was liberated by the American forces commanded by the late lamented General [George] Patton, the Brother Masons of the Camp of Buchenwald are proud of the fact that they did Masonic work in that death camp, running the risk of being hanged if their organization should be discovered. They believe that by their initiative and their action they kept up the morale of their Brethren, that morale which to us behind the barbed wire seemed to represent 80% of the life of man."

Another account of Freemasonry in action in Nazi prison camps was told by Pierre Fraysee to a member of The Philalethes Society.

Fraysee was a French Freemason who was arrested on July 26, 1943 by the Gestapo. He was accused of *gaullism* and espionage. He was trucked to a prison at Imperia, Italy, where he eventually met several other Masons. It didn't take long for them to know one another. An anti-fascist prison warden gave them permission to meet. Many lectures on Masonic history were told to mixed audiences. "These lectures and the exemplary conduct of the Masons," Fraysee said, "changed the opinion of Masonry of a good many non-Masonic prisoners."

The Masons were instrumental in aiding the seriously ill, "and in ameliorating the lot of the prisoners in general." The Masonic organization was formed into a lodge which held three meetings. They realized it was "clandestine," but they planned to inform their Grand Lodge of their activities when it was reorganized.

The Grand Master of the Grand Orient of Spain in Exile sent a telegram from Mexico to the United Nations. He outlined the cruelty of the Franco government, particularly as it pertained to Freemasons and their dependents. He asked that those imprisoned for the "crime" of being a Freemason be given "speedy relief."

The Vatican and "Catholic Clergy in Yugoslavia" were accused by D. Tomitch, a former delegate of the Grand Lodge of Yugoslavia, of murder and other atrocities. He said he had "ample evidence that many of the massacres of men, women and children of the orthodox and Jewish religions, were instigated and carried on with the active participation of the Roman Catholic clergy and that a million persons thus perished during the war in Yugoslavia. As in similar cases, the Masons were hunted down, imprisoned and slain wherever found." A number of monks and priests had been convicted, but the writer believed too many had escaped punishment.

The Philalethes for February 1947 proudly announced that Jean Julius Christian Sibelius had become a member of The Philalethes Society. He had been born at Tavastechus, Finland, on December 8, 1865. "He studied music in Berlin and Vienna, and is a member of the Musical Academy of Stockholm. He won universal fame by his music to the tragedies Knolema and King Christian II, and by the many splendid pieces which he composed, among them *Karelia* and *Finlandia.*"

Jean Julius Christian Sibelius

Sibelius composed many special compositions to be played during Masonic ceremonies. The Society was presented with a bound volume "containing manuscripts of Ritualistic music composed by our great Brother for use within tiled Masonic lodges." In 1947 a member of the Society said that Sibelius, at the age of 81, was confined to his home because of health, but "he still has many melodies in his head." Despite his poor health he had composed two more Masonic songs.

With peace established once again in Belgium, the Freemasons of Brussels reactivated the *Union des Families* which they had organized in 1911. Each Sunday the families met in a suitable recreational area, or in the picnic grove owned by the organization. The entertainment consisted of concerts, tennis, bowling, billiards and bridge. There was also dancing and amateur theatricals. There were always games for the children during these all-day affairs.

From the formation of the Philalethes, reading was encouraged. Before it published its own magazine, book reviews by Philalethes members were printed in other journals. This increased considerably after 1946 and the birth of *The Philalethes*. Among the books William H. Knutz recommended in February 1947, along with a brief synopsis, were: *The Holy Bible*; the Mackey/Clegg *Encyclopedia of Freemasonry*; Gould's *History of Freemasonry*; Newton's *The Builders*; the Mackey/Clegg *Jurisprudence of Freemasonry*; Preston's *Illustrations of Freemasonry*.

Knutz urged Masons to read the *Proceedings* of Grand Lodges and Grand Chapters, particularly the sections that dealt with "Fraternal Reviews." At that time there were many distinguished reviewers throughout the country. They kept the Masonic world informed about what was transpiring. Most of them "pulled no punches," but praised or condemned the action of other Grand bodies. Often the discussions on the printed pages were extremely animated!

Leo Fischer reviewed the book *A History of Freemasonry Among Negroes in America* by Harry E. Davis in March 1947. Fischer wrote: "That the historical legitimacy of this so-called Prince Hall Masonry is sustained by the evidence, is the argument of the author of the work herein referred to." In his conclusion Fischer said: "The legitimacy of this organization has been assailed, largely by prejudice or ignorance; but there is little doubt that it will sooner or later be generally recognized. In view of prevailing social conditions some time will pass before there can be anything more than an *entente cordiale*, though the realization of the latter may be closer than we think it is. In the meantime, seekers of truth and justice—and all Masons should be that—should at least familiarize themselves with the subject, and works like those of Bro. Davis are to be highly recommended."

It was reported that the head of the Catholic church in Switzerland sent a confidential letter to the ecclesiastic personnel in the country. He warned them against accepting aid from the Red Cross Child Relief, and especially "aid to the children of the Pestalozzi Village. The persons at the head of that movement are not catholics." He signed his warning *"In caritate Christi."*

The newspaper *Alpina* said the Grand Master of Swiss Masonry, a former Catholic priest, was the head of the relief funds. The paper pointed out that Swiss Masons always gave generously to charity without inquiring who received help. Catholics were treated as liberally as others. It added that the Swiss Masons had a better right to use *In Caritate Christi* than did the Catholic director.

During the late 1930s a French professor named Bernard Fay had been greeted and helped by leading Freemasons of the United States and Europe. He was writing a book that would be published by Little, Brown titled *Revolution and Freemasonry.* Earlier he had written *George Washington, American Aristocrat. The Philalethes* in March 1947 recorded: "Prof. Bernard Fay, who headed the anti-Masonic movement in France and was a very active 'collaborator' during the war, has been arrested and taken to the Fresnes prison, with various other individuals accused of intelligence with the Nazis."

Freemasonry In American History has this item from *The New York Times* of December 5, 1946:

Bernard Fay, former professor of American civilization at the College de France and writer on Franco-American relations, was sentenced to life imprisonment at hard labor today after his conviction on a charge of intelligence with the enemy. M. Fay has been charged with publishing documents and lists of the Freemasons for the Vichy (Nazi dominated) government. This had resulted, according to the prosecution, in deportation or death for thousands of them.

The prosecution had demanded the death penalty for Fay. The court sentenced him to life imprisonment at hard labor. Fay told the court: "I was glad to have in my hands the instrument capable of renovating the country. My mission was to organize a service for the detection of the Freemasons and masonic archives. To be successful in that work, I was obliged to have relations with the Germans, especially as they had an organization parallel with ours."

Fay claimed he wasn't an informer, but an "historian who was doing this for intellectual reasons." Many of the 60,000 names Fay turned over to the Vichy government appeared in numerous Catholic newspapers. Freemasons were hunted down, sentenced to concentration camps, or executed by firing squads.

In an article appearing in *The Trowel* of the Grand Lodge of Massachusetts in 1986, Henri J.A. Laprime wrote about the atrocities of the 40s. "The Vichy government made a decree, Aug. 12, 1940, prohibiting all secret societies. This decree was specifically aimed at Freemasonry. Adm. Charles Platon, a fanatic Calvinist member of the French Parliament, thought all Masons should be burned at the stake."

Laprime said a search was made for all Masonic lodges and members. Masonic property was seized in all occupied countries. In France all Masons were arrested. "The archives were centralized and placed in the custody of Bernard Fay, an historian and fanatic enemy of Masons." The head of state was given the power to eliminate Freemasons, "and until the end of the Vichy government many anti-Masonic measures were applied by Vichy and Berlin. The Gestapo took up residence at Avenue Foch in Paris and centralized all their anti-Judaic and anti-Masonic activities. Varieties of torture were carried out and those who proudly wore our symbolic apron were executed. Thousands of French Brethren died for the cause of liberating their nation."

Laprime continued: "In the Buchenwald camp more than 100 Masons like Charles Riandey, Sovereign Grand Commander of the Ancient and Accepted Scottish Rite of France . . . were all executed. The Nazi court of justice ordered the punishment of 6,000, among whom 549 were killed by the firing squad and 900 others deported to death camps."

What finally happened to Bernard Fay, the arch-enemy of Freemasonry? David G. Boyd, MPS, a lieutenant colonel stationed in Heidelberg, Germany, and Master of Alt Heidelberg Lodge No. 821 in 1987, was asked to do some detective work. He did, and filled in several blanks.

Bernard Fay was born in Paris on April 3, 1893. He studied at the *Condorcet* and the *Sorbonne* from 1907 to 1914. He was a volunteer in the Army Red Cross during World War I. He resumed his studies in 1919. He received an LL.D and M.A. from Harvard, then served as a professor at the University of *Clermont Ferrand* from 1923-33, then at the College *de France* from 1933 to 1945. He made several trips to the United States between 1919 and 1939. He was appointed the administrator of the French National Library in 1940 and remained there until his arrest in 1945. He wrote numerous books and many articles for various magazines. It appears his specialty was in the history of Freemasonry.

Henri Coston, who along with Fay, ran the anti-Masonic operation in France under the Nazis, said Fay escaped from the French penitentiary at St. Martin de Ré seven or eight years after he was sentenced to life at hard labor. How he managed to escape isn't clear. He returned to France and continued writing! Fay died in Tours on December 31, 1978. His funeral was held on January 4, 1979.

So well had Fay duped the Masonic world, well-known Freemasons often quote from his works even in this year 1988!

Were there German Freemasons in the Gestapo who remembered their obligations? Could be. The Germans raided the Grand Lodge of Norway and many of its lodges immediately after their occupation. The loot that wasn't destroyed was loaded and sent on its way to Berlin. The shipment disappeared and didn't reach its destination. With the defeat of the Nazis the stolen items were quietly returned to the Grand Lodge.

We've often heard: "If you want a job done, give it to a busy man." *The Philalethes* took note of this with the publication of a poem by an unknown author:

The Busy Man

If you want to get a favor done
By some obliging friend,
And want a promise, safe and sure,
On which you may depend,
Don't go to him who always has
Much leisure time to plan;
But if you want your favor done,
Just ask the busy man.

The man with leisure never has
    A moment he can spare,
He's always "putting off" until
    His friends are in despair.
But he whose every waking hour
    Is crowded full of work,
Forgets the art of wasting time,
    He cannot stop to shirk.

So when you want a favor done
    And want it right away,
Go to the man who constantly
    Works twenty hours a day.
He'll find a moment sure, somewhere,
    That has no other use,
And fix you while the idle man
    Is framing an excuse.

Memorial Day, once called "Decoration Day," was promulgated by the Grand Army of the Republic, Walter Quincke reported in *The Philalethes* for May 1947. A group from Chicago toured the battle-torn country around Richmond, Virginia, in March 1868. They noticed the many graves of Confederates decorated with fading flowers. General John A. Logan, then commander of the G.A.R., and a member of Benton Lodge No. 64 of Michigan, was told about what the group had discovered.

Logan issued an order, agreed to by his staff, to the many posts of the G.A.R. which read in part: "May 30, 1868, is designated for the purpose of strewing with flowers, or otherwise decorating the graves of comrades who died in the defense of their country during the late Civil War, and whose remains now lie in almost every city, village, hamlet and church-yard in the land. It is the purpose to inaugurate the observance with the hope that it will be kept up from year to year, while a survivor of the war remains to honor the memory of his departed comrades."

May 30 was chosen because it was on that date the last Union volunteer was mustered out of service.

The nation responded with vast throngs visiting cemeteries throughout the land. G.A.R. Posts paraded through city and village streets playing solemn music. It was an idea that has been followed to the present time.

Quincke wrote: "A nation can be only what its citizens make it, and the quality of the product is determined by the character of these citizens, and that character is determined by the ideals that control, and by the loyalty to these ideals of those who profess to follow and be led by them."

A member of The Philalethes Society in France reported on the activities of Franklin D. Roosevelt Lodge in Paris. It had been chartered in 1938, but the Grand Orient wouldn't permit the lodge to be named for a living person. The name then selected was changed on June 15, 1945 to that of the 32nd President of the United States. The day of the change of name was celebrated with festivities of every type imaginable. Brothers Verges and Dutoit "of the opera" sang "The Star Spangled Banner" and the "Marseillaise."

On the anniversary of the death of Roosevelt, April 12, 1947, the lodge held a memorial service for the late President. The Grand Masters of the Grand Orient and the Grand Lodge attended. So did representatives of the ambassadors of the United States, China and Greece. Over 1,400 other Freemasons were present to pay honor to the man who "by his indomitable energy and his ardent faith in our humanitarian ideal, saved civilization from servitude . . . and won an imprescriptible right to the gratitude of all free men."

Mrs. Eleanor Roosevelt, the widow of Franklin, was the guest of honor for the inauguration of the Franklin Delano Roosevelt Hall in Paris on December 9, 1948. Under an "Arch of Steel" she was led into the hall by the Grand Master of the Grand Lodge of France. She listened to the virtues of the late President being extolled, and it was noted that she had played an important role in his work for humanity. When she was introduced and rose to speak she received a standing ovation. She concluded by saying she would never forget the enthusiastic reception of the French Masons. The Grand Master ordered a "triple battery to be given in her honor." She then left to address the Society of United Nations.

The Freemason from New York who had defied the "doves" in Congress, who had flirted with impeachment, had saved freedom in Europe. For this he would be remembered and memorialized for years to come. It would be 1975 before much of the story of the courage of the 32nd President of the United States would be learned. This would come from "a man called 'Intrepid.' "

3. BUILDING
(1947–1951)

*I*n May 1947 the first of what would be many articles appeared in *The Philalethes* from the pen of Charles G. Reigner of Baltimore, Maryland. The President/Editor was still Walter A. Quincke and he reaffirmed: "It is the purpose of The Philalethes Society to raise Freemasonry to a higher plane of service, and Editor-Members of Masonic magazines, here and abroad, are privileged to reprint either in part or in full, any articles first published in *The Philalethes,* provided due credit is given as to their source."

The Mystery of the Dark Mountain, a western novel written by Lee Edwin Wells, who would become the "savior" of the Society, was reviewed. The Society continued its efforts to turn Freemasons into readers. This poem by an unknown author is further evidence of its goal:

Too Busy to Read

An hour with a book would have brought to his mind
The secret that took him a whole year to find.
The facts that he learned at enormous expense
Were all on a library shelf to commence.
Alas! for our hero; too busy to read,
He was also too busy, it proved, to succeed.
We may win without energy, skill, or a smile,
We may win without credit, or backing, or style,
Without patience or aptitude, purpose or wit—
We may even succeed if we are lacking in grit;
But take it from me as a mighty safe hint,
A civilized man cannot win without print.

It was learned that the six lodges in China that had been chartered by the Grand Lodge of the Philippines were reactivated as soon as the Japanese were driven out of the country. Lodges under the jurisdictions of England and Massachusetts also were revitalized. This wouldn't last long. Communism cannot permit any organization that believes in the freedom of man and of thought to exist.

Philip H. Coad of Ohio wrote in September 1947: "A number of the Craft papers have the appearance of being thrown together just before press time. They do not measure up to the style of the master craftsman." He felt this was sad, because "it is, in thousands of cases, the *only* contact the brother has with his fraternity." He spoke highly of a small weekly paper that had as

25

Walter A. Quincke

its motto, *"Our object is not so much to get more men into Masonry as to get more Masonry into men."* He deplored the "trash" "that clogs the news-stands or finds its way into the shelves of our libraries." The situation hasn't changed much over the years, except to become more permissive.

With the December 1947 edition of *The Philalethes* the addresses of new members were omitted. The reason: "To prevent the unauthorized use of the names of our members." Years later addresses were again added, but for the same reason this had to be discontinued.

The "First Inter-American Conference of Symbolic Freemasonry" was held at Montevideo, Uruguay, in April 1947, reported *The Philalethes*. Almost all the Central and South American countries were represented. Although the Grand Lodges in North America had been invited, none sent an official representative. This was one of many attempts over the years to establish a form of Masonic unity.

It was reported that, although Freemasonry in Spain had been legal for fifty-one years, under the dictator Franco, Freemasons were going to jail. Their crime? Being Freemasons! The minimum sentence was twelve years. It was believed 32,000 such cases had been tried by "special courts for the suppression of Masonry and communism."

Leo Fischer was disturbed because the lodges in America had "sadly neglected" music. He said they were leaving this to Scottish Rite bodies. He urged the "Craftsmen in the United States" to use "their gift of music for the benefit of Masonry." He continued: "The President of our Society, Bro.

Walter A. Quincke, is setting the Craft a good example in those respects. His numerous vocal and instrumental compositions include a number of Masonic pieces." Quincke was an accomplished pianist. Fischer highly praised the work of Jean Sibelius of Finland.

Lee Edwin Wells, FPS, from California, spoke of the trials of Freemasonry in the war-torn countries of Europe. He noted that members of The Philalethes Society were more aware of what had happened and was happening than most people. The reason? Because "our membership covers the world." Masons are not "divorced from world currents." He cited Hitler as an example. "He put Masons in concentration camps and hanged them. If we are so divorced from world events why has a church hurled interdicts and bulls against us for two hundred years? If we are only a social band of men, why then has revolutionary Russia banned us, and continues to do so wherever her power extends?"

Wells's answer? Because Freemasons believe in "Brotherly Love, Relief and Truth." No dictator "can tolerate these great principles that are the very heart of our Fraternity—the life blood of its tradition."

"Since the war," said Wells, "The Philalethes Society has gone through a reformation. We of the Executive Committee feel that the information we

Lee Edwin Wells

have, the papers that are written for us, should not be confined to the few. Therefore, we have opened the membership to every Master Mason in good standing in a just and legal jurisdiction, wherever it might be in the world. We realize that not all of us can write papers on Masonic subjects or devote our lives to research. But the knowledge gained by those who can is, of right, the property of *all* Masons everywhere. In every possible way we are trying to forward the great ideals and aims of the Craft."

With the beginning of the year 1948 John Black Vrooman, because of the pressure of other business, resigned as First Vice President. Lee Edwin Wells was elected to this office, an office he fortunately would be holding at the time of the Society's time of crisis. Leo Fischer was elected Second Vice President; Allister J. McKowen remained as Secretary-Treasurer; Quincke remained President and Editor.

Quincke strongly suggested members of the Society form study groups throughout the world. These groups were to be approved by the Executive Committee, but each group would be locally controlled.

The financial statement for 1947 was amazing. Dues received amounted to $549; fees from new members, $196; subscriptions, $132; total receipts, $1,171.54. From this amount $978.23 was spent—and this included the printing and mailing of eight twelve page issues of *The Philalethes*!

An article by the outspoken and brilliant Melvin Maynard Johnson, Past Grand Master of Masons in Massachusetts and Grand Commander of the

John Black Vrooman

28

Scottish Rite, Northern Masonic Jurisdiction, appeared in the July 1948 edition of *The Philalethes*. He took exception to some ultra-conservative Masonic leaders concerning the recognition of European Grand Lodges. They wanted the foreign Grand Lodges to prove they were legitimately descended; the state government was stabilized; the country had legalized Freemasonry.

About legitimacy he wrote: "Personally, I would rather be associated with a bastard who is himself a moral, upright good man than with one of legitimate birth who is a crook and a scoundrel."

Regarding stability: "It seems to me to be self-evident that the time to help with treatment and nursing is while one is sick and needs such help, instead of waiting until he is either cured or dead."

Johnson said concerning legality: "Few sovereign States, even of the English-speaking world, have expressly declared the legality of Freemasonry." He seriously added: "No American is a real Freemason, no matter what jewels he may wear, if he idly watches the destruction of Freemasonry and its ideals in other lands when he, with his brethren, has the opportunity of being a good Samaritan."

Johnson closed his remarks: "It is regrettable but true that there are those of official station in all large organizations whose action in important as well as trivial matters is governed by selfishness rather than that pure altruism which Freemasonry teaches. From this we are not exempt!"

Melvin Johnson was, in the opinion of many, one of the most dedicated Freemasons of his day. There were others who were disturbed by his bluntness. In this respect he was much like his friend Harry S. Truman, Past Grand Master of Masons in Missouri and the President of the United States. Johnson had the privilege of presenting Truman with the Gourgas medal, the first ever awarded. This was approved in 1943 while Truman was a Senator. For varying reasons Truman couldn't be present to accept it until November 21, 1945.

Leo Fischer continued to keep the membership informed about what was happening throughout the world through his translations. From a Dutch paper he learned that during the Japanese occupation of Java, Dutch Freemasons aided the Jesuit Fathers imprisoned there. While the Jesuits studied and worshipped clandestinely, Freemasons acted as their sentinels. An alarm was spread whenever discovery was imminent.

The magazine covered the story of the installation of the Duke of Devonshire as Grand Master of English Freemasonry. He was installed by the King with over 5,000 Freemasons present.

On the Antarctic Continent, on February 6, 1947, seven officers and petty officers in the U.S. Navy met as Freemasons. Lieutenant Commander F. G. Dustin told the story as he addressed the group:

My dear Brothers, we are gathered here today at the bottom of the world, a small group of men, representing the brothers of our respective lodges and our brethren all over the universe. We are members of an important function that our government has directed and assigned certain duties. I know you join in this feeling of pride I have as a citizen and as a Mason, that we, through our government are privileged to be standing on this virgin territory.

We Masons gathered here today are standing in a flimsy canvas tent. The canvas beats and strains. It is snowing and a blizzard is in the making. There are hundreds of feet of snow beneath us and around us as far as we can see. The elements in this area run wild and unharnessed. High velocity blizzards race across the unknown and then all is calm, but the rigors of this land have us not in fear. A great leader has placed the required tools in our hands and guides us with his knowledge.

Was this the first Masonic meeting held in Antarctica?

The Editor wrote a biography of John Black Vrooman for the September 1948 edition of *The Philalethes*. Among the many things told of Vrooman was his love of pipes. They were, and would remain, his "trademark" throughout his long Masonic career. Not too much later he would be considered "Mr. Philalethes" and "Mr. Mason" to thousands of Freemasons throughout the world. Through the pages of *The Philalethes*, which he would edit for years, he made a host of friends.

The January 1949 edition of *The Philalethes* found editor Quincke reminding his readers: "Most of the 'good luck' this year will fall to those who do not wait for it but proceed diligently to go after it." This could be said of any year or any situation.

Leo Fischer continued to keep his readers informed through his translation of news of "Freemasonry In Foreign Lands." Members of the District Grand Lodge of China, under the jurisdiction of the Philippines, talked about forming their own Grand Lodge. Its mother, the Grand Lodge of the Philippines, was continuing to prosper.

From Switzerland it was learned that the Grand Lodge Alpina survived World War I with but minor problems. With the rise of Hitler in 1933 the situation changed. The Swiss had always been influenced by the economic and political conditions prevailing in Europe, particularly France and Germany. Hitler's minions lost no time in condemning the democratic institutions in Switzerland. Those who supported freedom were among the first to be attacked. This meant Freemasonry was skillfully assaulted.

Dr. Gottlieb Imhof of Basel, Switzerland, wrote at length about Freemasonry under attack from 1937 to the fall of Hitler and Nazism. He said: "In those trying years of crisis the Swiss Grand Lodge ALPINA was the *only* Grand Lodge in Europe in which Freemasonry was being worked in the German language."

Leo Fischer

To combat the anti-Masonic propaganda raging throughout the country, the Grand Lodge took two bold steps. Its publication, the *Alpina,* had been an internal organ since 1874. It went public in 1938, and was published monthly! Then the Grand Lodge officers and other knowledgeable Masons were not only permitted, but urged, to discuss Masonic subjects in public! The citizens responded well. But "the traditional old enemy, the Roman Catholic Church, continued its two-century old struggle with unabated violence. It will probably never cease doing so."

Courageously that Grand Lodge celebrated its centennial on July 3 and 4, 1944. From reports it was a grand occasion. From the numbers of those participating, no one would know the membership in the country had declined by thirty-seven percent.

Throughout the war Swiss Freemasons helped the destitute in other countries. This continued long after hostilities had ceased. And with the close of the war, membership increased fairly dramatically.

An interesting "Arab Proverb" was published:

> He that knows not, and knows not that he knows
> not is a fool. Shun him.
> He that knows not, and knows that he knows not, is
> an honest man. Help him.
> He that knows, and knows not that he knows, is
> asleep. Wake him.
> He that knows, and knows that he knows, is a wise
> man. Follow him.

The President, reporting for the Executive Committee, said the year 1948 had been a good one for the Society, but more members were needed. The number of letters answered monthly averaged four hundred. Several Masonic periodicals were extolling the virtues of membership in The Philalethes Society. Costs were increasing at an alarming rate. About $1,500 would be required for necessary expenses, including the publishing of *The Philalethes*. Several Fellows had died, among them Charles Clyde Hunt of Iowa. To fill the vacancies, Philip Henry Coad of Ohio and Charles Gottshall Reigner of Maryland had been elected Fellows.

Lee Wells said that the formation of study groups had been a failure, but he urged the members to continue to try to make them viable. One was working in France and another being formed in Scotland. The membership of the Society totaled 245. With dues at $3.00 it would take an equal amount in donations to reach the necessary $1,500 to operate.

The inimitable Harold V. B. Voorhis, one of Freemasonry's most brilliant historians, particularly of the "little" Masonic bodies, answered an article in an earlier *Philalethes* that he considered erroneous. It concerned Albert Pike and the organization of the Rosicrucians, an association that came into the United States from Scotland in 1880. It is neither esoteric nor mystic, and has no association with the Rosicrucianism of the Middle Ages. This branch (*Societas Rosicruciana*) accepts only Master Masons on invitation, and specializes in Masonic research.

It appears that Pike was made an honorary 9th degree member and he was invited to accept membership "and the rank of Honorary Past Supreme Magus." Voorhis wrote: "Brother Pike became inadvertently placed in a position rather untenable, at least to him. In matters Masonic he was always unwilling to be just a member. He either became the head of a group or avoided it completely, but as a gentleman." Voorhis added: "He was very familiar with considerable Rosicrucian literature for one thing, because he used the works of Alphonse Louis Constant—in many cases without even changing the wording—in the preparation of his *Morals and Dogma.*"

Charles E. Holmes of Montreal, Canada, was elected a Fellow, and as his masterpiece wrote "Should Women Be Admitted to Masonry?" In 1948 the Society had received a letter from a lady teacher who, while residing at Algiers, Africa, had "attained high rank in the Craft," she claimed. She submitted many pages of arguments in favor of the rights of women.

Holmes found that the *York Manuscript No. 4* of 1693 referred to "he or *she* being made a Mason." Harry L. Haywood said that this choice of words was not accidental, that women were admitted to operative guilds. After Freemasonry had crossed the English channel to invade France, and this mixture of men and women "spread like wildfire among the nobility and intelligentsia." Meusnier de Querlon "wrote a play about it which was witnessed by 'everybody who was anybody' in Paris. As may be well guessed, it was a comedy, and was titled: 'Daphne's Suppers.' In this play the audience witnessed the organizing of a strike by all married women who agreed to deprive their Mason-husbands of their . . . conjugal rights until they had revealed the secrets of Masonry."

As early as 1730 "we find a record of the creation of a lodge of Adoptive Masonry to which women were admitted. But was this *real* Masonry? Of course not! It was an association with initiatory ceremonies and a ceremonial (it could hardly be described as a ritual), which that eminent French Masonic historian, J. M. [Jean Baptiste Marie] Ragon (1781–1862) has preserved for us."

"During the revolution of 1789 the lodges of Adoptive Masonry were 'en sommeil' (dormant) as were the Grand Lodges of the Grand Orient and the *Grande Loge de France* (Scottish Rite). As we all know Marie Antoinette, the Princess de Lamballe and many other noble women-freemasons perished on the guillotine, as did Louis XVI, who was a member of the Craft."

"No sooner did Emperor Napoleon ascend the throne than lodges were revived. Napoleon, as we know, had been initiated while in Egypt. It is therefore not surprising to find Empress Josephine attending a meeting of the Adoptive Lodge *Les Francs Chevaliers* of Strassberg which, at the time, was headed by Baroness Dietrich."

Holmes's conclusion? "I do not think it advisable for them to be admitted to take part in regular lodge work as we practice it. I am of the opinion that a happy solution would the fostering of women's groups. . . . Let the thinkers of Masonry seek a solution that will satisfy all members of the *genus homo.*"

The Grand Lodge of China was instituted in Shanghai on January 16, 1949. The officers were installed by Antonio Gonzales, FPS, of the Philippines. According to Dr. Hua-Chuen Mei the Chinese name of the Grand Lodge is *"Chung-Kuo* (China) *Mei-Seng* (the Life Beautiful—literally, Masonic) *Tsung-Hui* (Grand Lodge)." Mei added: "It may be said, however, that to the outside Masonic world, the Chinese name of the Grand Lodge is not now so important as its English title, since its Constitution, Regulation, By-laws and Ritual are all in English." The Grand Masters of Massachusetts and California quickly sent congratulations to the new Grand Lodge of China.

"The Mounties and Freemasonry" was the title of an article by John Gordon Hanna of Montreal in the August-September 1949 edition of *The Philalethes*. In 1873 the "Mounted Police Act" was passed by the Canadian Parliament. In the fall 150 men were sent across uncharted prairies to MacLeod, Alberta, which was named after the first Commissioner of the force. In a little more than a year these swift-riding, relentless officers stamped out the law-breakers. The way was paved for a westward invasion of settlers.

"Royal" was added to the name in 1905; in 1920 it became "The Royal Canadian Mounted Police." The force always had Freemasons, but it wasn't until the headquarters was moved to Regina that they could band together. In October 1894 North West Mounted Police Lodge No. 11 was instituted. "There were fourteen charter members, and membership in the Mounted Police was pre-requisite to membership in the lodge." Later the membership was so scattered it was necessary to permit "outsiders" to join. The "outsiders" eagerly petitioned and among its membership would be found judges, lawyers, clergymen, doctors, and all the learned professions.

In 1949, and today, Mounties were members of Masonic lodges throughout Canada. "Through the years the influence of Freemasonry has been strong among the 'scarlet riders of the plains.' And there is no doubt that the principles of the square, the level and the plumb rule have been carried by its members throughout the length and breadth of this fair Dominion of Canada of ours, and has aided them in upholding that proud motto of the Force: *'Maintiens le Droit.' "*

In the same September 1949 edition, the biography of James Fairbairn Smith, FPS, was published. He would prove a strong advocate of Masonic education throughout the years. He had established *The Masonic World* in Michigan in 1933, and continued its publication until he sold it forty-three years later. His writings were, and still are, Masonic gems.

James Fairbairn Smith

A facsimile of the petition of John Paul for membership in St. Bernard Lodge No. 122, Kirkcudbright, Scotland, adorned the second page of the October 1949 edition. According to an account by Walter Quincke, John Paul added the name of his uncle, William Paul Jones, an heir of Cadwallader Jones of Wales, who owned extensive property in Fredericksburg in Virginia. John Paul Jones was an active Freemason in Scotland, and then in the American colonies.

Jones, according to Quincke's research, was a frequent visitor in Fredericksburg Lodge No. 4. Ronald E. Heaton, FPS, and James R. Case, FPS, did an exhaustive research of the minutes of this lodge in 1975. They listed every member and visitor found in the old records. Jones' name does not appear among them. While fitting out the *Ranger* at Portsmouth, New Hampshire, Jones is said to have visited St. John's Lodge No. 1. He may have, but Gerald D. Foss in his *Three Centuries of Freemasonry in New Hampshire* (1972) doesn't record any Masonic visitations made by Jones.

This is not to imply John Paul Jones did not visit these and other lodges. In the early days of Freemasonry, and even today, records are not as complete as they should be. Secretaries aren't as meticulous as they should be; visitors and members often don't "sign in." Frequently signatures can't be deciphered, so secretaries ignore them. Then, also, there are many Masonic functions, such as celebrations of the Festivals of the Sts. John, where records of attendance are not maintained.

Without question, John Paul Jones was loved in New Hampshire. There's a "John Paul Jones" house in Portsmouth, and during his stay there he associated with many of the leading Freemasons. While outfitting the *Ranger*, Jones boarded with the widow of Captain Gregory Purcell, a member of St. John's Lodge No. 1. It's extremely likely that Jones did attend Masonic meetings and functions in New Hampshire.

Jones' body, on January 16, 1913, one hundred twenty-one years after his death, was placed in a crypt and mausoleum beneath the domed Naval Chapel at the National cemetery at Arlington. As Quincke noted: "No other United States Naval Commander has a tomb so imposing, a shrine so illustrious!"

In the same issue of the magazine, William H. Knutz of Illinois wrote about "Colonial Freemasonry." In his article he gave one of the many reasons it's often difficult to find who early members were. "Masonic membership of the early days is not always easily determined. Due to fires, dissolving of lodges or carelessness, minutes and records are often missing."

"The Birth of Kentucky's Grand Lodge" was the subject of an article by Albert C. Hanson, MPS, in the February 1950 issue of *The Philalethes*. The first Grand Master, William Murray, a member of Frankfort Hiram Lodge No. 57 of Virginia, was elected on October 16, 1800 and immediately installed. Hanson described the Grand Master as "probably the most accomplished scholar among all the eminent men of Kentucky at that day, a lawyer of strength equal to conflicts with George Nicholas, John Breckenridge, and Henry Clay, and in the rare gift of eloquence he surprised them." Murray, as Attorney General of Kentucky, "prosecuted inquiry as to the conspiracy of [Aaron] Burr, opposing Henry Clay and John Allen (Burr's counsel), both of whom afterwards became Grand Masters." (Burr had killed Alexander Hamilton in a duel. Burr fled, and attempted to found an independent country in Mexico and some western states. He was tried for treason, but acquitted for lack of evidence.)

The Grand Lodge of Virginia heartily welcomed its daughter into the ranks of the Grand Lodges. Sixty-five years later it wouldn't be as generous with another daughter, the Grand Lodge of West Virginia.

Alphonse Cerza, MPS, who would always be a strong supporter of Freemasonry against the unwarranted claims of anti-Masons, wrote about "Freemasonry and the Roman Catholic Church," in the same issue. He outlined the objections propounded by that church, and demolished them one by one.

Joseph Fort Newton died on January 24, 1950. Charles G. Reigner, FPS, extolled Newton's many virtues in the April issue of *The Philalethes*. "He carried on his work up to the end," wrote Reigner. "On the Sunday before his death he had conducted the service as usual at the Church of St. Luke and the Epiphany, Philadelphia . . . where he had been Rector since April 1938." Two days later he suffered a heart attack and died. "For breadth of vision, for clearness of thought, for simplicity and directness of expression, he stood head and shoulders above all other Masons of our time. He knew the *inner* meaning of Masonry. He shared the breadth of his knowledge with his Brethren in a number of books and in articles almost innumerable. Through every sentence he wrote there shines a transparent sincerity of thought, as well as love of the Brethren everywhere."

Newton was one of the few great men who didn't hesitate to give Freemasonry credit for much that he had accomplished as a Christian minister. In his autobiography, *River of Years,* he speaks of the Craft continually. Reigner noted: "In a national poll among the clergy held some years ago, he was selected as one of the five outstanding preachers in the United States." To this could be added England, and perhaps other countries, because over forty of his books had been published during his lifetime and many of these found their way into foreign countries.

In the June 1950 issue of *The Philalethes* Charles E. Holmes, FPS, continued to write about "Freemasonry in Foreign Lands." Under the subject of Japan Holmes wrote: "Freemasonry has followed the army of occupation into Japan, where it virtually did not exist as an organized body *prior* to the war. The first . . . lodge meeting was held there on January 6, 1950, when the President of Japan's parliament and four of its members were initiated."

"Several . . . lodges exist in Turkey, established by authority of the United Grand Lodge of England and the Grand Lodge of Scotland. The Altars of these lodges, which are 'regular,' bear three Volumes of the Sacred Law: The Bible, the Talmud, and the Koran, which are used in accordance with the candidate's professed faith. Some lodges do their ritualistic work in Hebrew, Arabic, and English. Co-existent are several lodges working under the Grand Orient of France, and quite a number have affiliated with the Grand Orient of Italy."

A portrait of Harold Van Buren Voorhis, FPS, adorned the cover of the January 1951 edition of *The Philalethes*. Even then the list of his Masonic memberships was extensive, and his writings even more so. By vocation he

Harold Van Buren Voorhis

37

was a certified gas chemist. He was a vice president for Macoy Publishing and Masonic Supply Co, among other things. Vee Hansen, who owned the company, having saved it from bankruptcy years earlier, said she had to terminate Harold's employment: "He spent too much time working for Freemasonry!"

The world-famous Harry Leroy Haywood, FPS, wrote on "Masonic Comity." His article is loaded with wisdom. "Freemasonry has something to offer the world which has nothing to do with Freemasonry. If a problem has been solved by an organization, a society, a fraternity, why should men go through the agony of solving it for a second time? If Freemasonry has found the answer to a question, why should any man labor to find the answer all over again? It is the contention of these paragraphs that Freemasonry long ago found the answer to the question which so bedevils the United Nations and the churches.

"That question can be stated in few words: how can a unity be established among many nations without destroying the identity and independence of those nations? How can there be religious unity without destroying the individuality and independence of all the religions? How can Presbyterians, Baptists, Greek Orthodox find a way to unite? . . . I believe Freemasonry has found the answer to such questions."

Harry Leroy Haywood

38

He spoke of the Constitutional Convention of 1787 which set up a federal government, leaving certain powers to the states. Of this he claimed: "One thing is certain: we shall always have the most costly political government ever devised because we shall always have to pay for fifty separate governments, one for each state and one for the nation."

Because of the statesmanship of the Masonic leaders after the Revolutionary period "we no longer are in danger of the nightmare of a single, national Grand Lodge at the one extreme, or, at the other, of a congeries of Grand Lodges behaving like atoms which repel each other, which could be nightmarish." Each Grand Lodge has, and makes, its own laws and all others accept and acknowledge this situation. Each shares its *Proceedings*, publications and acts with the others. Yearly the leadership meets to discuss mutual problems and triumphs.

"If a man is of the opinion that Comity could be more easily practiced among Grand Lodges than elsewhere, he does not know Grand Lodges; no other constituted societies in the world are more jealous of their independence and their sovereignty. If Comity can be worked among forty-nine Grand Lodges it can work anywhere. There is no reason why we should not have unity among nations, and among religions and denominations, without destroying the identity and independence of the nations and the religions."

Haywood doesn't mention it was The Masonic Service Association that proved representatives of Grand Lodges could meet together without the ghost of a National Grand Lodge appearing.

John Utzidil, MPS, wrote about Johann Wolfgang von Goethe for the January 1951 issue of *The Philalethes*. He said Goethe was initiated in the Lodge *Anna Amalia zu den drei Rosen,* Weimar, Germany, on June 23, 1780. On June 23, 1830, he was elected to Honorary Membership in his lodge for fifty years of service to the Craft, truth, and the uniting of "widely separated peoples in happy spiritual fellowship through the magic of poetry." For the occasion Goethe wrote and dedicated a poem to his lodge (the translation is by Frank H. Reinsch, MPS):

Fifty years today are over,
Neither joys nor sorrows last.
Fifty years so quickly over!
They have joined the solemn past.

But the urge to noble striving,
Brotherlove, and friendship true,
In our Bond age-long surviving,
Ever prove themselves anew.

They will always be resplendent,
Strewn like modest stars above,
Far and near with light benignant,
In the realm of right and love.

Let us then, with glad endeavor,
Try to dignify mankind;
Just as though we were forever
One in soul and heart and mind.

                                        Goethe
Weimar, 1830

In February 1951 Alphonse Cerza, MPS, started a discussion of Masonic literature, a discussion that would continue until his death in 1987. This would be one of his principal contributions to the Craft. He spoke of the classification system used by libraries. Under the Dewey Decimal System, devised in 1876 by one Melvil Dewey, Freemasonry comes under the general classification of "Sociology," which is numbered 300. Associations-Institutions is 360; secret societies, 366; Freemasonry, 366.1.

"Once you have the Dewey number at your command you can find in a library using this system every book on the subject of Freemasonry within a few minutes." Today, however, large libraries use the Library of Congress Classification System, which is a corruption of the Cutter System of 1891. Cerza believed a more "adequate and workable system" should be devised. He suggested a workable plan for the libraries of individual and large Masonic libraries.

Rick Gustafson, MPS, a professional librarian, resolved in 1987 he would endeavor to take Freemasonry out of the "secret Society" category. He received strong endorsement from the Executive Board of The Philalethes Society.

The growth of the Society was reported by the President in February 1951. It had grown from 40 in 1928 to 306 in 1950. So that it might be as effective as it should be, Quincke urged the members to let others know about its good works. "You may be surprised how many members of *your* lodge will want to support and share in our activities," he said. At the same time he suggested quality was more important than quantity; he wasn't interested in a large membership. He made it clear that subscription blanks would not be "sent helter-skelter through the mails." He wanted members who were impressed with the material the Society published.

Quincke recorded a large number of Masonic periodicals that were reprinting articles from The *Philalethes*. Volumes one and two had been exhausted. Surprisingly, he was able to report the financial condition of the Society was good.

A dispatch from China said the Communistic government of China "has officially recognized International Freemasonry as an authorized body in the Republic." Charles Holmes said: "We shall await developments with the greatest curiosity."

Later David W. K. Au, a Past Grand Master and member of the Society, wrote: "There is no truth to the report that the Communistic Government has officially recognized International Freemasonry as an authorized body in China. From the Communistic way of thinking anything 'International,' according to our interpretation, can only be Imperialistic." He did say: "Our lodges are meeting without interference."

The First Vice President of the Society, Lee Edwin Wells, writing in the February 1951 issue of *The Philalethes*, was concerned about the Grand Lodge of China. He feared "the Chinese Communists have taken the world to the very brink of another holocaust." He was also disturbed about what had happened, and was happening, to Freemasonry everywhere. "I think of the Greater and Lesser *Lights* that have been extinguished over the past three decades."

He added: "We must soberly look back and evaluate our Fraternity and ourselves. We must honestly weigh the value of our ideals and [those] of our fraternity and squarely face the part we have played in it.

"Are we 'pin' Masons? Do we feel that we can face persecution, perhaps death, as so many of our brethren have done before, for the basic ideas and ideals of our Fraternity? Or will we abandon it, since—to us—it was only another social aspect of our lives?

"Some three years ago, I tried very hard, in a speech delivered to a Lodge at Oxnard, California, to point ahead to this very problem that seems so close upon us now. I begged that new members, and old as well, be given a thorough grounding in the traditions and history of our Craft, that they may learn something more of its Symbols. Otherwise, we weaken ourselves; we may have many members but few followers, many 'pin' wearers, but few *living stones* that have made our Fraternity great. I am afraid that my warning fell on deaf ears."

Wells also feared Continental Masons didn't understand the American system of Freemasonry. In an attempt to rectify this, he had written an article on American Freemasonry. It appeared in *La Chaine d'Union* of Paris, then translated into Dutch and printed in *Algemeen Maconnick Tydschrift* in Holland.

It was reported that 214 lodges, many of them old and respected, had been closed in the Russian zone of Germany. There was great concern overseas about the number that would be eliminated as the Soviets captured more territory.

The controlled press of President Peron in Argentina was "printing violent attacks against Freemasonry." The media claimed Freemasonry in the United States was controlled by Wall Street. King Gustav V of Sweden had died and was succeeded by Crown Prince Gustav Adolf as "ex officio Grand Master of Sweden."

Alphonse Cerza was back with an article for August 1951. "Masonic Misinformation" was its title. He took on some of the myths then, and still, prevalent within the Craft. *Cathedral Builders* and *Comacines, their Predecessors and Their Successors* claimed the Roman Collegia of Artificers were the fore-runners of Freemasonry. Said Al: "The theory of the Cathedral Builders is a mere myth and should not be perpetuated by continuous repetition." The "schism of 1751" wasn't a schism at all, he said. The "Antients" Grand Lodge was formed by Irish Masons, not by defectors from the "Moderns."

The Rhode Island story of 1658, wherein a Masonic lodge was alleged to have been established, "cannot be accepted as true," wrote Cerza. It was claimed that John Moore was supposed to have "spent a few evenings in festivity with my Masonic brethren" in 1680. The letter he is supposed to have written was never found. "There can be only one conclusion," said Cerza, "that there never was any such letter."

As far back as 1950 *The Philalethes* had proven nine of the signers of the Declaration of Independence were Freemasons. This was substantiated later by Ronald E. Heaton, FPS, assisted by James R. Case, FPS. Yet many Masonic leaders were claiming as many as fifty were Masons. Again, Cerza tried to set the record straight.

All of George Washington's generals were *not* Freemasons. In fact, the majority of them did not belong to the Craft. Thomas Jefferson was *not* a Freemason. John Wesley, the founder of Methodism, was *not* a Freemason.

Cerza believed that it was because these myths were picked up by Joseph Fort Newton in his book, *The Builders*, that they were prevalent in the Masonic world. Cerza was also disturbed because whole works of Newton's were being plagiarized. They still are.

Cerza closed his article by saying: "Alexander Pope, in answer to his critics, once said: 'To err is human, to forgive divine.' Our purpose here has not been to criticize, but to urge more care in reproducing materials. If there is doubt regarding the stated facts, let this be known. When expressing an opinion, let it just be that and nothing more. If from pressure of other duties editors are compelled to use a pair of scissors instead of a pen, let them do so with discretion and first examine the material they intend to copy; also failure to give proper credit to author or source is *never* excusable, yet there are several Craft periodicals in circulation guilty of this inadvertence."

Harold H. Kinney, the Associate Editor, reported in August 1951 that the President and Editor, Walter A. Quincke "is now waging a gallant fight to overcome an illness that coupled with his efforts in behalf of our Society had reduced his vitality and energy to a low ebb." Quincke was expected to have a long period of recovery.

Walter didn't recover. Kinney wrote in December 1951: "The October-November issue of *The Philalethes* was scarcely off the press when a bereavement occurred world-wide in its import and interest to the Fellows and Members of the Society. It was the sudden death of our beloved President, Walter Albert Quincke, on Monday, October 29, 1951."

Kinney said Walter had, for years, devoted every waking hour to the work of The Philalethes Society. He had taken the Society from a "low ebb," to a steady growth. He produced a magazine whose influence had become "clearly manifest in the publications of Masonry throughout the world. Its Fellows and Members have become leaders in research and in the dissemination of authentic Masonic information." Walter Quincke had been much more than the chief administrative officer, he had been the Editor of the most prestigious Masonic publication of the day. "His life, however," wrote Kinney, "typified the ambition of a true and genuine Mason—to do something that shall benefit the world—'to bless with the glorious gifts of *Truth, Light, and Liberty.'* Thus the memory of Brother Walter's gentle nature, his humor and wit, his love of the beautiful, his thoughtful generosity, his unfailing courtesy, and his ideals of *perfection and brotherhood* shall continue to influence the lives of those who knew him. His writings shall bring enjoyment to those who seek *more light*, and they shall live again with him the golden moods and precious thoughts that are preserved in books such as *The Philalethes*."

From all over the country condolences were sent. When word reached the overseas members, many more messages of sympathy poured in. In the minds of most there was certainly the question: "Can The Philalethes Society survive this great loss?"

4. CHAOS
(1951–1954)

*B*efore the death of Walter Quincke another giant in the leadership of The Philalethes Society had left the scene. Leo Fischer, who had kept the membership informed about what was happening overseas, had died. The work and translations he had done would not soon be forgotten.

Others who would become giants within Freemasonry were beginning, or continuing, to work with the Society. Among them were Alphonse Cerza, Charles G. Reigner, Carl H. Claudy, James K. Remick, Robert J. Meekren, Elbert Bede, Allister J. McKowen, William Moseley Brown, Harold V. B. Voorhis, and Harold H. Kinney.

Allister J. McKowen notified the Fellows and Members of the Society that Harold H. Kinney, FPS, had been chosen Editor of *The Philalethes*. Kinney was a thirty-year member of Ocean Park Lodge No. 369, Santa Monica, California. He was a member of the York and Scottish Rites. By vocation he was a manufacturer "of electric musical instruments, and executive officer of the corporation."

The year 1952 marked the bicentennial year of the Masonic birth of George Washington. William Moseley Brown, who had written extensively

Allister John McKowen

44

William Moseley Brown

about George Washington, wrote about plans for Masonic celebrations during the year.

The Executive Secretary announced that as of January 1, 1952 the Editor of *The Philalethes* had also been elected International President. It was pointed out that Quincke had appointed Kinney his personal representative as well as Associate Editor. Kinney, therefore, was familiar with the goals of the Society and was in a better position to carry them out than was anyone else.

Dr. Roscoe Pound became a member of the Society in February 1952. The Editor was pleased to welcome him because he felt Pound could show new Masons some of the meaning behind the ritual. "Let us as individual members," he wrote, "as well as a Society, take the leadership in seeing that candidates receive instruction; that the forces that lie behind and beyond the ritual are *'brought to light'*; that the candidates are *shown how these TRUTHS can become dominant factors in their personal lives."*

Grand Master and Dr. Ing. Theodor Vogel, MPS, told his members on June 15, 1951: "The greatest and happiest, the most beautiful and wonderful time of German Freemasonry began when in 1945, after fifteen years of probation, we were allowed to work again. When we could recognize *the plan* which was made by the Supreme Architect of the Universe, when we became free of externalities, when we heard the inner voices again, when we could serve the distress, the hopelessness, and the despair of our people, when we became apprentices, fellows, and masters of the real *Royal Art*, and were allowed to recognize and realize the wish of many German Masonic generations, to collect the brethren in lodges again, of really growing together as a Craft." That's a long sentence that speaks volumes.

Vogel was happy to proclaim that "the deadly brutality of the criminals of 1933 has been stopped." He was proud to say there were 201 lodges and 153 Masonic clubs in Germany in 1951. Over a thousand men had joined the Craft during the year. He urged isolationism never again be practiced. "For the sake of our young people," Vogel said, "for the sake of our nation, *the fraternal chain has to encompass the world,* and German Freemasonry has to be a link in it which will be welcomed with respect and honor, and which will have a decisive importance."

Clifford W. Parkin, MPS, of Quebec, wrote an article for March 1952 which must have amazed many Freemasons. The Craft once met in English buildings adorned with "highly decorated signboards" swinging in the breeze. The word "Tavern" was on several of them. Even if the word was lacking, it was still a tavern. "We may well imagine the ground-floor interiors of these inns as well sanded and straw-strewn; with heavy ceiling beams, spacious fire-places, and leaded windows."

The description continued: "Those who frequented these taverns were garbed in a manner which would have astonished us if compared with our present restraint in dress. Distinguishing features were long coats and vests, the sleeve cuffs being extravagantly large, while the amount of lace on cravats hanging from the neck would have seemed effeminate to us of this age. Breeches, stockings, and shoes with prominent buckles were the leg coverings, while heads were adorned with wigs of amazing superfluity, topped by gaudily decked felt hats. It was then the custom of 'gentlemen' to carry swords as part of their customary dress. These were often used without hesitation when disputes became heated and insults exchanged."

Parkin said riots and bloodshed were frequent. He added: "This, incidentally, is one reason why the 'Old Charges' of our Craft place a ban on discussion of politics or religious denominational difference of opinions at our gatherings. Likewise why we are prevented from carrying any metallic objects at an important event in our ceremonial."

What brought about the revival of Masonry in 1717? The conditions then existing in England. The political, religious and moral atmosphere was a shambles. Ignorance, thievery and brutality were rampant. Education was reserved for the favored few. But there were those who were practicing humanitarian principles. Above all, men were seeking more freedom.

Christopher Wren, according to Parkin, was an honored master operative mason, respected by the craft and the intelligentsia. He was one of the founders of the Royal Society that was attempting to improve the sordid conditions of the day. But the lodges in London in 1716 felt they were being neglected by Wren. This could well have been because Wren died in 1723 at the age of 91! At any rate, a meeting was called to try to revive masonry in London. The meeting was held at the Apple Tree Tavern in Charles Street, Covent Garden, London, in 1716.

From this meeting had come the "annual assembly and feast at the sign of The Goose and Gridiron in St. Paul's Churchyard on June 24th of 1717." It was the Festival of St. John the Baptist, "a patron saint of the medieval craftsmen." In England, it was "Midsummer Day," also referred to as "the high noon of the year, the day of light and roses." The era of Speculative Freemasonry had begun.

It was the Reverend John Theophilus Desaguliers, a close associate of Wren's, Parkin writes, to whom the new era is indebted for its ultimate success. It isn't known if he was in at the beginning. Nothing is heard about him until 1719 when he became the third Grand Master. His subsequent work earned him the appellation of "Father of Modern Speculative Masonry."

The Editor published an outline for the study of Freemasonry, because the young Mason "is entitled to more than" a mere introduction to the ritual. Much of the proposed study came from the pen of Robert I. Clegg, and was published in the excellent *Builder* magazine, a publication of the defunct National Masonic Research Society at Anamosa, Iowa.

The plan called for a study of: 1. Ceremonial Masonry (the ritual and ritual work of the lodge); 2. Symbolical Masonry (the meaning behind the ritual); 3. Philosophical Masonry (history and philosophy); 4. Legislative Masonry (the Grand Lodge and its laws; the lodge and its functions); 5. Historical Masonry (all other aspects of Freemasonry).

"How Ancient Is Freemasonry?" asked Clifford Parkin in April 1952. "Extravagant statements," he said, "should be considered in the knowledge that TRUTH is one of our cherished and essential tenets." Engaging in "spanning gaps by building mental bridges" with vivid imagination should be avoided. "Many have heard that truth is stranger than fiction," he wrote, "but they will not risk a recital falling flat by telling an unvarnished tale."

"If we, as upholders of the great principles of our institution wish to continue as well instructed brethren, let us firmly beware of being misled," Parkin continued. Over enthusiasm can be dangerous, and we should be careful not to mix legends with facts. He noted that this had been one of the Reverend George Oliver's problems. "He had accepted without hesitation many crude theories from previous writers (who probably knew as little as he did on the subject)." The value of Freemasonry "is not to be determined by its ancientness, but in the possibilities which it affords us" today and for the future.

The Editor, Harold Kinney, wrote: "The Temple of Freemasonry is erected upon the cornerstone of *service to others*. Before a candidate is permitted to pass between the Pillars of the Porch he must avow his desire to be of service to his fellowman. . . . If each member of our Society were to daily exert his God-given *talents for the welfare of others,* the faculties, powers, capacities, and accomplishments represented in our membership would be a most potent force for good, felt in every hemisphere of the world."

Death struck again. The President and Editor had died after a short illness on July 21, 1952, at the age of 57. Lee E. Wells, the then President of The Philalethes Society told part of the tragic story in February 1954:

There is a tradition of the Craft that tells of the confusion and chaos in the Temple caused by the untimely death of the Master Workman. The trestleboard was empty of design, nor was there the sound of tool, the building stopped. Then, the tradition continues, a craftsman was appointed to take the place of the Master Workman and eventually the Temple was completed and dedicated to the service of the Grand Architect of the Universe.

In the past two years, unfortunately, the Philalethes Society has followed a similar course. Our beloved brother and President, Walter P. Quincke, was called to the Supreme Lodge above and he was succeeded ably by Bro Harold H. Kinney. The work of the Society continued without interruption. Then Bro. Kinney also died, very suddenly.

The work of the Society stopped. There were no designs upon the trestleboard, and there was confusion and chaos. Bro. Allister McKowen, then Secretary-Treasurer, recovered all the Society's files, records and possessions from Mrs. Kinney and still has them in his possession. The First Vice President [Wells], because of pressing personal problems, could not assume the executive position, and, in fact, did not know if he should, awaiting word from the Secretary. The Second Vice President was a resident of Canada and in no position to take over the work so abruptly left by Bro. Kinney.

Time passed, a period during which no one Fellow or Member felt that he, personally, should take the initiative. Then, in April of 1952, Bro Wells and Bro. Bede held a conference with an idea of exploring the means of re-activating the Society once again. Later, in May, Bro. Wells conferred personally with Bro. Harold Voorhis in New York and Bro. Alphonse Cerza in Chicago. It was the opinion, as expressed by Bede, Voorhis, and Cerza, that the Society definitely should be re-activated. They knew that many members and Fellows had written to Bro. McKowen and received no reply. Each of them had in turn received queries and could not answer them. Their own questions to Bro. McKowen went without answer.

The task of reviving the Society was, and is, a tremendous one. After repeated requests and directives, Bro. McKowen has not given a report on the files, records, possessions, and moneys of the Society that he has received. Bro. Wells had, fortunately, a duplicate membership list, but it dated from just before the death of Bro. Quincke. The immediate problem, therefore, was to appoint pro tem officers, contact each and every Fellow and Member as shown on the old membership list to confirm address, membership, and willingness to continue within the bonds of the Society.

To this end, Bro. Wells assumed the Presidency. By directive, he immediately appointed Bro. Alphonse Cerza of Chicago [Illinois] as First Vice President with the duty of contacting all members in the Central and Southern sections of the United States. Bro. Arthur Triggs of Oakland [California] was appointed Second Vice President with the duty of contacting all members in the West and Southwest. Bro. Lawton E. Meyer of St. Louis [Missouri] was appointed Secretary.

The story became even more horrible. William Major Brown of Oklahoma City was soliciting dues and fees from members of the Society. Thinking this had the approval of Meyer and John Vrooman, Wells appointed Brown as Treasurer of The Philalethes Society. It was quickly learned that Brown planned on printing *The Philalethes* as a supplement to his *Masonic Review.* Objections poured in from all over the country. *The Philalethes* wasn't to be a supplement to anything. So Wells appointed Alphonse Cerza as Editor and asked Brown to send the Society's funds in his possession to Chicago. "Brown stated he would release none of the Society's funds for the purpose of publication in Chicago. Thereupon, and most regretfully, Bro. Wells sent a directive to Bro. Brown which read in part:

"It is therefore with deep regret that I must ask for your resignation as Treasurer of The Philalethes Society. The funds in the Oklahoma Bank may remain there until transferred to some other institution. You will take steps to release the funds.

"I further, regretfully, request that you cease and desist all activities for and in the name of the Society, including correspondence and publication."

The order was sent by registered mail on December 12, 1952.

"It has always been a weakness of the Society from its very inception that it was a 'one man' organization," continued Wells. To prevent another chaotic situation, Elbert Bede was appointed chairman of a committee to draw up a Constitution for the Society.

The Editor, Alphonse Cerza, now a Fellow of The Philalethes Society, included an obituary for Harold Hile Kinney.

Carl H. Claudy, FPS, Executive Secretary of The Masonic Service Association, wrote to Cerza on January 18, 1954: "No news that I have had recently gives me the satisfaction incident to learning of your willingness to take over the editorial duties of the *The Philalethes* magazine.

"The Society should not be allowed to die. Too much hard work went into it; too much good was done by it; too much inspiration flowed from the pages of the magazine.

"If you and those who will work with you can keep it alive and rebreathe into it the spirit of service in which it was conceived, you will perform a great and important task for those brethren to whom the study of Masonry and the real understanding of its principles are an important aim in life."

With the February edition John Black Vrooman started a regular column called "Bureau of Masonic Information."

The former Executive Secretary visited Cerza prior to the May issue of the magazine. He went over the work of the Society of previous years, evidently breaking his long silence. The books and records in his possession were turned over to Cerza for safe keeping until "the permanent officers of the Society have been elected."

Wells, in the meantime, had found much of the old correspondence pertaining to the Society. From this he had concluded the Society was founded "to be a loose-knit correspondence group." As others came into the circle Cyrus Field Willard, one of the founders, suggested there be "forty immortals," now called "Fellows." The title was intended to honor Masonic editors, writers and serious students of Freemasonry. Shepherd carried on this theme after the death of Willard.

With the death of Shepherd, Quincke took over the helm and "infused an entirely new idea into the Society. He made the qualifications for membership very liberal so that even the beginning Mason who was interested in his Fraternity could join with us in receiving Light. We became international and gained the respect of the best Masonic minds around the world." Kinney carried on the same theme.

One factor the committee to draw up a Constitution was faced with was the question of "irregular" Masonry. It appeared the majority of the Fellows and Members weren't concerned with the subject. They claimed they were not having *Masonic* communications with one another, so the subject shouldn't be considered. They recognized, however, there were jurisdictions that took the proposition extremely seriously. In the interest of harmony, therefore, the Constitution would insist on permitting only "regular" Freemasons to be members of the Society.

William Major Brown supplied the President with the names of the members who had paid their dues to him. Cards from the Society were issued to them. Brown said he would hold the funds in Oklahoma until permanent officers were elected.

Along with the June edition of *The Philalethes* went the Constitution prepared by Elbert Bede, William Moseley Brown and Laurence R. Taylor. Included was a list of suggested officers to be balloted on. These were not made a part of the edition because they were to be returned for counting to Bede.

The October edition of the magazine brought forth a complete change in the leadership of The Philalethes Society. Alphonse Cerza had been elected President; Arthur H. Triggs, First Vice President; Elbert Bede, Second Vice President; Lawton E. Meyer, Executive Secretary; John Black Vrooman was not only the Treasurer, but began his long tenure as Editor of *The Philalethes*.

Why was the work of Lee E. Wells not rewarded by making him permanent President? Because he didn't want the job, it appears. It was claimed he had said his work as a full-time professional writer had to come first.

There may be more to the story than meets the eye. According to Albert L. Woody, FPS, who said in 1987: "I can tell you from personal knowledge that it was conceived by Al Cerza one day in my shop, and that Al engineered the reorganization with the assistance of Lee Wells and the others. There was one other who tried to get hold of the Society, but Al was successful in avoiding that."

With this first-hand information, what Wells reported to the membership

Alphonse Cerza

when he took over the reigns, falls into place. That Wells was a "professional writer" is unquestioned. Over the years he wrote over forty books, some under the name of Richard Poole and other pseudonyms. But did he claim he wanted to devote full time only to his novels? At any rate, after the results of the election, the Society lost track of him. Attempts to find him, or something about him, during 1987 proved futile. According to the best information obtainable, Wells was suspended, for not paying his dues, by his lodge in California in 1955, a year after the election that made Cerza the new President of the Society.

Early in 1988 it was learned a book entitled *Gun Vote at Valdoro*, written by Richard Poole, had been published by Doubleday in 1969. A phone call to the publisher's editorial department brought the information that Lee Edwin Wells had died. But when and where the publisher didn't know. From the Virginia State Library came information about a book titled *Indiana Authors and Their Books*. This led to the Mystery Writers of America with headquarters in New York City.

Priscilla Ridgeway of the Mystery Writers found Wells's original application for membership. She also found he had moved to San Diego, California, before he dropped his membership in the MWA in 1980. Captain Frederick Kleyn, Jr., U.S.N., and Secretary of the San Diego Chapter of The Philalethes Society took it from there. He learned that Lee Edwin Wells had died in that city on April 29, 1982. The long search was over.

Wells was born on June 1, 1907 in Indianapolis, Indiana. He became a Master Mason in North Park Lodge No. 646 in that city on February 26, 1944. He demitted to Centre Lodge No. 23 on August 1, 1945, shortly after he had become a member of The Philalethes Society. In 1950 Wells moved to the Los Angeles, California, area and affiliated with a lodge there. In 1955 he was dropped by that lodge from its membership. As far as can be determined, he never again was re-instated. *The Philalethes* for June 1988 carried a story entitled: "The Savior of The Philalethes Society: Lee E. Wells."

In writing of Wells in October 1954, Cerza said: "As a professional writer, and one whose time was not his own, he called on those whom he knew would accomplish the purpose sought; contacted key men in all parts of the country, and set the wheels in motion that resulted in the writing and adoption of a Constitution and By-Laws, and the selection, nomination and election of permanent officers who would take over the reins of the Society, and make it active and aggressive in Masonic research.

"Little credit has been given this ardent Mason for his work. His personal and professional obligations preventing him from accepting the Presidency of the Society, which he so richly deserved, he stepped down from that position and continued his labors for the good of the Society, without thought of personal advancement or honors. . . [the Society's] present state of activity will be forever a monument and tribute to his devotion and love of Masonry."

Cerza, the new President, reminded the members that "the officers and committee members are employed at full-time occupations. The services they render the Society were without compensation and during their spare time." Cerza strongly suggested there had been enough talk, and it was now time for aggressive action. It was time to "CREATE MASONIC ENLIGHTENMENT."

Cerza's closing paragraph as President should be repeated in this, the 60th year in the history of The Philalethes Society:

"The Society has served a useful purpose for many years. This was possible through the cooperation of the Fellows and Members. Your officers cannot do the work by themselves. The help of all is needed. You can help in one or more of the following ways: write articles if you are literarily inclined, pay your dues if you have not done so, recommend Masons to membership, make constructive suggestions to your officers, correspond with other Members, and suggest the names of Members of the Society who should be given the title of Fellows when vacancies occur. Let us know in what field your interest lies so that we may labor together for the success of the Society and the benefit of the Craft."

The dark days for The Philalethes Society had ended. Would this be forever?

5. REBUILDING
(1954–1956)

*J*ohn Black Vrooman told his readers: "What is needed now more than anything else, is ORIGINAL material with verified data, facts, dates and conclusions." He said there were many areas needing extensive research. One topic he wanted covered was "The Vigilantes," the law enforcement agency "in places of lawlessness" in the Old West. He believed many of them were Freemasons.

The President, Alphonse Cerza, appointed members of the Society as representatives in several states and foreign countries. He wanted the Society to grow so it could be more beneficial to Freemasonry in general.

William Moseley Brown reported on his journey to foreign climes. He said all was well with Freemasonry overseas and it was growing stronger than ever where freedom existed. Wherever he traveled he was received warmly by the Masonic leadership.

The Executive Board, for the first time, established a category known as "Life Fellow." Named were Robert J. Meekren, a Fellow with a "varied and exact knowledge of ritualistic matters"; James M. Clift, Grand Secretary Emeritus of Virginia (Clift died on October 16, 1954, before he could be informed of this honor); Arthur C. Parker, "known for his Masonic dramas, and bringing something of practical value to the Masonic student" (Parker died on January 1, 1955, shortly after being notified of this award); and Harry Leroy Haywood, "one of the world's greatest Masonic students." Haywood was further commended for making "simple the lessons so eagerly sought after" by all Freemasons.

Cerza and Vrooman brought out a subject as relevant today as it was in 1954.

The common cry of writers everywhere is: "Why should I write when no one seems to read or care for my efforts?" That there may be a better spirit of cooperation, a truer interpretation of our objective—the purpose of The Philalethes Society—ONE WHICH IS FOR FREEMASONS WHO SEEK LIGHT, AND FREEMASONS WHO HAVE MORE LIGHT TO IMPART—we need to bring a closer and more intimate spirit of discussion and inter-change of ideas between our members everywhere.

It is not enough to have articles published in our magazine. We must have discussion of these Masonic topics by author and reader, by student and researcher. If there is a difference of meaning—an amplification of ideas and an exchange of opinions can be the best means of closer and better understanding—

of a better fellowship and greater appreciation of the efforts of those who have the interests of the Craft at heart.

Too often Masonic endeavors are unappreciated, unsung and barren of community activity. The Philalethes Society, above all else, needs to cultivate and sponsor a closer union, a greater understanding between its component members.

When an article appeals to you, write the author and tell him so. He will appreciate your words of praise. If you disagree, tell him wherein you do not see eye to eye with him. Get closer to your fellow-students and help make The Philalethes Society that close-knit unit it deserves to be.

Amazingly, in 1988 there are still Masonic leaders who make wild claims about the number of delegates to the Constitutional Convention who were supposedly Freemasons. As early as 1954 *The Philalethes* debunked this. It also proved the number of Washington's generals who were Master Masons were fewer than had been often reported. Since then two Fellows of The Philalethes Society, Ronald E. Heaton and James R. Case, researched and published the truth through several editions of *The Philalethes* and more fully through The Masonic Service Association.

Lawton E. Meyer

Many other myths have been uncovered by researchers writing for *The Philalethes*. Many of these will be found within these pages.

The Executive Secretary, Lawton E. Meyer, wrote fondly of the need for books. "Books are the Prophets, the idea-kindlers and the spiritual helpers of Life," he said. "And as they constitute the veriest democracy, let them not be gaudily-garbed as a soliciting harlot, (though not as well-thumbed), but let them be bound in simple dignity—as Franklin or Pitt." He suggested "books should never be left too long on the shelves, they should come out and mingle with the people. As pearls take on lustre from the vitality of the wearer, so does a book come alive as it becomes one with the reader."

"Masonic week" in Washington, D.C., was mentioned in the pages of *The Philalethes* for the first time in February 1955. This was when the Grand Masters, Grand Secretaries, and many of the Allied Masonic Bodies got together for annual meetings.

"Montana Vigilantes" was the first article to appear after the plea by the Editor for information about the law-enforcers of the Old West. It was written by Myril J. Greely, MPS. "3-7-77! This was the secret sign of our Montana Vigilantes! Wherever this sign appeared [it] meant the death sentence to the recipient. There was no escape. Capture and death was inevitable and certain!"

Gold was found at Grasshopper Creek, later named Bannack, and in 1862 the rush was on. In April 1863 a number of Freemasons in Bannack requested a dispensation for a lodge from the Grand Lodge of Nebraska. The dispensation was granted but the lodge never met. In November 1863, however, the same Grand Lodge granted a dispensation for a lodge to meet at Nevada City. Utah Lodge U.D. existed for seven months. Virginia City Lodge, a product of the Grand Lodge of Kansas, was more successful in December 1863. A year later it received its charter. In 1866 Montana had its own Grand Lodge.

Shortly after Virginia City Lodge requested a dispensation from Kansas, a group of men met. They took the following oath (as actually recorded):

We, the undersigned uniting ourselves in a party for the laudible purpos of arresting thieves & murders & recover stollen property, do pledge ourselves upon our sacred honor each to all others do soleminly swear that we will reveal no secrets, violate no laws of right & never desert each other or our standard of justice so help us God, as witness our hand & seal this 23 of December A D 1863.

Were these early vigilantes Freemasons? According to Greely's information all but one of the twelve men who signed this oath were members of the Craft. Moreover, he added: "More than a thousand and possibly 2,500 men had taken the secret oath of the Vigilantes. Freemasons? Yes, and justly so!

You and I—how proud we are of our heritage!"

William A. Thaanum, MPS, added to the story of the vigilantes of Montana in August 1955. Much of the lawlessness in and around Bannack in 1862 was caused "by a young man named Henry Plummer, of prepossessing appearance and, as we would now say, a good mixer. He ingratiated himself into the favor of the miners and other townsfolk, so that when the office of sheriff became vacant . . . Plummer was chosen to assume the duties."

Then trouble increased. Plummer "gathered under his command as well organized and as ruthless a band of desperadoes as any of the masterminds of systematized crime in the history of the West. They had means of recognition, passwords, an oath with the penalty of instant death if unfaithful or guilty of treachery to the group, and wore identifying apparel and style of hair and whiskers."

They were divided into groups of road agents, informers, secretaries, messengers, and lookouts. The settlements were at the mercy of this "law enforcement officer" and his thugs. Hundreds of murders and other atrocities were attributed to them. One of these, the torture-murder and robbery of a young man brought the people together. The formation of the vigilantes was the result.

The vigilantes cleared the territory of the thugs. Plummer, the leader, "and four of his associates were hanged at the same time in Bannack and it was not long before the people of Bannack and Alder Gulch communities were able to go about their common affairs and their necessary travel to and from the different towns without interference from road agents and their ilk."

Thaanum believed most, but not all, of the vigilantes were Freemasons.

He also mentions a Masonic funeral that took place on November 2, 1862. W. H. Bell knew he was dying. He told a friend he wanted a Masonic burial. When the day arrived a call was made for the Masons in the community to gather together. "The response was so surprising that they had to adjourn to a more commodious place." The author asks: Was it because of this large turnout, and the respect for the Masonic organization, that of the known 103 persons murdered by the Plummer gang, "not a single Mason was among this number?"

Which spelling is correct: "Demit or Dimit?" Harold V. B. Voorhis investigated. He found 53 of 203 Grand bodies used "demit"; 112, "dimit"; 30, neither. His exhaustive research produced this conclusion: "In view of the evidence here presented, the writer is of the opinion that the correct English usage should prevail regardless of the current usage by Grand Bodies, and [even though] the evidence shows a greater usage of the word DIMIT, such evidence should be stricken out of this discussion, and that the decision should rest on the findings of men of letters, namely, the adherence to the original and only correct form, that of DEMIT."

Cecil H. Ellis, MPS, was highly critical of former presiding officers who refused to "Lay that Gavel Down." In his closing paragraph he wrote: "It is often said that the 'Pasts' are the backbone of a lodge or other Masonic body. Let us be content to be just the backbone and support but, let us permit the head, and the arms, and the legs (whom we have regularly elected to office) do the running of the lodge or body, and let us 'Pasts' remain in the background, rendering advice and assistance when necessary, but never interference."

"Freemasons' Hall in London, England, or the Masonic Peace Memorial, as it is called, was erected as a Masonic Headquarters for the English Freemasons and as a monument in memory of the Brethren who gave their lives in the First World War," wrote Alfred A. Northacker, MPS. "The cornerstone was laid on July 14, 1927, by Field Marshal H.R.H. The Duke of Connaught, K.G., Most Worshipful Grand Master. He also enjoyed the privilege of officially opening the building on July 19, 1933."

Within the 151 rooms is the museum housing the "finest collection of Masonic treasures and curios in the world." The Grand Lodge library was started in 1837, and is now in Freemasons' Hall. It "contains literally thousands of valuable volumes, historical and otherwise." Among these is Dr. James Anderson's 1723 *Book of Constitutions*.

Nine new Fellows of The Philalethes Society were named in October 1955. Roscoe Pound, Dean of the Harvard Law School, and Deputy Grand Master of the Grand Lodge of Massachusetts, headed the list. The others were: George Stirling Draffen of Scotland, Edward J. Franta of North Dakota; Frederick William Eyre Cullingford of North Carolina; Laurence R. Taylor of Indiana; Henry Wilson Coil of California; Francis Joseph Scully of Arkansas; Jose Oller of Panama; and John C. Hubbard of Oklahoma.

For several months a proposed seal for the Society had been displayed on the cover. The members had submitted their suggestions concerning the "decoration" adorning the insignia. The October 1955 cover contained the results. Wisely the members had rejected the unnecessary adornments. It wouldn't have a square, triangle, "G", or unsightly flame. A book would take the place of the "G" and delicate smoke replaced the flame.

The Editor had asked the members what they would like to see in *The Philalethes*. Carl H. Claudy, FPS, was blunt (as usual): "Cut down the evangelical, the religious, the inspirational, and give us more *fact* stories, history and intelligent interpretation of symbols." Robert H. Nisbet, MPS, suggested: "Let's confine ourselves to Craft Masonry, never mind the 'sideshows.' "

"Though I may not be deeply interested in a particular phase of Masonry," wrote John Vanderwood, "someone else is, or it would not be something to enjoy, evaluate and sift. Each one must be accepted, because all Masonry does not go to the same depth."

Louis LeGrand, MPS, of South Africa said: "The magazine is one of the finest Masonic publications that I have come across, and I come across a good few." He pleaded with members of the Society to continue writing for the magazine, and encourage those who were hesitating to get started.

Norman C. Dutt, MPS, was in the U.S. Navy and acted as a roving reporter for the magazine. He had written about Freemasonry in Hawaii earlier, and in December 1955 Robert G. Cole, MPS, elaborated on what Dutt had said. "King Kalakaua was the second king to serve his lodge in the East," Cole wrote. "In 1874 the king made a tour of the United States. . . . King Kalakaua visited lodges in Washington, New York and Boston. On January 15, 1875, he visited Oriental Lodge in Chicago" and the lodge room was filled to overflowing; so much so, the doors had to be closed to prevent a crush.

At the age of 55, Lawton E. Meyer, FPS, Executive Secretary, died on Christmas morning 1955. He had worked faithfully since the reorganization of the Society in 1953. He had served with the Marines in World War I, and was twice decorated for bravery. He was a member of Tuscan Lodge No. 300 in St. Louis.

Another Masonic stalwart, Harry Leroy Haywood, FPS-Life, died suddenly on February 25, 1956. His accomplishments, especially in the literary field, were staggering. Much that he wrote will be quoted until time shall be no more. Laurence R. Taylor, FPS, wrote: "So long as there are eyes to read and souls to respond to his gentle pen and gentler heart, Brother Haywood's presence will live among us." Haywood became a Master Mason on June 7, 1915 in Acacia Lodge No. 716, Webster City, Iowa. "From that date until his death he was a devoted and dedicated Mason." His funeral rites were conducted by the lodge to which he belonged at the time of his passing, Mizpah No. 639 of Cedar Rapids.

Following the death of the Executive Secretary, Arthur H. Triggs resigned at the end of December as First Vice President. Masonic bodies in California were demanding more of his time. The Executive Committee convinced John Black Vrooman he should resign as Treasurer and take over the duties of Executive Secretary. Dr. William Moseley Brown of North Carolina (and Virginia) was elected First Vice President. Elbert Bede remained as Second Vice President, and Delbert C. Johnson of Missouri became the new Treasurer.

The reorganized Philalethes Society had proven it had come of age. Its Constitution and Bylaws had worked. Although key officers had to be replaced, they were, and the business of the Society continued uninterrupted.

Through its officers and members The Philalethes Society could continue the search for truth.

6. DEVELOPING
(1956–1960)

*L*aurence R. Taylor, FPS, wrote for the second issue of *The Philalethes* in 1956: "Freemasonry has lost a devoted son. Harry Leroy Haywood, learned scholar, author and teacher of Masons, entered the Lodge Celestial on February 25, 1956 at Cedar Rapids, Iowa. His spirit now joins the select and illustrious company of our Craft's immortals." Taylor concluded: "Few men will be more deeply enshrined in the hearts of those he served."

It has been claimed that a "prophet is without honor in his own country" (often "state" is substituted). This wasn't so with Harry Leroy Haywood. In the "Hall of Masonry" included in the Grand Lodge Library building of Iowa, a memorial to Haywood's memory was placed. It was an eight foot round table made of special-cut oak with a built-in globe that adorned the center of the room. A bronze plaque with the words "More Light" was embedded on it. On it were these additional words: "In Memory of HARRY LEROY HAYWOOD, A Peerless Teacher of Masons, All things that in Creation are . . . from dust to man and seraphim belong to God's Freemasonry. Presented by Midwest Conference on Masonic Education."

Carl H. Claudy, Harold V. B. Voorhis, Reginald V. Harris and Ray V. Denslow were elected Life Fellows in June 1956. Each had performed outstanding service for Freemasonry in varying categories.

"Why should we look in the Bible for source data for a Dionysian or Samothracian mystery ritual," wrote Harold Voorhis, "for that is what our Hiramic Legend is." Nowhere in the more than one hundred "Old Charges" written prior to 1717 can anything be found pertaining to this Legend, Voorhis said. Nor can anything about it be found in any of the works of the English scholars prior to 1717. It didn't appear until some ten years after the formation of the Grand Lodge of England.

Voorhis continues his discussion in depth, then concludes: "The Hiramic Legend is a very ancient Greek Legend, proved by its use under several names, many centuries ago. It was introduced into Masonic Lodges about 1725–30 by James Anderson, John Theophilus Desaguliers and others— superimposed upon the theme of the building of King Solomon's Temple, then a very popular subject in England.

"During the course of the next hundred years the lectures (really the degrees) were revised several times and the present three degrees developed to a point where their early adoption is clouded because of the removing of recognizable points which would have easily given us the needed clues to their origin. It must be pointed out, again, that trying to find the basis of our

Plaque honoring H. L. Haywood

system in the Bible has resulted negatively because it came not from the Old Testament, but from Grecian legends."

No one took issue with Voorhis during the months that followed.

Melvin M. Johnson took exception to what William A. Thaanum had written in April 1956. According to Thaanum there is no such thing as *the* "ranking Mason" in any jurisdiction. "Rank in Freemasonry is merely a courtesy," said Thaanum, "and in the final analysis, however many degrees he has received by his own petition; however many honors have been given him by the ballot of his brethren . . . no Brother can claim that he outranks even the latest initiate in the ranks of Master Masons."

Wrote Johnson: "The Most Worshipful Grand Master of a Grand Lodge is, in his territorial jurisdiction, the 'ranking Mason' of his Grand Lodge and of Freemasonry. . . . Under the prevailing law of our Fraternity, the Grand Master could suspend from membership even the Sovereign Grand Commander of the Southern Jurisdiction if he should be in St. Louis and should commit a heinous offense." Several others agreed with Johnson. So did Thaanum, in part, after he had reflected on the subject.

Thaanum, however, noted that jurisdictions vary in enforcing Masonic laws drastically. Not all jurisdictions permitted a Grand Master to have the powers Johnson had enumerated. Thaanum wanted Johnson and his readers to know the Mason a local newspaper had called "the highest ranking Mason in the state" wasn't the Grand Master. He wasn't even a Past Grand Master; he was an officer of an appendant body.

Alphonse Cerza debunked more myths. Martin Luther of religious fame was not a Freemason; neither was Alexander Hamilton of revolutionary war fame. Theodore Roosevelt never sat in a Masonic Lodge with Elihu Root, his Secretary of State—Root wasn't even a Freemason! Which, according to Cerza, makes the story suspect of Teddy sitting in a lodge over which his gardener presided.

The Philalethes continually supported the Pusan Masonic Club of South Korea. This club, composed mainly of American servicemen, had taken under its wing the care of destitute children. In 1951 the Freemasons in Korea had laid the framework for a children's hospital. With so many Masons in that country during the "police action," monetary support was readily available. As a consequence the hospital grew and became fully functional. "Now that the bulk of the American armed forces has left that peninsula, the job must be carried on from the United States," said Colonel and Brother Roger M. Crosby. *The Philalethes* endorsed the plea for financial assistance.

The Executive Committee announced the election of seven new Fellows in December 1956. They were: Melvin M. Johnson of Massachusetts; Ray Baker Harris of the District of Columbia; William F. Spaulding of England; Wendell K. Walker of New York; James R. Case of Connecticut; McIlyar H. Lichliter of Massachusetts; and Harry W. Bundy of Colorado.

"Freemasonry in Free China" was the topic Hugo V. Prucha, MPS, covered. "In 1951, because of the advances of the communists, the M.W.G.M. ordered the suspension of all Grand Lodge and of all subordinate Lodge activity," he wrote. "In 1953 when some of the former members were united once again in Taiwan, activities were resumed." He said that he, an American Mason, "felt right at home" during the work of the lodge he was visiting.

Vrooman told his readers in February 1957: "The Philalethes was once called THE ROYAL SOCIETY OF FREEMASONRY, and all of us have learned well the lesson that it is not possible to rest on past laurels, but that each of us must do something to make the *present* and the *future* equally worthy of support and Masonic activity."

"The Montana Highway Patrol emblem includes the numbers 3-7-77," once again Vrooman reminded his readers, and that this is an "old Vigilante warning advising lawless persons that they would occupy graves *three* feet wide, *seven* feet long and *seventy-seven* inches deep."

Death took another member of the Executive Committee on October 29, 1956. The Treasurer, Delbert C. Johnson of Missouri, was buried with Masonic rites by Rolla Lodge No. 213. G. Andrew McComb of Cleveland was appointed to fill the vacancy.

The Executive Committee established an award called the "Certificate of Literature" in an attempt to encourage good writing for *The Philalethes*. James R. Case received the first Certificate for his literary Masterpiece entitled "The Hamilton Bi-Centennial." (In operative times a mason craftsman's competence was demonstrated by cutting a master's piece in stone; now the word is used in connection with a sample of the work of a Masonic student.) In this article Case pointed out that Alexander Hamilton was never a Freemason.

It was announced this contest for the Certificate of Literature would be extend into 1957. Actually, it has been continued every year since, although there have been some years in which no Certificate was awarded. This wasn't because there were no articles deserving of the award, it was because there has been an "unwritten" perception that a winner can win but once. In those years that none was awarded it was because the committee making the selection wouldn't settle for "second best." A previous awardee had the best articles, in the opinion of the committees. So they authorized none.

In 1955 a few members of the American Lodge of Research of New York loosely organized a Workshop during the meetings of the Allied Masonic Bodies in Washington. These were continued in 1956 and 1957 under the sponsorship of The Philalethes Society with assistance from the Lodge. It was evident that there were many Masons present interested in furthering their Masonic knowledge. It was also evident that the feature had to be better organized. James R. Case was appointed to work on plans for the 1958 meeting.

The office of Executive Secretary had reached a point where Vrooman needed assistance. James K. Riley of St. Louis, Missouri, was appointed Assistant Executive Secretary, making official the work he had been doing for several months.

"After the candidate has been raised," wrote Alphonse Cerza, "Masonic literature should be placed in his hands so that he who can read may do so; he should be encouraged to read so that he may gain understanding; and with this understanding we will be creating a new and better Mason." Years later he encouraged Allen Roberts to write *The Craft and Its Symbols* as a presentation volume for this reason.

"I don't know all them big words, but I learn 'em, and someday I'll be a Mason," said a middle-aged man of Grecian background after he had been raised, according to Warren Fowler Mellny. This touched Mellny deeply. When he was called on to speak he used as his topic "Someday I'll Be a

Mason." He confessed "I have not always been a Mason, in its whole sense. Figuratively I have been a member." As he pondered this thought he concluded this is the case with far too many—there are many members, but too few Master Masons.

A giant among giants died on May 28, 1957. Carl H. Claudy, FPS-Life, author and Freemason-extraordinary, passed away in the District of Columbia. He is remembered for his excellent books and other writings. Few remember that it was he who saved The Masonic Service Association when, during its darkest hour, he took over the helm as its Executive Secretary in 1929. His story, and that of the Association, is told in *Freemasonry's Servant*.

As many great men had before and since, Carl Claudy was a high school dropout. As with all who attain greatness, he never stopped studying. His numerous books, articles, and accomplishments attest to that. He worked in Alaska prospecting for gold; as a traveling salesman; and a manufacturer's representative. He edited a science magazine, and his editing continued with other publications. He was a newspaper reporter, a photographer, and especially a freelance writer. In World War I he served as a major in the reserves. After he became a Freemason he devoted much of his life to furthering the aims of the Craft. Before his death he was perhaps the most decorated Freemason in the country, if not the world.

Carl H Claudy

Claudy's association with The Masonic Service Association began in 1923, and he served as an associate editor under Joseph Fort Newton, editor of *The Master Mason.* When the MSA had almost become extinct, with only seven member Grand Lodges left, the Association turned to Claudy for its salvation. He took the job of Executive Secretary for one-tenth the salary of his predecessor, and brought it back to life.

"What is Truth?" asked Roscoe Pound, FPS, in his "Masterpiece." "Cicero wrote," said Pound, "that on which all men are agreed must of necessity be true." Pound added: "But what all men agree upon may be only the fashion of thinking of the time and place." He continued: "Truth is a word of at least nine meanings of which the most significant are: Conformity to fact, exact accordance with what is or what has been, or what shall be; conformity to fixed starting points for reasoning; and righteousness—conformity to absolute or postulated standards of conduct. It was used in this sense in St. John's Gospel and in Paul's second Epistle to the Corinthians.

"Jesus used the word in the third sense. Pilate, as an Epicurean, thought of the first sense in terms of the origin and constitution of the physical universe, as to which Epicurus was thoroughly skeptical. As Mrs. Browning put it, Lucretius 'denied divinely the divine.' "

It was noted in October 1957 that Freemasonry played an important role in the dedication of the Harry S. Truman Library in Independence, Missouri, on July 9. The principal speaker was Chief Justice Earl Warren, a Past Grand Master of Masons in California. The parades featured Masons, and Masonic and political dignitaries from all over the country and world were present. They were there to pay tribute to the greatest Freemason of the twentieth century.

G. Andrew McComb, the acting Treasurer of the Society, was elected a Fellow.

The officers elected to govern the Society during the 1958–60 triennium were: William Moseley Brown, President; Elbert Bede, First Vice President; Charles Gottshall Reigner, Second Vice President; G. Andrew McComb, Executive Secretary; and James R. Case, Treasurer.

The Editor reported: "The Society is in the best shape it has been in since its birth. Activity, co-operation, contact, *work,* Masonic information and the exchange of ideas, and best of all—a co-ordination of effort, have brought the Society to a place in which it has the opportunity to *serve,* to amalgamate and to take its proper place in Masonic service."

Jan Jean Sibelius, MPS, an honorary member of the Grand Lodge of New York, died September 20, 1957.

Another Masonic giant was lost to the Craft. Melvin Maynard Johnson died on December 18, 1957. McIlyar H. Lichliter, FPS, wrote of Johnson:

"He had earned many titles and had worn them with distinction, but one title outshines them all—'FREEMASON.' "

Unlike many who rise to prominence in appendant bodies, Johnson's first love remained Ancient Craft Masonry. In the Grand Masters' Conferences he supported Symbolic Masonry as superior to any appendant body. In his position as Grand Commander of the Northern Masonic Jurisdiction of the Scottish Rite, he used his influence to support and work for Freemasonry in general.

In some circles he was praised and in others condemned for his support of Harry S. Truman. It was Johnson who backed Truman in his fight to force the Southern Jurisdiction of the Scottish Rite to return the 33rd degree to Ray V. Denslow, FPS. The full story of this episode will be found in *Brother Truman*.

It was Melvin Johnson who saw the need for assistance, monetary and moral, for those suffering from what is commonly called "schizophrenia," a mental disorder. In 1934, under his leadership, the Northern Masonic Jurisdiction of the Scottish Rite became the first organization to support the fight in this field. Before his death Johnson received many Masonic and civic awards for his service to his fellowman.

Allen Cabaniss, MPS, Grand Orator of the Grand Lodge of Mississippi, was named the winner of the second Certificate of Literature. "The Importance of the Fellowcraft Degree" was judged to be the best article for 1957. *The Men's House*, by Joseph Fort Newton, was highly recommended. Newton was termed "a Masonic Pioneer." Vrooman added: "His fresh, simple and straight forward way of giving his message has made his work endure far beyond ordinary lengths."

" 'Father' Taylor, one of the stalwarts of anti-Masonic days," wrote Vrooman, "whose prayer, 'Oh, Lord, Bless this Glorious Order; bless its friends; yea, bless its enemies, and make their hearts as soft as their heads. Amen.' was a rallying-cry to all who wanted a firm belief in Masonic principles."

The out-going President, Alphonse Cerza, pleaded with the members to continue working for the Society and Freemasonry. "The officers cannot do a good job without the help of the members," he rightly stated. The Executive Committee elected Cerza as a Life Fellow at the conclusion of his term of office.

The new President, William Moseley Brown, reminded the members that articles are always welcome for consideration in *The Philalethes*. The magazine "is *not* one which carries reprinted material. Certain types of articles are frankly not suitable for our purposes and those submitting them have to be notified accordingly."

The Philalethes for April 1958 covered the story of the third Masonic Workshop held in conjunction with the meetings of the Allied Masonic Degrees. It was held in the Statler Hotel in the District of Columbia on February 21. For the first time the presiding officer was the President of The Philalethes Society, William Moseley Brown. James R. Case, FPS, was the chairman. The Society had finally been recognized as *the source* for Masonic education. It would remain so to the present day.

The Workshop focused on "Masonic Bibliography." Papers were presented by Ronald E. Heaton, MPS, Ray Baker Harris, FPS, Wendell K. Walker, FPS, and Ward K. St. Clair, FPS. Each was a specialist in the field he covered. Harold V. B. Voorhis, FPS-Life, related some of the pitfalls to be found in Masonic research. Dr. William L. Cummings, MPS, suggested bibliographies were lacking in the English language. He cautioned his listeners not to "rely too much on Masonic Encyclopedias more than 50 years old, which are often inaccurate; [and not to] start out with preconceived ideas, attempting to reconcile the facts with these ideas—don't twist data."

The largest attendance to date was recorded. Forty-three Fellows and Members of the Society registered, thirty-four others were present. This would grow year by year.

Morton Deutsch, MPS, wrote a book titled *Whence Came You.* He covered some of his research for his book in an article called "Masonic Research." Among other things, he said he had actually found "the Lodge of the Holy Saints John of Jerusalem." He couldn't believe the stories he had heard about this being symbolic, or mythical, were true, so he set out on a quest to find it. "I did find 'it,' and its ruins still standing in Jerusalem in 1892, and corroborated the find by an actual photograph," he wrote. "The Masonic writer of today must be bold in his speculation. He certainly cannot expect to find records waiting for him, when our ancient enemy delighted in burning the same."

The following month, under "Recommended Masonic Reading," an unsigned author cautioned those who might read *Whence Came You.* "A combination of some deep thinking and much unverified and questionable facts, makes this work appear as a result of having slipped through the sieve of separation of fact and fiction. . . . The author has put together enough material for half a dozen books, without taking the time to check the truth and authenticity of what he has written."

William R. Denslow's *10,000 Famous Freemasons* was justly commended as a *must* volume for every Masonic library. The first volume was published by the Missouri Lodge of Research in 1957. Harry S. Truman, a Past Master of the Lodge and 33rd President of the United States, wrote its Foreword. There were to be three more in the series. No Masonic researcher would be caught without the set. So much in demand did it become that when it went out of print, Macoy Publishing and Masonic Supply Co. of Richmond, Virginia, took it over and has kept it in print.

The Grand Lodge of the Philippines issued a formal statement on July 8, 1958 agreeing "the Grand Lodge of Japan is now in Fraternal relations with the Grand Lodge of the Philippines, thus approving its request for fraternal recognition, with exchange of representatives." An unhealthy situation had been finally resolved. The way had been paved for recognition by other Grand Lodges.

"The Dead Sea Scrolls" found in the Judean desert near the Dead Sea in 1947 were examined by Ralph R. Walters, MPS. He searched for a Masonic connection with the Essenes, a connection that had been at least suggested by Albert Pike and Mackey and others. He could find none, but he didn't rule out the influence of the Essenes as developed by some of the founding fathers of the Craft.

Cerza told something of "the astounding story of Leo Taxil" who was named Gabriel Antoine Jogand at birth. Taxil spent his early life in a reformatory operated by the Jesuits, and developed "a great antagonism to the Church with special emphasis on clericalism." His flexible imagination produced a book entitled *Private Love Affairs of Pius IX,* "and [Taxil] was fined because of the obscene material contained in the book." His further activities earned him the reputation "of being the most dangerous enemy of the Roman Catholic Church."

In 1881 Taxil petitioned Freemasonry. With some hesitation he was accepted, but he didn't last long as an Entered Apprentice. After attending three meetings he was expelled. He then "recanted" and returned to the Church, informing the hierarchy he would write anti-Masonic books, a shrewd move to gain acceptance in the Church he had renounced. This he proceeded to do, even though his wife continued to turn out anti-clerical material.

Taxil created a "Miss Diana Vaughan, of Charleston, South Carolina, who was presented in 1895," wrote Cerza. "She was represented as having been born in 1874 as the daughter of the devil. Though really non-existent, Leo Taxil presented to his reading public copies of her memoirs in which she recited how she was dedicated to the devil when she was ten years of age, was initiated in an American Lodge, and was later wedded to the devil. Month after month she issued copies of documents which were represented as being true and recited the events of these satanic lodges."

So true did the material appear, "Diana" received thousands of letters praising her for her work. "She" sent a contribution to Cardinal Parocci who was to conduct an "Anti-Masonic Congress" in Trent in September 1896. This Congress was attended by a large number of the Catholic hierarchy. A German delegate who saw through the hoax was denounced as being a tool of the Masons. Taxil held a meeting in the hall of the Geographical Society in Paris on Easter Monday, 1897. He told the large crowd "that Diana Vaughan was non-existent and that for twelve years he had been fooling the Roman Catholic Church." Taxil had to be protected from the angry mob by police. The Church remained unusually silent about the hoax. And its damage lives on as Taxil's story still surfaces occasionally.

The Philalethes for October 1958 announced that Dr. Charles H. Pugh of North Carolina, and Dr. William L. Cummings of New York had been elected Fellows of The Philalethes Society. The President spoke with justifiable pride about the service the Society had rendered during the past thirty years. "Others planted and we have reaped!" he said. "Those who preceded us have builded better than they knew. . . .

"As we observe our thirtieth anniversary, let us all rejoice together at the progress which has been made, the contributions which our members have given to the great Fraternity of which we are avowedly a part, the opportunities for service which have been ours, and the acceptance of our Society by the leaders of Masonry all over the world. There has also been a 'union of hearts' and a welding of spirits among our members, all for the good of Masonry and of mankind. For what is the object of our Fraternity if it is not to serve men for the glory of God and the advancement of brotherhood. . . . How sorely is the realization of this purpose needed just now! With all our rejoicing, let us in humility render thanks to the Supreme Architect of the Universe for all His blessings to us and to our Brethren wheresoever dispersed upon the face of the globe!"

Brown noted that the membership had grown to "more than 500 strong, and with its Fellowship of some of the most outstanding Masons of the world." He called upon members of the Society, in groups of two or more, to celebrate this thirtieth year to hold birthday celebrations throughout the land. This would be done and the response was greater than anyone could have suspected. He asked for a doubling of the membership during the next two years so the Society, through its magazine, could be a leader in the spreading of truth. He praised the Workshops which had now "become the special responsibility of The Philalethes Society."

He concluded: "It has been my experience that most of us do not have to go too far in Masonic study before they are 'bitten by the bug,' so to speak, and become inveterate students of the history, jurisprudence, symbolism, and philosophy of the Craft. Each of us *must* have a 'philosophy of life.' How helpful are the teachings of our Fraternity in the formulation of that philosophy!"

"Someone said many years ago, 'The person who knows how to read and does not read, is no better than the person who does not know how to read,' " wrote Cerza in the December 1958 issue of *The Philalethes*. "There is a great deal of wisdom in those words. The purpose of reading is threefold: To secure facts, to receive pleasure, and to find inspiration."

Cerza cautioned his readers to check what they read. Most "old Masonic books are not necessarily reliable. Some things improve with age, but not books written with imagination rather than facts." He felt too many well-meaning Masons with poor judgement and little experience had produced books that have misled the unwary. He suggested book reviews be studied. He recommended the following Masonic authors as authoritative: "H.L. Haywood, Carl H. Claudy, Roscoe Pound, Melvin M. Johnson, Joseph Fort Newton, William Moseley Brown, Charles C. Hunt, and Ray V. Denslow."

The Editor of *The Philalethes*, John Black Vrooman, found some correspondence written prior to the formation of The Philalethes Society. George M. Imbrie wrote to Cyrus Field Willard on January 15, 1927: "You and I would never have joined the Masons had we not learned something of its philosophy. Should we form a society on the same lines you suggest, would it not be almost a counterpart of the old Royal Society [of England] of the old days?

"Therefore, is it not possible that these men [of the old Royal Society] became philosophers through their connection with the old Masonic society?" Evidently Willard, and then Robert I. Clegg, agreed and The Philalethes Society was born.

During the annual meeting of the Executive Committee in February, James Case resigned as Treasurer to devote more time to research. Ronald E. Heaton of Norristown, Pennsylvania, was appointed to this position. Heaton was the financial officer of the Synthane Corporation and would retire shortly after this appointment. He, along with Case, had become an expert in the Masonic history of the Revolutionary period.

George C. Marquis of Missouri wrote a letter which was published in the February 1959 issue of *The Philalethes*. He had recently heard that George Imbrie had been the first President of the Society. (Actually, Willard was the first President, Imbrie was the first Executive Secretary.) He told how Imbrie was scheduled to give the lecture of the Most Excellent Master degree in a Chapter at Harrisonville, Missouri. Marquis met Imbrie while the latter was waiting to give the lecture. "George immediately arose and advanced toward me," said Marquis. As they met in the center of the room, "George put his hand on my shoulder, then fell against me, and was unable to speak. We laid him on a sofa in the room and called a physician. George never regained consciousness, and died in the hospital in Harrisonville that night."

Ronald E. Heaton was declared the winner of the Certificate of Literature for 1958. His "Some Conjectured American Freemasons" was deemed the best article for the year. The President appointed John Black Vrooman as Executive Secretary, *pro tem.*, to replace G. Andrew McComb who had resigned.

The meetings of the Allied Masonic Degrees moved from the Statler Hotel to the Hotel Washington in February 1959. On the 20th the President of The Philalethes Society conducted a business meeting. Then the fifth annual Workshop was convened with Dr. Charles G. Reigner, FPS, Second Vice President presiding as the chairman. The subject discussed was "Source Materials in Masonic Study."

Those present learned source material may be found almost everywhere. Newspapers, periodicals, state records, libraries, tombstones, histories, clipping services. Even books not Masonic in nature, as well as journals and other papers, often contain important Masonic information. The richest source is the well stocked Masonic library.

William J. Whalen, an anti-Mason, published a book entitled *Christianity and American Freemasonry.* Cerza wrote: "It bears the official approval of the Roman Catholic censor and the Archbishop of Milwaukee. . . . This book sings the same old tune in a different pitch. In a clever way the author congratulates the Craft for its many benevolences, he praises the many fine men who have been Masons, but is opposed to the so-called "secret aims" of Freemasonry. He infers these aims are so secret that most Masons have never heard of them! It never occurred to him that if they are so secret they do not, in fact, exist."

Whalen updated his 1959 tome in 1986. It was obvious from his personal correspondence with me and others that he had in no way changed his opinion of Freemasonry. It was he, more than any other person, who convinced the Catholic Bishops that they should prohibit Catholic men from petitioning Masonic Lodges. He claims Freemasonry is incompatible with Christianity, a theme many fundamentalist religions have adopted. It was he who, through the Catholic Bishops' report, caused some Grand Lodges, or Grand officers, to endeavor to change or do away with the age-old symbolic penalties recited by initiates into Freemasonry. Without question, Whalen has had an adverse influence on American Freemasonry far surpassing that of any other person of the twentieth century.

Bliss Kelly, MPS, said "Penalties are Self-Inflictive." In discussing the penalties one should take into account the rules of grammar. "When this is done," he wrote, "it is at once clear that all these penalties are self-executing. No Mason is to execute any penalty upon anyone, and no Lodge, officer or group is to perform any act which would carry out any penalty. Each candidate binds himself under no less penalty than having certain things done to himself—no one else is to do it. *Each member is to execute the penalty upon himself.*"

Lee E. Wells was making a name for himself as a professional writer. Several of his books had been published, and more would be. The Executive Committee, evidently in recognition of Wells's efforts to revitalize the Society, elected him a Life Fellow.

In 1927 *The Cabletow*, the official publication of the Grand Lodge of the Philippines, had printed "The Masonic Editor's Vow." It reprinted it in 1959. Vrooman thought so highly of it he ran it as his editorial in the April 1959 issue of *The Philalethes*. Here it is:

THE MASONIC EDITOR'S VOW

I am firmly resolved: To write only that which is clean and true and for the best interest of the Craft; to endeavor to instruct and enlighten the readers of my paper; to let brotherly love, tolerance and charity guide me in my judgment of persons, things and events; to be temperate in expression, show fortitude under attack, display prudence in dealing with questions of moment, and endeavor to do justice to all, whether friend or foe.

I will not mock or belittle that which others firmly believe to be right, just and holy, nor will I hurt the feelings of any person, great or small, if I can help it.

I will not allow my judgment and policy to be influenced by mercenary motives, but will proceed without fear or favor and prefer honest poverty to ill-gained affluence.

Towards my colleagues of the press I will ever be courteous and honest, abstaining from borrowing their thoughts and ideas and copying their work without giving due credit in each case, and I will do all I can to bring Masonic journalism to that high level which it should and must occupy.

Throughout the years each Editor of *The Cabletow* has fulfilled this vow. The publication is one of the better Masonic journals still being published. Each Editor of *The Philalethes* has, perhaps unknowingly, followed this vow without exception. The Society has indeed been fortunate in the caliber of the men chosen to edit its official publication.

In the 1960s colleges and universities in the United States were hotbeds of discontent. Drugs, alcohol, and promiscuity were rampant. Speakers with other than "ultra liberal" viewpoints were unwelcome at many of these institutions of "higher learning." Even in this enlightened year of 1988 the same situation is far too often prevalent. It may come as a surprise to learn there are students on the other side of the picture.

In 1897 a Square and Compass club was formed at Washington and Lee University at Lexington, Virginia, according to *The Philalethes* for August 1959. This club received a charter from the state of Virginia on May 12, 1917 under the name of "Square and Compass Fraternity." During "the next eleven years fifty-seven Collegiate Squares (chapters) were established." In these about five thousand men were initiated, "including fifteen college and university presidents, many Grand Lodge officers, professional men, and important public officials." The name was changed in December 1950 to "Square and Compass—Sigma Alpha Chi."

At Tri-State College, Angola, Indiana, Sigma Mu Sigma was founded in 1921. The founders were "three Knights Templar, who with nine other Master Masons received a charter from the State of Indiana. In 1924 the National Council of Sigma Mu Sigma received its charter from the United States Government." Nine more collegiate chapters were formed. This fraternity "received the Highest Interfraternity Scholastic Rating."

The two fraternities were united on August 3, 1952, "in the Masonic Temple, Angola, Indiana. The name became "Square and Compass—Sigma Mu Sigma." The first Grand President elected was Dr. Harry K. Eversull; the first Grand Secretary was Dr. William Moseley Brown, FPS, soon to become President of The Philalethes Society.

This fraternity's purpose? "To thoroughly indoctrinate the college men of America with the traditions of our American Heritage, through ritualistic and fraternity-conducted educational programs devoted to a more comprehensive understanding of the Rites of Initiation and our American Way of Life."

The Philalethes for August 1964 carried "Collegiate Freemasons" by Almond Fairfield, MPS. The article covered the history of fraternities connected in some manner with Freemasonry. He substantiated Vrooman's earlier work. Fairfield went a step further: "The Masonic Lodge established by Williamsburg Masons in 1751 received a new constitution and charter from England in 1773. This might have had some influence upon the founders of Phi Beta Kappa who met in the Apollo Room of the Raleigh Tavern that stood some three hundred yards from the Williamsburg Lodge Hall."

"The Collegiate Order of the Golden Key was first conferred at the University of Oklahoma, March 21, 1925," Fairfield added. Several Grand Lodge of Oklahoma officers and Past Grand Masters were the recipients. "The ritual was written by a college Mason for college Masons with the purpose of giving them a comprehensive understanding of the Rites of Initiation and of Masonic philosophy." According to Fairfield, "the Order of the Golden Key is the only one that remains strictly Masonic by limiting its initiates to Master Masons."

Fairfield also mentioned that Freemasons in England and America had been early supporters of public education, long before others took up the cause. He told the story of three men armed with a mall and chisel who were working on a cathedral. The first was asked what he was doing. "I'm carving this stone," said the first. The second replied, "I'm earning a penny a day." The third exclaimed, "I'm building a cathedral!"

David R. Lane, MPS, wrote in an article entitled "Why Masonry Must

Teach By Symbols": "Our institution leaves every member free to find what light and truth he can, and if what he finds does not happen to coincide with what some other Brother has found, that is all right with Masonry." To aid the "plodder and the genius," he said, is to teach through symbols. "Masonry is not alone in the use of symbols to convey truths. Men have been using symbols as far back as we know anything about civilized peoples. All the early religions made use of symbols. Christianity makes liberal use of them today."

Normally Alphonse Cerza ignored Masonic books he considered unworthy for the thinking Freemason to read. This wasn't the case with *Freemasonry, a Sleeping Giant* by Charles Van Cott. He tore it apart! He felt so strongly about its contents his review deserves to be recorded in full.

This is a book of 352 pages which contains apparently a reproduction of articles formerly published in the author's magazine *Masonic Inspiration.* The jacket, in several colors, contains the Masonic emblem, and contains some sensational statements such as "Startling—a Bombshell Report," and "Critical Review of U.S. Masonry." It also states that it is "six great books in one," but a reading failed to disclose what "six" books are meant; and in my opinion, the word "great" is a gross exaggeration.

I have seen a number of copies of the author's leaflet or magazine. Each of those which I have seen have glaring headlines designed to attract attention in the sensational manner of some newspapers. The material in the book is not arranged in logical order. The items often have no relation to one another as they appear page after page and one gets the impression that the author at random picked out items from his magazine and threw them together to fill the pages. While the author has an engaging style, writes pithy sentences as adopted by the professional news writer, his facts are not always correct, and he states so many personal opinions that fact and opinion is not easy to differentiate.

In my opinion this book will do a great deal of harm. The author has appointed himself the champion of the Craft to accomplish things which are foreign to Freemasonry. He has stirred himself to a pitch of apparent fever and wants to use the Craft as a vehicle to impose his views on the community. He urges that the Craft engage in battle with the Roman Catholic Church; this is a violation of the Ancient Landmarks. Many of his suggestions are political in nature; these also are in violation of Masonic law. The publication of the book is a private business venture by the author; the use of the Masonic emblem for such purposes is questioned. The few items in the book that are of interest are so few that it is not worth while wading through the rest of the material. It is regrettable that one who has such talent should waste it in such an effort.

Continuing a long tradition, the cornerstone of the extension of the East Front of the United States Capitol was laid with Masonic rites. The ceremonies took place on July 4, 1959. The honors were performed by the Grand

Lodge of the District of Columbia. The Editor of *The Philalethes* noted: "The first record of a cornerstone laying by a Masonic body is found in *Mist's Weekly Journal,* May 26, 1722, the affair being in connection with the building of St. Martin's-in-the-Fields at London, England."

The laying of a cornerstone by Freemasons is an innocent practice and can cause no problems, right? Wrong! The dismissal of the Architect of the Capitol was demanded. The Archdiocese of Washington, D.C., refused the invitation to be present on July 4. Why? "We simply do not feel that a Catholic priest could participate by giving a benediction for a ceremony in which the Masons perform quasi-religious rites." Were the heated objections correct? Perhaps the words of President Dwight D. Eisenhower, not a Freemason, answers this.

> Finally, we gather on the Fourth of July, as our forefathers did at Independence Hall, more than ninescore years ago, to emulate them as they pledge their common adherence to basic principles, and their common obligation to uphold these principles regardless of differences of opinion, even of policy.
>
> So long as we never waver in our devotion to the values on which these men began the building of the Nation, no differences of partisan policy or partisan feelings can cause America to falter on her upward course.

Cerza observed: "What lesson can we learn from this incident? This cornerstone and Independence Day, 1959, bring to the front a problem which will re-appear in the days to come. It is fitting that we face it here and now as Americans and Masons." He outlined some of the history of the laying of cornerstones by Freemasons.

"It might well be construed that the hierarchy of this church is not in sympathy with the principles of Americanism," continued Cerza, "which is supported by history and tradition. It is to be noted that three clergymen took part in the ceremony; they found no difficulty observing the Masonic ceremony because it is clearly not a religious service."

Cerza added: "The enigma of the Roman Catholic Church can be understood only if one considers that this organization has a dual aspect. The friction between this church and others does not arise because of the religious beliefs, or ceremonies, or practices of the devoted members in and out of the clergy class but rather in the determination of hierarchy to impose its political and social views on the rest of the community. The mystery disappears when one recognizes that the leaders of this church are acting not only as clergymen but as politicians and social minutemen."

"I am afraid," Cerza concluded, "that future historians writing the history of this era will state that in our great concern for the Bolshevist menace we overlooked an insidious movement within our gate, burrowing at our very foundation, while hiding behind a religious cloak of respectability."

Carl R. Greisen, Grand Secretary-Recorder of the "York Rite Bodies" of Nebraska, was elected a Fellow of The Philalethes Society on August 20, 1959. He was immediately thereafter elected Executive Secretary, a position he would fill with distinction for a number of years.

The founder of the Order of DeMolay, Frank S. Land, died after a short illness on November 8, 1959.

In his editorial for February 1960, Vrooman cautioned the Society against taking on the promotion of various pet projects. "As we have often stated," he wrote, "one of the objectives of the Society is to have a medium through which its members may interchange and develop their ideas and research in Freemasonry. Ours is a group whose sole objective is to help each other to better understand and spread the principles of Freemasonry."

Alphonse Cerza listed ten criteria for the would-be writer to ask himself: 1. Do I really have a desire to write on this subject? 2. Do I have the ability to write? 3. Is the subject I have selected of general interest? 4. Is my desire to write merely to see my name in print? 5. Is my subject too broad? 6. Is the subject I have selected one that has been overworked? 7. Is the subject I have selected likely to add something to the readers' knowledge? 8. Have I verified all the facts which I will include in the manuscript? 9. Am I merely stirred up over this matter and merely trying to 'sell' my opinion? 10. Am I trying to connect up Freemasonry with some other group?

During the Workshop in D.C. in February 1960, William R. Denslow spoke on "Pitfalls and Pratfalls in Compiling Masonic Biographies." In his office, he said, he had cabinets full of Masonic biographies and for more than eight years much of his time had been spent with them. He quoted Thomas Carlyle as having said: "History is the essence of innumerable biographies. . . . Biography is by nature the most universally profitable, universally pleasant of all things; especially biography of distinguished individuals."

"If history is to be accurately presented, minute care must be exercised in the recording of biographies," Denslow added. "Inaccurate biographies mean inaccurate history. The nineteenth century was notorious for Masonic journalism in the United States. Scores of Masonic magazines and journals were published, each trying to make larger claims than its contemporaries. The rule-of-thumb for claiming Masonic membership for distinguished individuals was, 'If you saw it in print, it's true'; and the more often it was reprinted, the truer it became."

Denslow had learned all the "tricks of the trade" it would appear, for he continued: "Another favorite dodge was the use of quotes to escape responsibility and yet lend an air of authenticity." Most erroneous statements come from "after-dinner speakers" who like to drop names. Again he quoted Carlyle: "I hate quotations. Tell me what you know!"

Francis J. Scully, FPS, told those attending the Workshop about "Compiling Masonic Biographies." He suggested ways to obtain them: From the family; Masonic *Proceedings*; Obituary notices in newspapers; Masonic libraries; Masonic publications and books; Masonic scholars and writers. He urged everyone to prepare his own biography and keep it with his important papers.

Roscoe Pound was awarded the Certificate of Literature for 1959 for his article "What Is Law?"

Shortly after William R. Denslow spoke, his father, Ray Vaughn Denslow, received special recognition from the United Grand Lodge of Germany through its Grand Master, Dr. Theodor Vogel. It was a timely commendation. On September 11, 1960 Ray Denslow died. The Masonic world lost a great Freemason, one whose friendship spread around the globe.

Ray Denslow had been an advisor and mentor to Harry S. Truman from the moment Truman entered the "line" in the Grand Lodge of Missouri. In fact, Ray, a Republican, supported Truman, a Democrat, for the first step of the rung to become Grand Master. Throughout his Masonic career, Truman turned to Ray for counsel. It was little wonder that Truman appointed Ray to head a commission to go overseas to study the Masonic difficulties in Europe following the close of World War II.

John Vrooman said Ray Denslow's contributions could be summed up in four categories. "First and foremost, it was in the field of the *human side* of Freemasonry that he shone the brightest. No man was too humble or too obscure to be contacted and helped by him when the need arose. . . . [Second] Ray Denslow excelled in his ability to read and analyze human character. . . . [Third] was in the field of Masonic research and study. . . . [Fourth] was his continued, myriad and amazing writing. Masonically, there are few, if any, who have excelled this brilliant and understanding Mason in contribution to the literature of Freemasonry."

Ray Denslow had created and published *The Royal Arch Mason* magazine and had a subscription list of over one hundred thousand. So well did he build its foundation it has continued. His son, William, followed where his father left off. When his eyesight began to fail, the magazine was turned over to Jerry Marsengill, Editor of *The Philalethes*, to edit. It still has a circulation of over one hundred thousand.

Cerza highly recommended the second edition of the book by Bernard E. Jones, *Freemasons' Guide and Compendium*.

In an article entitled "The Right to Speak," Cerza condemned the censorship imposed by the Roman Catholic Church on its adherents. He spoke highly of several Catholic clergymen who defied "the rule of Rome." He retold the story of the four chaplains who gave up their lives to help soldiers when their troop ship, the *Dorchester*, was torpedoed by a German submarine in February 1943. A chapel to honor these four men of God was erected in Philadelphia. In 1951 men of all faiths were invited to ceremonies to memorialize the occasion.

"One of those invited to the banquet held when the chapel was about to be completed was a Congressman named John F. Kennedy," wrote Cerza. "He accepted the invitation to attend the banquet at a hotel in Philadelphia. He was invited as a leading Roman Catholic layman. Two days before the affair Kennedy called Dr. [Daniel A.] Poling and advised him that he could not attend. He gave as his reason that Cardinal Dougherty, of Philadelphia, had advised him not to appear. Kennedy was told by Dr. Poling that the affair was at a public place, not at a church, that men of other religious groups were attending, and that there was nothing sectarian about the affair. Kennedy stated that he understood all this, but yet could not attend. . . . It was necessary to prepare new programs so that it would not be necessary to mention the incident and embarrass the Congressman.

"Later, when the dedication ceremonies were to take place, General James O'Neill, Deputy Chief of Chaplains of the United States Army, accepted an invitation to attend as a member of the Roman Catholic Church. A few days before the dedication he too called Dr. Poling and informed him that Cardinal Dougherty had advised him not to attend the dedication.

"Brother Truman, then President of the United States, attended the dedication ceremonies. He spoke with feeling about the four heroes and this fitting memorial in their honor. He was speaking in the spirit of Masonry and Americanism when he said: 'These four chaplains obeyed the Divine Commandment that men should love one another. . . . This is an old faith in our country. It is shared by all churches and all denominations . . . the unity in our country comes from this fact.' " Cerza asks: "Is our American way of life going to be changed slowly and indirectly by a religious power whose beliefs are foreign to our fundamental principles?"

Dr. Daniel A. Poling, editor of the *Christian Herald* and pastor emeritus of Marble Collegiate Church in New York City, said: "I have found that the outstanding Christian leaders in the great churches of American today, have been and are members of the Masonic fraternity." This clergyman in the Dutch Reformed Church was from a Masonic family. His great-grandfather, grandfather and father were Freemasons. His son, also a clergyman, was a member of the Craft. So wrote A. Warren Cate, MPS, for the February 1963 issue of *The Philalethes*.

Poling became the Chaplain of the Chapel of Four Chaplains in Philadelphia in 1948. His son, Clark V. Poling, was one of those four Chaplains who gave up his life to help save those who were aboard the *U.S.S. Dorchester.* At the time he became a Freemason he said: "I arrived at the decision that Masonry is a vital and dynamic force in America, and in the world, for everything high and worthy to which my life has long been committed. And there is something more. Masonry occupies, in my opinion, a unique position of opportunity and obligation in the human order today."

In the December 1960 issue of *The Philalethes* James R. Case revealed who the only Masonic governors were during the founding period of the United States. As of the 4th of July 1776 there were three: Archibald Bullock of Georgia; Richard Caswell of North Carolina; and Henry Laurens of South Carolina. There were two as of October 19, 1781: Nathan Brownson of Georgia, and John Hancock of Massachusetts. On April 30, 1789 there were five: George Walton of Georgia; John Hancock; John Sullivan of New Hampshire; Alexander Martin of North Carolina; and Thomas Chittenden of Vermont. Case places a "?" after the name of Thomas Nelson of Virginia and John Eager Howard of Maryland.

Concluded Case: "It can be seen that never at any time during the period between the Battle of Lexington and the day when the Republic was born was there a time when *all* of the governors of the thirteen, states, or states-to-be were Freemasons. . . . The *total* does not even reach thirteen."

During the year a bonus booklet written by Ronald E. Heaton titled *Valley Forge Yesterday and Today* was distributed to the members. This was another indication the Society had developed past the dreams of its founders. The membership was over 600 and growing.

7. EXPANDING
(1960–1962)

*I*t's unusual for a newspaper to carry anything favorable concerning Freemasonry. The *New York Post* for December 22, 1960 did when it ran Leonard Lyons' column "The Lyons Den." *The Philalethes* carried it in full.

SOCIAL NOTE: Gregory Ratoff's friends who attended his funeral here this week were surprised that it included a Masonic ritual too. Ratoff, a true cosmopolite who was at home in all the capitals of the world, somehow didn't appear to be a joiner of anything except Actors Equity and the Screen Directors Guild. Darryl Zanuck explained it.

Years ago Zanuck went on a six week hunting trip through Canada. His companions were several directors—Raymond Griffith, Lloyd Bacon and also John Adolphi—whose credits included the George Arliss film, "The Man Who Played God." Adolphi suddenly suffered a heart attack and died. Zanuck decided to bring the body back to his widow, so that she could collect his insurance without having to wait years until there'd be a "presumption of death."

It was a six-day trip back to the base. Zanuck had the body packed and repacked in ice, constantly, until they reached their base at a village called Revelstoke. The coroner first wanted proof of identity. The man's pockets produced a Masonic card with his photo. The coroner convened a jury of villagers, who certified the cause of death.

The next day Zanuck and his friends accompanied the coffin to the railroad station, where they boarded the train back to California. And at the station, in this tiny Canadian town, they found 100 men in Masons' regalia waiting to bid good-bye to the dead Hollywood director they had never met, and of whom they knew nothing except that he was a Mason. Zanuck told this story to Ratoff, who insisted: "I must join the Masons."

"A new day has dawned," said John Black Vrooman in February 1961. "Another *Triennium* of The Philalethes Society has been ushered into the history of our Society.

"New faces, new ideas, the utilizing of old officers and their ideas, and the blending of the old and the new into a workable unity, bring a bloom to the cheeks of the new cycle."

Elbert Bede of Oregon, eighty years young, took over the helm of the Society as the President. Dr. Charles Gottshall Reigner of Maryland was the First Vice President, and Robert H. Gollmar, Second Vice President. Greisen remained Executive Secretary and Heaton, Treasurer.

The new President set forth some of his plans and thoughts in a special column.

Benjamin Elbert Bede

It has occurred to me that we have in our Society the cream of Masonic students and editors, yet we are not acquainted with one another. I know short biographical sketches of our members would be of interest to me, and I imagine they would be to the entire membership. If our exchequer was in condition to finance a booklet containing such biographies, I should seriously suggest such a booklet as one of the bonuses we hope to give in addition to our magazine.

I regret there is not sufficient space available in our magazine for such a project. I should welcome letters from the membership giving me their ideas on this subject.

What we are able to finance depends entirely upon our income from joining fees and annual dues. We should look forward to providing three or four bonus publications each year, but at present we are financially handicapped. . . .

We should, wherever possible, get our magazine into Masonic libraries that have reading rooms. Some members may wish to make gifts of such subscriptions.

I cannot too strongly urge our members to be regular attendants at their Craft Lodges, and always they should be prepared to make short speeches unexpectedly. Members of Philalethes are presumed to be prepared to spread Masonic light. They should be quick to accept invitations to make formal addresses on Masonic subjects.

Know your Philalethes Society and its work and be ever ready to tell others about it.

William Moseley Brown, the immediate Past President, was elected a Life Fellow of the Society. He also became the Grand Abbot of the Society of Blue Friars, a position that had been held by Ray V. Denslow at his death.

A far-reaching announcement was made by Harold V. B. Voorhis at the opening of the Workshop on February 24, 1961. Henry Wilson Coil, FPS, of California, had completed his *Encyclopedia*. It would be published by Macoy Masonic Publication and Supply Company. This would replace Mackey's as the standard reference work for Freemasonry.

President Elbert Bede opened the Workshop with a brief business meeting. Charles K. A. McGaughey, MPS, took over as the chairman. Charles F. Gosnell, MPS, and Conrad Hahn. MPS, Editor of publications for The Masonic Service Association, presented papers. Over 200 interested Masons were present.

Ronald E. Heaton, Treasurer of the Society, was elected a Fellow, not only for his financial work but for the excellence of his Masonic research. Through his efforts, all who cared to read would learn who the actual Freemasons were among the Founding Fathers of the United States.

Carl R. Greisen, the Executive Secretary, was elected President of the Masonic Relief Association of the United States and Canada. This association was organized in 1885 to add strength to the the few similar local groups then operating to relieve distressed Masons. It concerns itself mainly with Freemasons away from home who need assistance. Its work is little known among the rank and file members, but its services are invaluable to the Grand Lodges of the two countries.

The Editor, John Black Vrooman, told the membership in June 1961: "It is with pride we announce that a booklet, *The Masonic Fraternity, Its Character, Customs, Ideals and Traditions*, written by the late Ray V. Denslow, FPS, will be sent at an early date to each member. . . . Another splendid bonus [will be] given the membership, this being *The Degrees of Masonry*, by Dr. Charles Gottshall Reigner, FPS, First Vice President."

The Editor also stated: "It Seems To Me That as this country brings to mind the conditions, happenings and background of the War of the

Rebellion—the American Civil War, that it can be well said that Freemasonry played a large and important part in determining the final outcome. Worshipful Brother Allen E. Roberts, MPS, has made an outstanding contribution to this phase of our national history, and the first of his articles, written especially for *The Philalethes*, appears in this issue."

Vrooman was referring to "Masonry Under Two Flags." The series ran for ten months. Later it became a book published by The Masonic Service Association under the same title. It won for Roberts the Certificate of Literature for 1961.

The Philalethes reported that George E. Bushnell of the Northern Masonic Jurisdiction of the Scottish Rite testified in Philadelphia. He was a witness in a case concerning a Prince Hall Masonic group and "a bogus organization." A portion of the testimony is recorded:

Q. Judge Bushnell, you have already defined and distinguished the word "clandestine." Is there any other Negro Masonic body in the United States that the Northern Masonic Jurisdiction of the United States of the Supreme Council recognizes as being legitimate other than Prince Hall?

A. No, sir. . . . We know that Prince Hall is legitimate.

Q. Are you in a position, Judge, to tell me why?

A. We know that they are legitimate in their origin. We know that they are right in their philosophy. We know that they are trying to benefit mankind. We know that a lot of these other groups are just commercializing Masonry and preying on their fellow citizens and adding to the misery of the world and we don't want to have any part of it.

Robert H. Gollmar, the Second Vice President, was elected a Fellow of The Philalethes Society in June 1961. He was a Past Grand Master of Masons in Wisconsin and the Foreign Correspondent for that Grand Lodge.

The death of Laurence R. Taylor, FPS, a long-time worker in the field of Masonic education in Indiana, was noted in June. At the same time a prepublication offer was noted by the Missouri Lodge of Research for its forthcoming book, *House Undivided: The Story of Freemasonry and the Civil War*.

The Philalethes for August 1961 carried an editorial written by James Fairbairn Smith, FPS, in his *Masonic World*. "Masonic education," wrote Smith, "is being experimented with all over the country. . . . Above all, some have made the devastating blunder of assuming that we wanted to be educated. This was a tragic error for we have no more desire for mental pablum than we have for a stiff dose of jalap. We want to be amused and, perhaps, stimulated but never educated."

Much of the balance of Smith's opinion is worth absorbing:

What we want is something direct, startling, breathtaking, that piques our curiosity, flatters our vanity, or gives us a mental jolt; and boil it down in capsule form. We like to be told that fourteen Presidents of the United States were Masons; that Stoney Creek Lodge No. 7 alone, kept the light of Masonry burning in Michigan for eleven years during the anti-Masonic period. . . Masonic historians have, by a sort of diabolical consent, written the driest, dreariest lot of stuff and overlooked really interesting episodes and personalities. There is an inexhaustible fund of romance and glamour in the story of our beloved Craft that our history writers have not recognized at all. . . .

We suggest that the phrase "Masonic Education" be thrown into the waste basket, next that all heavyweights with the bulging foreheads should be kept off the committee as should all word-mongers, phrase-makers, forty-minute sermonizers, pedants, dry-as-dusts, and "literary fellars." A good committee might be made up of a newspaper man, a publicity expert, a scenario writer, a mechanic, and an old-fashioned tiler. The tiler knows the likes and dislikes of the rank and file and the ante-room is surely the real clearing house for ideas, criticisms, and good suggestions. The scenario writer should be able to judge dramatic values and popular reactions. The newspaper man could present the material in a concise, readable, and understandable style. The mechanic could be used as a test tube upon whom all plans could be tried out. The Publicity man would dress up the material and put it over. To this, a successful salesman might be added, and a Past Grand Master to serve as the voice of conservatism.

Lastly, since the fellows who duck educational programs are, also, those who watch TV, attend movie shows and read the daily paper, it might be well to entitle our endeavor "The Romance and Glamour that is Freemasonry."

These are the methods that are guaranteed to get Masonic Education out of the clouds and down where the average Mason lives.

Members of the Society were filling many important offices throughout the Craft. Many more would serve Freemasonry in influential capacities throughout the years. In October 1961 *The Philalethes* informed its readers that Charles K.A. McGaughey, MPS, had been selected General Grand Secretary of the General Grand Chapter, Royal Arch Masons, International. McGaughey had spent a life time working for Freemasonry; he would continue to do so through this position to this day.

William R. Denslow, the author of *10,000 Famous Freemasons, Freemasonry and the American Indian,* Editor of *The Royal Arch Mason,* and writer of many valuable articles, was elected a Fellow of The Philalethes Society.

Avery Allen and his anti-Masonic works was the topic of an article by William T. Hastings published in the December 1961 issue of *The Philalethes.* It would appear that Allen had once been a member of the Craft. His anti-Masonic works, however, seemed to be based on the legitimate works of Webb and Cross, along with anti-Masonic material he found in the writings of others.

There were 706 Members and Fellows on the roster of the Society as of December 31, 1961, *The Philalethes* reported in April 1962. The Workshop was a resounding success. Its theme had been "Methods and Tools for Masonic Research." The panel for the discussion period consisted of Harold V.B. Voorhis, William Moseley Brown, Allen E. Roberts, Ray Baker Harris and John Black Vrooman. The Chairman was Charles F. Gosnell, one of the speakers, along with Conrad Hahn and Bruce H. Hunt.

Hunt said: "As Freemasons we must look beyond the tiled precincts of our mother lodges. We cannot and must not confine our thoughts to the political boundaries of our Grand Lodges. The universality of Freemasonry must become vivid and real in our minds. Our brethren in far and distant lands are but a few hours away! Their problems must become our concern also. There must be unity between Masons wheresoever dispersed throughout the habitable world."

A mythical story had been circulating concerning the Lodge of the Holy Sts. John at Jerusalem. It had been claimed it was located over Clerkenwall Gate in London. Harry Carr of England was asked to research the truth. He reported: "Most of the quotation is pure imagination run riot. The Gate still spans the road, and we have records of the room (now called the library) having been used as a lodge room from circa 1750 to circa 1880. The building is now the headquarters of the Order of St. John (non-Masonic), and has had no Masonic connections for approximately 80 years.

"There are no secret passages, no gavel of King Richard, and it is extremely doubtful if its Masonic history goes back any further than circa 1700, though Lodges of a kind have met there as far back as the Great Fire."

William R. Denslow, FPS, the immediate Past Grand High Priest in Missouri, and recently appointed Junior Grand Steward of the Grand Lodge, wrote about leadership for the August 1962 issue of *The Philalethes*. He believed most of the Craft's problems could be solved with hard work and improved officers.

"We need better leadership in Masonry," said Denslow. "Unless we have effective officers, your Masonic bodies will decay." He strongly advocated a shortening of the time required to reach the top. A good man cannot take the time necessary from his personal life "doing little but attending hundreds of meetings—none of which call for his ability, leadership or imagination. His life is full and demanding, and he cannot visualize attending *do-nothing* Masonic meetings for that length of time. The incentive is not worth the goal."

Denslow believed the civic organizations were able to develop because Freemasonry "left a vacuum." Lodges had grown to unthinkable numbers. "Freemasonry lost much of its impact when it became so large that the traditional *Table Lodges* were disbanded," he said. When Lodges were small "they met in small taverns, and each meeting included a dinner. It was an intimate affair, and the ties of friendship and brotherly love were strongly cemented."

The President, Elbert Bede, appointed Frank H. Wilson, MPS, chairman of a new Publicity Committee. His first job was to send every Masonic publication in the world articles about The Philalethes Society.

Information gathered from officers of the Society helped Raymond D. Reel, MPS, form the Sarastro Masonic Club in Vienna, Austria. This was the first, and only, Masonic club authorized in this country. There were eleven lodges in the city, but all of them worked in the German language. English-speaking Freemasons found it difficult to communicate Masonically. The Austrian Grand Master gave the group every assistance possible, even providing it with a fine place to meet and build a library.

"In this city 'on the beautiful blue Danube'—the 'city of wine, women and waltzes'—there are no English language media. . . . Both this city and this country are more than 95% Catholic. It's even said to be 'more Catholic than the Pope!' Therefore, you never find any mention of Masonic activities. Neither do you find any Masonic insignia worn by native Masons."

The Philalethes for February 1963 carried the talk Allen E. Roberts, MPS, presented at the Northeast Conference on Masonic Education and Libraries in Maine. It was titled "The Writer of History in the Future of Masonry." He asked: "Why are you and I Masons? Is it not because Freemasonry is what it is? It has to be, because there is no 'glory' attached to what we do for the Craft. Most of the time our own organization doesn't even recognize our efforts with a slight pat-on-the-back.

"If we were to utilize our same efforts for a service club the newspapers would play it up. So would our communities. What we do for Freemasonry is relegated to the archives."

Roberts added: "The writer of history has a definite and firm place in the future of Masonry. We must portray Masonry in its true light. Either he has failed in the past to present the true story of Masonry, or there have been too few Masonic historians. Something has gone wrong for men who can attain the highest offices in appendant bodies, and even Grand Lodges, and want to change Freemasonry. What is the answer?

"I believe it's in telling the real story of Freemasonry. And that is where the Masonic historian enters the picture. But his task in not an easy one—if he is to be a true historian."

Roberts suggested writers should add "warmth" to their narratives. He believed those few outside of Freemasonry who have read Masonic books have read, for the most part, "trash." He noted Masonic writers and editors actually work for nothing other than "Master's wages." He said it was long past time to make the wages fit the expertise of the craftsman. And "the writer remains a craftsman. No button can produce words or phrases. They must come from the mind shaped by the spirit."

He concluded: "Make no mistake. Writers are available. All they need is your backing. Readers are available. Hundreds of Masons, young and old, are hungry for good Masonic books. Make the books available and they will be purchased."

The membership at the end of 1962 was reported at 874, the highest number ever.

The expansion and development of The Philalethes Society had continued along with those of the small Masonic bodies that met in Washington each February. There was strong evidence Freemasons were seeking truth and information. While Masonic membership throughout the country was declining, these research groups were growing.

Could the Society continue to conquer the trend?

8. MATURING
(1963–1966)

*T*he theme for the Workshop in February 1963 provoked a lengthy discussion. "Masonic Research" in its many forms was covered by the chairman, Allen E. Roberts, Alphonse Cerza, Wendell K. Walker, and Dr. William L. Cummings. Several who attended considered it "one of the best Masonic Workshops ever attempted by the Society."

Many of them said most members of The Philalethes Society are "more interested in getting Masonic information and a knowledge of Freemasonry" than in research. This was conceded, but it was pointed out that without researchers there would be little knowledge to impart. Both the "receiver" and the "sender" play vital roles.

Norman C. Dutt, MPS, was awarded the 1962 Certificate of Literature for his article about "The Lewis Freemason."

Anti-Masonry by Alphonse Cerza, a publication of the Missouri Lodge of Research, was made available through this Lodge. It would later be reprinted and distributed by Macoy Publishing and Masonic Supply Company of Richmond, Virginia.

The June 1963 issue of *The Philalethes* announced that Allen E. Roberts of Virginia, Kenneth F. Curtis, the long-time chairman of the membership committee, and Jerry R. Erikson of California, noted for his research and publication of sports and political personalities who were, or are, Freemasons, were elected Fellows of The Philalethes Society. It was also noted that LeRoy Gordon Cooper, Jr., the well-known astronaut, had received the degrees of the York Rite at Cocoa, Florida.

Andrew J. White, Jr., a Past Grand Master of Masons in Ohio and Grand Secretary of the Grand Lodge, who would become a member of the Society, wrote a devastating article opposing Masonic funerals. His article in the June 1963 issue of *The Philalethes* would provoke heated discussion, pro and con, for months.

In the same issue, Harold V. B. Voorhis, along with Edwin G. Sanford, a former employee of the Grand Lodge Library of Massachusetts, recorded the backgrounds of Rob Morris and Robert Macoy. Both had been instrumental in the formation of the Order of the Eastern Star. Fictitious information had been circulated about both for years. This was an attempt to set the genealogical record straight.

Rob Morris' actual name was Robert Williams Peckham. He was born August 31, 1818 in New York City; died July 31, 1888 in La Grange, Kentucky. Robert Macoy, founder of Macoy Publishing and Masonic Supply

Company in New York City (still in existence under the same name in Richmond, Virginia), was born in Armagh, Ulster County, Ireland, October 14, 1815; died January 9, 1895 in Brooklyn, New York. The article goes into great detail in listing their marriages and children. It doesn't deal with their Masonic backgrounds, nor does it give any reason for Morris adopting a new name.

In October Alphonse Cerza said he had been asked how to get Masonic books placed in public libraries. He suggested Lodges should purchase and present them; and members should donate them to the libraries after they had read them. He noted that libraries depend on reviews from certain publications to determine what they should purchase. Legitimate Masonic books are rarely reviewed by the media. To offset this Cerza asked his readers to let others know Masonic books are available, then see that they were borrowed regularly to create a demand for acquiring more Masonic books.

New officers for the Society were named in December 1963. Dr. Charles Gottshall Reigner became the President; Judge Robert H. Gollmar, First Vice President, and William R. Denslow, Second Vice President. Greisen and Heaton remained in their offices.

"An Ideal Masonic Publication" was a paper presented by Denslow at the Midwest Conference and reproduced in the December 1963 issue of *The Philalethes*. He didn't mention *The Philalethes*, but did call attention to the excellence of his own magazine *The Royal Arch Mason*. In his paper he said: "If a heraldic emblem could be considered appropriate for certain Masonic editors, I would suggest a pair of scissors and a pot of glue, rampant on a field of yellow! For they are the 'clip-artists.' Their publications, seldom, if ever, contain an original article. The first test of a good publication is the amount of original material it contains."

Denslow later said: "The featuring of local personalities and minor events can be the 'kiss of death' to any Masonic publication on a state level. An editor must remember that his reader is not interested in 50-year pins, the secretary who has served 40 years (why didn't they get rid of him instead of bragging?), the posed group picture and the meaningless listing of full Masonic titles. The place for these is in the publication of a local Masonic group where everyone knows the subject and is interested in reading about him."

He quoted "that 'gadfly' of Freemasonry, Dwight L. Smith of Indiana." Smith wrote in the 1961 *Proceedings* of his Grand Lodge: "Time out a moment while I sound off: Why so many Grand Lodges are interested in sending their publications into the home of every Master Mason in the jurisdiction is far too deep for me. With one or two notable exceptions, there is not a Masonic publication in the United States that I would want cluttering up the living room of my home. Look over the entire field of Grand Lodge publications in the nation and what do you find?" They are "imitators,"

Smith claims, and he would like to see a national publication "that every Master Mason could welcome into his home with pride."

The Editor of *The Philalethes* called attention to the New York World's Fair scheduled to open in 1964. He said the "New York State Masons are financing and building a Masonic Pavilion dedicated to brotherhood." It would display many rare and valuable Masonic relics loaned by several Grand Lodges and individual lodges throughout the country.

The Philalethes noted with horror the assassination of the President of the United States, John F. Kennedy. Vrooman wrote: "The American way of life has been to fight the battle of public life with ballots, not bullets, and whatever our outlook on the matter of politics, we assert, fervently, that we must let the law take its course, and fight the battle in traditional and orderly fashion. Whatever our politics or religion, this has been a demonstration of anarchy, not law."

Alex Horne, MPS, wrote about "The Doctrine of the Perfect Youth" for February 1964. He noted that this "doctrine" had been somewhat liberalized since World War II, and particularly after the Korean conflict. He called attention to the action of the Grand Lodge of Indiana. A dispensation had been granted to form Bartimaeus Lodge whose only purpose was to confer degrees on candidates of other lodges who had "serious physical handicaps."

Masonic pavilion, New York World's Fair

91

The officers of this lodge are drawn from surrounding lodges; it merely acts as a "specialized degree-conferring Lodge working in behalf of other Lodges near Indianapolis."

The Editor said he had received two new excellent publications: *More Light*, published at Beirut, Lebanon, "full of Masonic information," and *Masonic Digest* of Johannesburg, South Africa.

Dwight W. Robb, MPS, examined the Masonic life, or non-Masonic life of Sir Christopher Wren, as many had done before him. He noted that in 1716 Wren was 85 years old, and he died in February 1723. He came to the same conclusion as had most of those who had studied Wren's life—there's no definitive confirmation of his connections with Freemasonry. Robb claimed: "modern authorities are inclined to accept his membership in our order." He doesn't name these authorities. Robb added: "In 1729, Christopher Wren, Jr., son of Sir Christopher Wren, was Master of the Lodge at the Goose and Gridiron Ale-house (now Lodge of Antiquity, No. 2) and it is thought by several Masonic students that the son might have been confused with the father."

Reigner, the new President, said he had been a member of The Philalethes Society "since the days of Walter A. Quincke. During these years I have observed with growing enthusiasm the progress the Society has made. The improvement in our magazine has been truly remarkable. Our membership

Charles Gottshall Reigner

92

has grown apace—so that now we number well over a thousand Masons who seek light and have light to give."

Gollmar, the First Vice President, cautioned: "In the field of scholarship we should emphasize accuracy. The weeds in the garden of Masonic literature have, through the years, been amazing in their number and hearty growth. We should constantly strive to cut them back without becoming dry or stilted and without unnecessarily limiting the right of every Mason to interpret the symbols for himself."

"I become more and more disgruntled as I listen to that part of the ritual which deals with the 47th Problem of Euclid," wrote Gilbert L. Biller, MPS, in February 1964. "Each time I deliver this myself, I am impressed with its lack of meaning, its wealth of misinformation, and Masonry's neglect of the most important factor involved in the exposition of this section."

Biller said: "Pythagoras, so far as Masonry is concerned, is a legendary character, and any Masonic reference to him is almost entirely fictional. Pythagoras lived from 582 to 506 B.C. He was the founder of the science of numbers, the numerical inter-relation of musical tones, and geometry. (Euclid lived circa 300 B.C.)" Biller wonders how the 47th Problem of Euclid could be ascribed to Pythagoras! He also wonders how Pythagoras could have been raised to a non-existent degree. It was Archimedes, a later Greek mathematician, who, when he determined how to confirm that silver isn't gold, cried: "Eureka, signifying in the Greek language, I have found it."

To explain his motive in writing "A Critique On the Pythagorean Theorem" Biller concluded: "I have no quarrel with Masonry in its insistence that the ritual remain intact and without change through the ages. [But it has been changed countless numbers of times!] To use myths, allegories, parables, symbols, etc. is fine. But material such as cited above is so obviously erroneous that it has no rightful place in Masonry. As it reads now, this passage is false and misleading, and should be deleted."

With the February 1964 issue of *The Philalethes*, Roberts's series on "Masonry Aids Reconstruction" began. It was, and would remain, his argument that the solidarity of Freemasonry, North and South, helped curb the animosity of the war. Throughout the series he produced dramatic accounts to prove his thesis.

Edwin P. Clark, MPS, was concerned with the "Public Image and Public Relations" of the Craft. "It seems obvious that if the public is to get an unequivocal image of Freemasonry," wrote Clark, "then we've got to decide just what Masonry is and is not. Furthermore, this image must be developed on a national level, for the image of Freemasonry in New Jersey must also be the same as the image of Freemasonry in California. If the type of man we desire is to be attracted to Freemasonry, that attraction must be developed within his ever-changing environment."

Also concerned with the same topic was Howard W. Moore. He indicated this in a paper presented at a Chicago meeting of The Philalethes Society and printed in the April 1965 issue of *The Philalethes* under the lengthy title of "Public Relations and the Image of Masonry as Interpreted in Our World Today." "What is public relations?" asked Moore. "Simply defined, you can say—*Good* public relations is a well-planned, effective program of telling a story of your organization, its objectives or purpose, its many activities and accomplishments.

"I would rather define it as communications with a purpose—to mold favorable public opinion and develop a climate or acceptance conducive to furthering your aims. Public opinion has become the most powerful force we know—it is the only force that counts in the realm of ideas. . . . Freemasonry, if it is not going to follow the declining path of other respected fraternal orders, must adopt a program of favorably influencing public opinion."

The Executive Committee met February 28, 1964 without John Black Vrooman. He was ill at his home in St. Louis, Missouri. The Workshop was held in the evening in conjunction with the American Lodge of Research of New York. By dispensation, the New York Lodge was permitted to hold the meeting in the room of Lafayette Lodge No. 19 in the Masonic Temple in the District of Columbia. In spite of the heavy snow storm, 175 were present.

Reigner, the President of the Society, related some of the history of the Society. "The history of Freemasonry in France in the Eighteenth Century is crowded with Rites and Bodies of various kinds," said Reigner. "In 1773 there was established in the Lodge of Amis Reunies in Paris what was called the *Rite des Philalethes*, a word coined from two Greek words which mean, literally translated, 'Love of Truth.' " With the death of the founder, Savalette de Langes, the Rite came to an end.

Although there was no direct connection between the Society and this Rite, Reigner used it "to demonstrate that the name *Philalethes* has been known in Masonic history since the latter part of the Eighteenth Century." He then spoke about the early days of the Society. Other papers presented included "Masonic Research Groups" by Harold Voorhis, and "Washington and His Masonic Contemporaries" by James R. Case.

Norman C. Dutt was elected a Fellow; Andrew J. White, MPS, received the Certificate of Literature for 1963.

An interesting item was included in a box in the April 1964 edition, but who originally wrote it wasn't mentioned.

Are You Equal to This Planting?

Plant five rows of peas: Preparedness, Promptness,
Perseverance, Politeness, and Prayer.

> Then three rows of squash: Squash Gossip, Squash
>   Criticism, Squash Indifference.
> And five rows of lettuce: Let us be Faithful, Let
>   us be Unselfish, Let us be Loyal, Let us Love
>   One Another, and Let us be Truthful.
> But no garden is really complete without turnip:
>   Turn up for Church, Turn
>   up with a Smile, Turn
>   up with a New Idea, Turn up with Real
>   Determination.

In answer to a query about Admiral Farragut, Gerald D. Foss, Grand Historian of the Grand Lodge of New Hampshire, supplied an account from the minutes of Old St. John's Lodge No. 1 of Portsmouth. It reads:

August 17th 1870. Masonic Hall, Portsmouth, N.H. Wednesday August 17th A.L. 5870-A.D. 1870.

A Special Communication of St. John's Lodge No. one of this City was held here this Forenoon at 11 o'clock to attend the funeral of our Deceased Brother ADMI- RAL DAVID G. FARRAGUT who died at this Navy Yard at Noon of last Sunday. A large Number of Members and Visiting Brothers were present and a Lodge of Master Masons was opened; and after the Usual Services in the Hall a large procession was formed conjointly with St. Andrews' Lodge.—Then accompanied by the Portsmouth Cornet Band and escorted by DeWitt Clinton Commandery of Kts. Templar we joined with a Grand Naval Procession just landed from Three U.S. Steamers with many Distinguished Army Officers which Procession was also joined by other various Societies and Companies and our City Government; the whole making a Very Large and Imposing Procession; which being escorted by Two Battalions of U.S. Troops, Heavy Artillery and Marines, proceeded Sol- emnly through our more Important Streets to Saint John's Church; where appro- priate Religious Services were performed by the Rev. Dr. Montgomery of New York City; the friend and former Chaplain and Pastor of the Deceased. Then to a Tomb within the Grounds of the Church was the Body Committed with the Rites of the Episcopal Church and with the Rites and Appropriate Formalities of our Order; our Most Wor. Grand Master John R. Holbrook [a member of St. John's Lodge] officiating. After which Fifteen Volies (sic) were fired by the U.S. Troops formed in front of the Tomb. From the Tomb we returned to this Hall where the Lodge was closed in Proper Form.

Geo. P. Edny, Secretary

In June the Editor quoted Edward Everett Hale:

> I am only one,
> But I am still one.

95

I cannot do everything,
But still I can do something;
And because I cannot do everything
I will not refuse to do the something that
I can do.

Alphonse Cerza asked: "Is Ritualistic Work Enough?" He concluded the answer is a resounding NO. He believed the Freemasons interested in working with the ritual were in the minority. Because this was so, they "should be cultivated as precious members who help maintain the very foundation of the Craft." He wanted serious thought given to the needs of the majority. "Let us cultivate the student and the administrator and fit them into the fabric of the Craft so that all may benefit," he pleaded.

"Many of us will recall *The Builder,*" wrote Reigner in the June 1964 issue of *The Philalethes*, "the outstanding magazine published by the National Masonic Research Society [of Anamosa, Iowa] from 1915 to 1930. Dr. Joseph Fort Newton, the author of that stimulating book, *The Builders*, was also the first editor of the magazine. His successor as editor was Harry Leroy Haywood, whose writings on Freemasonry over a period of years are well known to us all. Brother [Robert I.] Clegg was a contributor to *The Builder* and to other Masonic magazines. He organized a number of Masonic Study Clubs—the forerunners of our Masonic Research Lodges of today."

In 1987 The Philalethes Society made *The Builder* available on microfiche to anyone interested. So also was another magazine edited by Joseph Fort Newton, *The Master Mason* of The Masonic Service Association. Earlier, every issue of *The Philalethes* magazine had been copied to microfiche.

Why didn't Lyndon B. Johnson receive more than the Entered Apprentice degree? A letter from Brooks Hays, who was listed as having attained the thirty-third degree of the Scottish Rite, was printed in the June issue. The Editor considered it a "reasonable and logical reply and answer." The letter read:

THE WHITE HOUSE
WASHINGTON

March 9, 1964

I am writing to thank you on behalf of the President for your letter with reference to his Masonic ties.
President Johnson received the Entered Apprentice degree on October 30, 1937, the ceremony being conducted by the Johnson City, Texas, Lodge No. 561. After receiving this degree, Mr. Johnson found that his Congressional duties, upon which he entered in 1937, took so much of his time that he was not able to

pursue the Masonic degrees. It was his considered judgment that it would not be fair to the fraternity to proceed with the degrees since it would be impossible for him to be active as a Master Mason. He regretted this very much and I can assure you that he has maintained the same interest in and admiration for the Masonic order that inspired him to apply for the degree back in 1937.

The President's tremendous public responsibilities as a Member of Congress, Vice President, and as President, which have engaged him since 1937, have prevented his realizing his hopes of completing the Masonic degrees, but he trusts that he will someday find it possible to receive the degrees. In the meantime, he maintains an appreciation of the teachings of Freemasonry, particularly as reflected in the statesmanship of many of his predecessors.

If we contrast this statement with the dedication and Masonic work of Harry S. Truman, one of Johnson's predecessors, it appears strange. But one must take into account that Truman was a Freemason before he became a politician. Truman knew, and loved the Masonic ritual. And he, while a Senator, was elected Grand Master of Masons in Missouri. He always stated this was more important to him than his election as President of the United States! He knew well the teachings of the Craft; Johnson didn't, and Johnson didn't realize how these lessons might have made him a better man and a better President.

Memorials to Ray Baker Harris, FPS, and Robert J. Meekren, FPS, were carried in the June issue of *The Philalethes*. Harris was best known for his work with the Scottish Rite of the Southern Jurisdiction. Meekren, an Englishman who became a Canadian Freemason, was one of the early Fellows of the Society. He was a frequent contributor to *The Builder.*

The August 1964 issue of *The Philalethes* found Cerza writing about "Freemasonry and Shakespeare." He recorded several illustrations of the writings of Shakespeare he believed would be of interest to Freemasons.

Now . . . Whence Come you? (Merry Wives of Windsor, Act 4, Scene 5).

Let's part the word. . . .

No! I'll not be your half. (Love's Labour Lost, Act 4, Scene 2, 5).

They whisper one another in the ear; and he that speaks doth grasp the bearer's wrist. (King John, Act 4, Scene 2).

I am a Brother of a Gracious Order late from the sea. (Measure for Measure, Act 3, last Scene).

The singing Masons building roofs of gold. (Henry V, Act 1, Scene 4).

Both are at the Lodge. (Titus Andronicus, Act 2, Scene 4).

This is a Worshipful Society. (King John, Act 1, Scene 1).

You have made good work, you and your apron men. (Coriolanus, Act 4, Scene 1).

What! My old Worshipful Master. (Taming of the Shrew, Act 5, Scene 1).

Where is thy leather apron and thy rule? (Julius Caesar, Act 1, Scene 1).

Come swear to that. Kiss the book. (The Tempest, Act 2, Scene 1).

The profound Solomon. (Love's Labour Lost, Act 4, Scene 3).

I will, as 'twere a Brother of your Order. (Measure for Measure, Act 1, Scene 4).

I have ever squared me to thy counsel. (The Winter's Tale, Act 3, Scene 3).

Guard the door without. Let him not pass. (Othello, Act 5, Scene 2).

I have not kept my square, but that to come shall be done by rule. (Antony and Cleopatra, Act 2, Scene 1).

They never meet, but they do square. (A Midsummer Night's Dream, Act 2, Scene 1).

Lambskins to signify that craft being richer than innocency. (Measure for Measure, Act 3, Scene 1).

I thank you good Tubal. (The Merchant of Venice, Act 3, Scene 1).

As Cerza said, statements similar to the foregoing are plentiful in the works of Shakespeare, and this caused some to believe he was a member of the Craft. But isn't it more logical to suspect that Masonic ritualists of yesteryear incorporated his phrases into the ceremonies and ritual of Freemasonry?

Roscoe Pound, FPS, considered by many as the world's greatest legal scholar, died on July 1, 1964. Pound was born in Nebraska in 1870. He was educated in that state before traveling to Harvard University. He was a prolific writer. The bibliography of his writings fill more than 245 printed pages! How did he do it? Alphonse Cerza described the desk Pound designed: "An unusual piece of furniture used for most of his lifetime, 37 feet in outer circumference with a hole in the middle. The Dean entered through this space by lifting up a flap of the desk. He occupied a swivel chair in its center, spinning around whenever necessary to pick a reference book from the open shelves inside. These shelves contained well catalogued books and papers. . . . A typewriter was sunken in at the proper level, so that when once seated he could reach any department of his work without getting up." What might he have accomplished had the personal computers of today been available to him!

Pound became a Master Mason in Lancaster Lodge No. 54 in Lincoln, Nebraska in 1901. It is claimed he learned the catechism of the first degree on his way home from the lodge. He was Master of the lodge in 1906, Grand Orator in 1906–08, and was later elected an Honorary Past Grand Master. He later affiliated with several other lodges and became prominent in the Grand Lodge and Masonic circles in Massachusetts.

Henry Emmerson of New York was elected a Fellow in August 1964. Voorhis said there were then five Fellows from foreign countries; the other 35 from American jurisdictions. Conrad Hahn and Bruce H. Hunt were elected Fellows in October, and Elbert Bede was named a Life Fellow.

Cerza, in a guest editorial concerning secular politics, said those who do not vote are "passive traitors." He asked his readers to remember: "Bad public officials are elected by good citizens who stay home on election day."

The President, Charles Reigner, wrote: "Always we need to go behind the ritual in the effort to find fundamental truths we can apply in our own lives and actions. Masonry, like life itself, is always in the *process of becoming*. It is ever beckoning us on to a deeper understanding of the spiritual aspects of life and the high ideals which it sets before us. In that never-ending quest, each Mason has a part."

The Editor saluted the Virginia Craftsmen for cementing "International good will and friendship." This traveling degree team had traveled to Scotland to exemplify the Virginia ritual in four Scottish Lodges. It was done to repay those Scottish Freemasons who had helped Babcock Lodge No. 322, Highland Springs, Virginia, celebrate its fiftieth year. On that occasion over 6,000 Master Masons had been present in the Richmond Arena to witness the exemplification of the Master Mason degree as it is conferred in Lodge Glasgow, Scotland. The Scottish Masons returned to Virginia twice more; the Virginia Craftsmen returned to Scotland in 1987.

Judge Robert H. Gollmar, First Vice President, in a paper presented at the Midwest Conference and reproduced in *The Philalethes* referred to that Scottish visitation. "One more suggestion for the broadening of Masonic Education: In the October issue of *The Philalethes* Brother Vrooman notes that the Virginia Craftsmen and their ladies . . . have just returned from a visit to Scotland where they conferred a Master Mason degree in full form. Last year a Scottish Lodge came to Richmond and did the same.

"Masonic visitations are not a new idea. Along both borders of our country, Lodges have visited back and forth for years. Within our country, visitations ranging from next door neighbor Lodges to jaunts across several states have been common. I suggest that such visitations are Masonic Education and should be recognized as such.

"I suggest further that if the exchange of students between countries is considered education, the exchange of Masons between countries could be equally Masonic education."

Vrooman was disturbed. "By what right does government interfere in civic and fraternal affairs?" he asked. "More and more we are finding that the Government of the United States, through agencies, commissions and committees, has been making unwarranted intrusion into fraternal, social and civic groups, their leaders and their members, to the extent that the intrusion and interference in which they have no business are becoming obnoxious and a nuisance."

He noted that at least one Grand Master had issued an edict forbidding any member to answer any questionnaire. "Let's keep government out of fraternal and civic endeavor!" Vrooman concluded. He suggested the leadership do what The Masonic Service Association proposed: request the Congressional representatives to make it clear the Civil Rights Commission had no right to invade the privacy of organizations.

The Masonic "penalties" were again under attack it was noted in *The Philalethes* for December 1964. A proposal was made in the United Grand Lodge of England to change the wording from "under no less a penalty . . ." to "ever bearing in mind the ancient penalty. . . . " Vrooman believed this might make the situation more "harmonious." The debate would continue throughout the Craft. The arguments pro and con would prove "harmony" difficult to achieve.

Part six of "Freemasonry Aids Reconstruction" covered "The Impeachment Trial of Andrew Johnson." The nasty affair, with its anti-Masonic and political overtones, was covered at length. Included was a chart depicting how each of the fifty-four Senators voted in the "trial" that should never have been. Johnson, the Freemason from Tennessee, was acquitted by one heroic Senator.

That Senator was Edmund G. Ross. President John F. Kennedy praised Ross highly in his *Profiles in Courage*. Ross' story is told by Ben W. Graybill, MPS, in an article appearing in the April 1974 issue of *The Philalethes*. Ross has been made a Master Mason in Topeka Lodge No. 12, 1859. This may have been the reason he became the junior Senator from Kansas in 1866. The governor, Samuel J. Crawford, had early affiliated with Topeka Lodge.

Senator Jim Lane could no longer stand the harassment at home and in Washington for his support of President Johnson, and on July 1, 1866 he took his own life. The governor called Ross to his office and informed him he was to be the new Senator. As Graybill said, the Radicals in the Senate knew the vote for the impeachment of the President would be close, so they pulled every dirty trick in the book to influence those who might support Johnson. Without question, many who favored Johnson's views wouldn't risk committing political suicide to support him. The Radicals went to work on Ross.

"The Radicals did not overlook a single approach in their attempt to influence Ross," wrote Graybill. "In reply to a telegram from Kansas, signed by '1,000 and others' demanding he vote for the conviction of the President, Ross said: 'I do not recognize your right to demand that I vote either for or against conviction. I have taken an oath to do impartial justice according to the Constitution and laws, and trust that I shall have the courage to vote according to the dictates of my judgment and for the highest good of the country.' A 21 year old girl, Vinnie Ream, a sculptress engaged to carve a life sized marble statue of Lincoln, was approached in an effort to get her to use her influence with Ross. She and her family lived in the same rooming house where Ross was staying. When she refused she was subjected to gross indignities.

"It was a dramatic moment in the Senate of the United States on May 16, 1868, when Chief Justice Salmon P. Chase, presiding at the trial, called for the vote of Senator Ross, saying 'Mr. Senator Ross, how say you, is the respondent, Andrew Johnson, President of the United States, guilty or not guilty of a high dismeanor, as charged in this article of impeachment?' There was no sound and hardly a movement as Ross rose to cast the decisive vote, saying, 'Not Guilty.' With these two words his political career ended. He returned to Kansas where he and his family were socially ostracized and ignored. . . . Thus a great man, a Kansas Mason, chose to sacrifice an eminent future by practicing the Cardinal Virtues of Masonry, Temperance, Fortitude, Prudence and Justice."

Although Andrew Johnson left the White House he remained an interested and loyal American citizen. He had never approved of Ulysses S. Grant, his successor, and refused to ride in the same carriage with Grant to the inauguration. Johnson told his Tennessee friends: "When I accepted the Presidency . . . I did not accept it as a donation, or as a grand gift establishment; I did not take it as a horn of plenty, with sugar plums to be handed out here and there."

In March 1875 Johnson returned to Washington—as a Senator from Tennessee. But he didn't have time to stop the corruption in the Capitol; he suffered a fatal stroke at his home during the congressional recess in July. His family acceded to his wishes and let the Masonic fraternity he loved make his funeral arrangements. His Greenville Lodge No. 119 performed Johnson's last rites.

The Philalethes for February 1965 carried an article stating "Oldest Masonic Lodge Building Is In Halifax, North Carolina." This was shown to be false in 1975 in an article written for *The Philalethes*, the *Masonic Herald* of Virginia, and in *Freemasonry in American History.* Royal White Hart Lodge of North Carolina, the lodge in question, received a warrant from the Grand Lodge of England ("Moderns") in 1767, becoming No. 413 on its list. During its early years it met at Anthony Troughton's tavern. In 1772 it moved to William Martin's Ordinary, at the sign of the Thistle, and there it remained. Attempts were made to build a hall without success until December 15, 1821 when at last it did meet in its own building. It has met there ever since.

The oldest Masonic building in the United States is Masons Hall in Richmond, Virginia. This was erected in 1785 and was the home of the Grand Lodge of Virginia for several years, as well as Richmond Lodge No. 10. Richmond-Randolph Lodge No. 19 later joined with Richmond Lodge as a joint owner, then the former purchased it outright. In 1987 it was still the home of Richmond-Randolph Lodge and Richmond Royal Arch Chapter No. 3. (For a complete discussion see *Launching the Craft* by Thomas C. Parramore and *Freemasonry In American History* by Allen E. Roberts.)

"The Masonic Transition Period" by Dwight W. Robb, MPS, covered some of the background of early Speculative Masonry. "The Lodge of Edinburgh (Mary's Chapel) No. 1, is probably the only 'surviving Masonic body which can boast the possession of its minute-books as far back as 1598,' " wrote Robb.

"The first volume covers the period from 1598 to 1686 and it shows that on 'The 3 day off Joulie 1634' three 'gentlemen-non-operative' members were initiated. This is the 'earliest record of the admission of non-operatives in the whole of Scotland' before 1736, when the Grand Lodge of Scotland was formed."

The other two Lodges covered by Robb were Lodge Mother Kilwinning No. 0, and Aitchison's Haven Lodge which "initiated their first non-operative member in 1672." Robb added: "The oldest records of The Masons Company of London that have come down to the present time, is an account book whose first entry bears the date of 1620."

The Editor, John Vrooman, noted that the President, Dr. Charles Reigner, had been elected Chairman of the Committee on Educational Institutions, Synod of Virginia, Presbyterian Church. William E. Yeager, a Past Grand Master of Masons in Pennsylvania, had become Chairman of the Grand Lodge Committee on Masonic Culture (Education).

Bliss Kelly, MPS, didn't agree with the Editor's stand on Masonic penalties. "It must be admitted," wrote Kelly, "that the 'terrible penalties' of these obligations are the things which impress candidates and make them realize the solemnity and importance of Masonry. Without them, or with merely a reference to them as 'ancient,' Masonry becomes becomes 'milk toast,' without backbone or substance sufficient to maintain its importance."

Also in the February 1965 issue, the Reverend Forrest D. Haggard, MPS, wrote about "The Man, the Church and the Lodge." "I cannot say that I see a conflict between Freemasonry and the Church," he wrote. "The ideals and purposes of the Masonic Fraternity are in harmony with the spirit and goals of the Church." He concluded his paper with: "We live in a dark and troubled age. The forces of evil are combined against the forces of good. Even good words, like the word 'square,' for example, have been twisted around by the perverted minds of a sick generation until they stand for just the opposite of their original intent and purpose. In this kind of a world we need the most solid support of a good community. The support that encourages honesty, courage, loyalty and faith, and that puts human meaning into these words. That support is an uncrushable triangle so joined that, no matter how tumbled or twisted, it forms a solid base on which to stand. That triangle may be formed by the union of the Man—the Church and the Lodge."

The Order of DeMolay had been covered in the pages of *The Philalethes* over the years. The April issue featured more of the work of this youth organization.

William E. Yeager was elected a Fellow of The Philalethes Society in June 1965.

In January 1965 the *Saturday Evening Post* ran an article that appeared to imply that the Ku Klux Klan held a meeting in the Masonic Temple of Indiantown Lodge No. 165, South Carolina. The Grand Master took exception to the article and wrote the publisher. He explained that the ladies of the Rehobeth Pentecostal Holiness Church had secured the Lodge dining room to cook and serve lunch as a money-making project. He asked that the magazine set the record straight. It promised to do so.

Alexander H. Buchan, Grand Secretary of the Grand Lodge of Scotland, answered a query about John Paul, who later became John Paul Jones: "From the records of our Lodge St. Bernard Kilwinning No 122 in Kirkcudbright (1765–1796) it is shown that a petition for membership was received from Captain John Paul of the 'John' of Kirkcudbright on 27th November 1770 and that he was then duly admitted and recorded in the Minutes as having been 'entered.' It is interesting to read that at the end of the minute, confirming the identity of the intrant, there is a note 'Paul Jones entered.' At a later date he is recorded as having been 'passed' but there is no minute showing that he was raised to the Master Mason degree nor have we any information of his further interest in Freemasonry in Scotland. . . .

"It is known that John Paul Jones referred to his Lodge in France and this is generally believed to refer to Lodge 'The Nine Muses' (Les Neuf Soeurs) in Paris. This Lodge absorbed much of the literary, artistic and scientific talent of that time. . . . Paul Jones was also associated with the Mother Lodge of the *Rite Ecossais Philosophique,* an offshoot of the Grand Orient of France founded in Paris in 1776."

"Masonically Speaking" was the title of an article by Charles F. Adams, MPS, in the December 1965 issue of *The Philalethes*. It was based on the talk he gave during the Workshop in February. "Will you not agree that some of the most interesting speeches you have heard, if accurately transcribed from a tape recording, would make a literary composition of very questionable merit?" he asked. "And that many dull and uninteresting speeches, were, in fact, read from a manuscript of a very excellent quality?" He strongly suggested the reading of manuscripts not be substituted for plain speaking. Write the manuscript, if it's to be printed, but don't read it, he cautioned.

William Moseley Brown, FPS, a Past President of The Philalethes Society, died on January 8, 1966. Brown had served his country and Freemasonry well. He had become a Master Mason in Mountain City Lodge No. 67, Lexington, Virginia, in 1922. He served in World War I as a private and was discharged as a major; in World War II he left service as a Lieutenant Colonel. He ran for Governor of Virginia as a Republican (a fatal decision at that time!) and he also ran for Congress. In Freemasonry he served as Grand Master, Grand Commander, and Grand High Priest in Virginia. In 1934 he served as Grand Master of the Allied Masonic Degrees. He was Grand Abbot of the Society of Blue Friars, and he served as National President of the National Sojourners in 1942. He wrote many lodge histories, the bicentennial book on George Washington for the Grand Lodge of Virginia, and *Freemasonry in Virginia* in 1936, the only history of that Grand Lodge ever published.

"I Will Save Washington" was the title of "an Historical Narrative" by Allen E. Roberts, FPS, in the February 1966 issue of *The Philalethes*. It concerned the bloodiest battle of the War Between the States, Antietam. General George B. McClellan took a Federal Army in disarray and turned the Troops of Robert E. Lee away from what could easily have been a Confederate victory in Maryland. The story covered many instances of brotherhood in action by Freemasons who remembered to practice without their lodges those lessons learned within.

McClellan, an Oregon Freemason, has never received the credit he deserved. After the first Battle of Bull Run, he took a disoriented army and built it into a fighting machine. Then a two-fold attack was planned to capture Richmond, Virginia. It failed, but only because "Stonewall" Jackson and Robert E. Lee had out-foxed Abraham Lincoln. Lincoln, fearing the Confederates were about to invade Washington, held back the support that was supposed to join McClellan on the outskirts of Richmond. McClellan was "fired." Even so, because he took unauthorized command at Antietam, he did save Washington, but still received no plaudits for his heroism.

"The Development of Masonic Leadership" was the title of an article by Joseph Farwick, MPS, in the February 1966 issue of *The Philalethes*. It was adapted from a paper read at the Midwest Conference. "The fact remains that, being the largest user of personnel, we have the least amount of training for our leaders," said Farwick. "How can this be rectified? By devising some method of regular training programs for lodge officers. In industry there is the production of material goods—in the . . . lodge, dedicated Masons [are required] to carry out such a program—dedicated to *building character,* the principal interest of our Craft." He suggested every Master be reminded he must wear three hats: that of the ritualist, the administrator, and the sociable Brother.

In his paper prepared for the Workshop in February 1966, and printed in the April issue of *The Philalethes*, William E. Yeager, FPS, said: "The

William E. Yeager

purpose of Freemasonry is to prepare, educate, and train its members for the higher relationships of life. Initiation should fit them for a life long association with men who are concerned with the rights and responsibilities of the individual, the mystery of man's relationship to God and his fellow man. In thus shaping and molding the character of its initiates it can contribute to the improvement and advancement of humanity.

"Freemasonry has survived all the vicissitudes that have beset it over the centuries because of what it is and what it stands for—a philosophy of life so simple that all men can understand and subscribe to it—a way of life which the individual Mason may readily translate into his everyday activities."

Alphonse Cerza was awarded the Certificate of Literature for 1965. He was, two days later, chosen the Blue Friar for 1966. It was noted that J. Edgar Hoover, Director of the Federal Bureau of Investigation, had been awarded the Grand Cross of the Scottish Rite, Southern Jurisdiction.

Frank H. Wilson of Massachusetts was elected a Fellow of the Society. For many years he acted as the Public Relations committee for The Philalethes Society.

In the June 1966 issue of *The Philalethes*, Alphonse Cerza called attention to a biography of Giuseppe Garibaldi, "one of the world's outstanding fighters for freedom." Cerza said Garibaldi "became a Mason in *Les Amis de Patrie* Lodge of Montevideo, Uruguay, about 1844; later he affiliated with Tompkins Lodge No. 471 of Stapleton, New York. In 1860 he became Grand Master of the Grand Lodge of Italy. . . . The latest of many biographies is *Garibaldi and His Enemies.*" Cerza said it was a fine biography "but like many biographies of great men who have been Masons, the Masonic affiliation is ignored."

In August a memorial to G. Andrew McComb, a former Executive Secretary of the Society, was printed. His funeral had been held on April 23, 1966.

The October 1966 issue of *The Philalethes* carried several noteworthy items. In memoriam to Dr. William Leon Cummings, Harold Voorhis wrote: " 'Doc' Cummings will never be replaced as a Masonic historian. His uncanny memory of odds and ends paid off over and over again. All Masonic historians will miss him. Hundreds of other Brethren will mourn his loss. Freemasonry has lost one of the pillars of the present century of Brethren."

The same issue announced the death of another Masonic stalwart, Ward K. St. Clair, who had died on September 12, 1966. And Dwight L. Smith was named a Fellow of The Philalethes Society.

In December it was announced that the officers for the next three years would be Robert H. Gollmar, President, William R. Denslow, First Vice President, and Andrew J. White, Second Vice President. Greisen and Heaton remained Executive Secretary and Treasurer. And Charles Forhands Adams was elected a Fellow.

9. FOUR DECADES
(1967–1969)

In February 1967, the new President, Robert H. Gollmar, said the magazine would continue to be improved and that the meetings for all interested Freemasons would be continued each February. He wanted to make the Society even more international in scope, and he would like to see more members meeting as groups. He predicted the Society would never be large, but he wanted it to have a small, steady growth. He was particularly anxious to have the Society continue to explore the problems encountered in Freemasonry. "We should always be ready to help Masonry wherever the written or spoken word will assist," he wrote in closing.

As many Masonic historians had before him, and more since, Alphonse Cerza pointed out that no one knows how old Freemasonry is. In his first article, "Our Masonic Heritage," he began a series on the history of the Craft to commemorate the 250th anniversary of the formation of the Grand Lodge of England. He said that while the Roman Collegia of 715 B.C. resembled Freemasonry, a resemblance is all it was. The Essenes, a religious group prominent in the time of Christ, also had some resemblance to Freemasonry. So did many other organizations of long ago, and some do today. But there has been nothing to connect any of them with the Craft.

The Editor noted that Bruce H. Hunt, MPS, of Missouri had been elected General Grand Recorder of the General Grand Council of Royal and Select Masters in October 1966. Charles K.A. McGaughey, MPS, of Kentucky, continued as General Grand Secretary of the General Grand Chapter of Royal Arch Masons, International. Both hold these positions in 1988. There always would be Philalethes members in positions of leadership throughout the world.

Signs of the times! The February 1967 issue of *The Philalethes* reminded the members: "DON'T FORGET **Your Zip Code Number** is needed to complete your address. Without it your magazine WILL NOT be sent. Send it NOW."

The Philalethes reported in April that the Masonic Workshop had produced the liveliest participation to date. The topic concerned Freemasonry taking part in community affairs.

Harry Gershenson, MPS, concluded: "There can be no doubt as to the obligation of Freemasons to take their place in the affairs of their communities. By the same token, until the Grand Lodge laws are altered, it is very difficult, if not impossible, for Masonic lodges to do so as a unit." This brought about a discussion of the differences in the laws governing the Grand Lodges of the country.

Wylie B. Wendt, FPS, disagreed with Gershenson. He made it clear that individuals should work for their communities, but lodges should not. His reasoning? "Freemasonry is not a religion; it is not a service club; it is not a reform institution; it is not a spectacular public show; it is not a forum." He based much of his arguments on the booklets written by Dwight L. Smith.

In Summing up, Cerza covered several points raised by the two speakers. He concluded that Freemasonry, rightly, mainly through its appendant bodies, has been serving the community for many years. He strongly suggested the lodges and Grand Lodges become more involved in community affairs, and let the world know it. His final word: "And I want to leave this parting thought: We best can worship God by serving our fellow men."

Ross Hepburn, FPS, New Zealand, was named the winner of the Certificate of Literature for 1966 for his articles about Freemasonry in New Zealand. It was noted that James D. Carter, MPS, of Texas, and Allen E. Roberts, FPS, of Virginia, were named the new Blue Friars. It was the first time in many years that two Blue Friars could be chosen. This can only occur when the membership falls below twenty. Roberts' paper, "Freemasonry Works in Mysterious Ways," was printed in *The Philalethes*.

The June 1967 issue of *The Philalethes* carried a reprint from the *Daily Quincy Herald* of Illinois for September 26, 1867. It was titled "Unusual Cornerstone Laying For A Great Railroad Bridge." It covered at length the ceremonies at Quincy for the bridge crossing the Mississippi River. It took the "ferry-boat *Quincy* and the steamers *Huron* and *Jesse* to carry the "imposing processions" to "pier No. 5 of the bridge, already partially crowded with eager ones, . . . making full 2,500 present in Mississippi midwater, of which there were about 1,000 Masons, to witness the ceremonies attendant upon the greatest work of the kind entered upon along this magnificent stream."

The event was recorded in full. The paper reported: "During this impressive ceremony the immense audience remained hushed—silent—attentive." The entire party returned to shore and in the depot of the C.B. & Q. Railroad the orator delivered his address, which was recorded in full. The orator gave a history of the laying of cornerstones by Freemasonry, then recounted some of the history of the Craft.

Cerza recommended the first volume of *Freemasonry Through Six Centuries* by Henry Wilson Coil, FPS. It was published by the Missouri Lodge of Research, with the second volume to follow a year later.

Much has been written over the years about Masonic involvement in the "Boston Tea Party." Fortunately, a first-hand account appeared in the August 1967 issue of *The Philalethes*. It was written by Dwight W. Robb, MPS, and was titled "Masonic Extracts From an Unpublished Diary of John Rowe." For the record, Rowe was a Loyalist and the last Provincial Grand Master of the Saint John's Grand Lodge of Massachusetts, having been appointed in 1768 by the Duke of Beaufort of England.

Robb recorded Rowe's recollection of the events leading up to the historical event day by day. Those to whom the shipments of tea were consigned continually petitioned the governor for assistance. The governor vacillated. The shipments arrived. An angry crowd met at Faneuil Hall, determined to keep the cargo from landing. The ships were ordered to tie up at Griffiths Wharf. Rowe's diary told of what followed:

"A Number of People Appearing In Indian Dresses went on board the three Ships Hall Bruce & Coffin. They Opin'd the Hatches, hoisted Out the Tea & flung it Overboard, this might I believe have been prevented. I am sincerely Sorry for the Event. Tis said near two thousand People were present at this Affair.

"18 December Saturday. The Affair of Destroying the Tea makes Great Noise in the Town—tis a Disastrous Affair & some People are much Alarm'd. I Can truly Say, I know nothing of the Matter nor who were Concerned in it. I would Rather have Lost five hundred Guineas than Capt Bruce should have taken any of this Teas on board his Ship."

A search for tea that had drifted ashore was made and when found, burned. Turning Boston harbor into a giant tea pot brought the enactment of the "Boston Port Bill" by the English Parliament. The port of Boston was closed; British regiments were sent to the area to "suppress riots." Rowe remained a Loyalist and continued to "drink to the Kings Health."

In this first-hand, eye witness account, Rowe, a Freemason and Loyalist, wrote nothing about the Green Dragon Tavern, St. Andrews Lodge, Masons, Masonry, or Freemasonry. He named not a single participant in the "Boston Tea Party." And to this day not a single participant has been truthfully named.

Andrew J. White was named a Fellow of the Society in June.

In October 1967 the President of the Society offered some advice for new writers. "It is often easier to start with a small job than to plunge into a large one. In writing, it is easiest to write about the things you have had personal acquaintance with. Before a Masonic writer attempts an involved philosophical article, he should look in his own Masonic backyard."

It was announced in December that James D. Carter of Texas had been named a Fellow of the Society. He had recently completed the first volume of the history of the Southern Jurisdiction of the Scottish Rite. For some unknown reason, Carter wasn't permitted to carry on the task of completing this history.

Jerry Marsengill, MPS, of Iowa, who would later become the Editor of

The Philalethes, wrote his first article for the magazine. The title of the paper published in December 1967 was "And the Grinders Cease."

Benjamin Elbert Bede, always known as "Elbert," was buried with Masonic rites by his mother Lodge, Ashlar No. 209, on October 28, 1967. He had spent his life publishing and writing. His writings, often on the lighter side, carried unforgettable messages. One of his favorite magazines was the *Oregon Freemason* which he published and edited for several years although it never was a profitable venture. He served The Philalethes Society well as its President. Those who shared his philosophical comments during the meetings of the "little Masonic meetings" in the District of Columbia were always refreshed. Those who knew him loved him. He had been a "Mason's Mason" for more than a half century.

Allister John McKowen also died in 1967. He was one of the first to join The Philalethes Society. He served the Society as its Executive Secretary from 1946 to 1954. His business activities were such that he had to cease taking an active part in the Society when it was reformed.

In February 1968 it was noted that Charles K.A. McGaughey and Benjamin W. Ela were elected Fellows.

Goodly Heritage, the history of the Grand Lodge of Indiana written by Dwight L. Smith, FPS, its Grand Secretary, was highly praised by Cerza.

William S. Conaway, MPS, discussed "The A,B,C's of Masonic Leadership" in the February 1968 issue of *The Philalethes*. He classed Masonic leaders under several categories: The absent leader; the barking leader; the critical leader; and the discussing leader.

"The mentally absent leader is present at all of the meetings of his group—if not in mind, at least in body," wrote Conaway. The physically absent leader "probably doesn't do as much actual harm as type one. . . . All he has to lose by being absent is opportunity—opportunity to bring life to the organization which he was elected to lead."

". . . In order to be a Barking Leader, cussing is not absolutely necessary; although it probably helps, since we all know that barking at a man is a good way to get him do any assigned task, especially when the pay consists of the proverbial corn, wine and oil." The critical leader "is the leader who feels that he has the God-given duty to criticize; not anything that might help, or help his Brother to better ritualistic work," or to become a better man.

The discussing leader "believes in discussion" for every subject. "All Masonic leaders are afflicted with this topic. This one is good for several hours or several days, depending on the number and lung capacity or those who think they are authorities, and that includes every Mason, from the youngest E.A. to the M.W.G.M. who presides in the Grand East."

Bruce H. Hunt, FPS, covered "Why Freemasons Lay Cornerstones" in

February 1968. He gave some of the history of the laying of cornerstones in this country and abroad. "Primarily," he wrote, "Freemasonry is a building Fraternity—not that it is now engaged in the actual erection of buildings or other structures—but because it was, originally, made up of men who made their living by working upon the great cathedrals and other monuments of antiquity."

Hunt closed with: "The symbolism of the Ancient Craft is based upon the science of architecture, and thus will exist as long as the planet revolves upon its axis. It is in recognition of this origin that Freemasons are delegated to perform the time-honored ceremonies of cornerstone layings upon important public buildings."

Walter M. Callaway, Jr., MPS, wrote his first article for the February 1968 issue of *The Philalethes*. It was titled "A Masonic Debt to Hitler." He covered the despicable character of the German dictator. Because Hitler outlawed Freemasonry, Callaway took notice of Freemasonry. It actually caused him to petition a Lodge and made him seek more and more light in the Craft. Callaway would later be the first recipient of the highest award the Grand Lodge of Georgia offers. Because of the excellence of his editing of the Georgia *Masonic Messenger,* he was later elected a Fellow of The Philalethes Society. Then he was made a member of the Society of Blue Friars.

In his column for April 1968, the Editor, John Vrooman wrote: "It Seems To Me That—the impact of Masonic Week in Washington was the greatest stimulant that Freemasonry in this country has received in many years. It emphasized thought, planning, action, and above all, it allowed the leaders of the Craft to sit down together to talk over our mutual problems, exchange ideas of good value, and return to our respective homes with new visions for the continued improvement of Freemasonry. Thank God for such vision! . . .

"Developing Masonic Leadership was the theme of the 1968 Masonic Workshop, and was one of the outstanding meetings of any yet held. The important thing was the audience participation, which was stimulating and provocative. Everyone who made comment on the two fine papers read, was emphasizing the need for, and the importance of developing leadership that could and would make it possible for Freemasonry to progress."

The President thanked "Brother Allen E. Roberts who had prepared a splendid Workshop program. He presided during the Workshop, and did an outstanding job. My thanks, too, to Brother Joseph A. Batchelor and Brother Ben G. Gustafson for their excellent papers. These papers stimulated the best discussion from the audience that I have ever seen at a Workshop. . . . My deepest thanks, too, to the some two hundred members who attended the Workshop, who listened courteously and with interest and participated."

Dwight L. Smith, FPS, was elected to the Society of Blue Friars and presented a paper titled "The Young Man Who Lisped." It was published in the April 1968 issue of *The Philalethes*.

Someone suggested the Society form a book club to make Masonic books available at a discount. A request for opinions went over with a dull thud. The proposal has never again surfaced. However, in 1983 Anchor Communications was formed and did offer members of the Society good Masonic books at a sizable discount.

Bob M. Stow of Missouri, who had been editing the column "Notes, Queries and Information On Items of Masonic Research" for several months, was named a Fellow of the Society.

The October 1968 issue of *The Philalethes* commemorated the Fortieth Anniversary of The Philalethes Society.

John Black Vrooman wrote about much of the early years of the Society in an article titled "The Development, Growth and Philosophy of The Philalethes Society After Forty Years." He said: "The whole story . . . since its formation on October 1, 1928, is not to be found in the mere recital of a narrative of events and landmarks . . . the real story behind its phenomenal growth and influence is in the sterling character, philosophy and leadership of the men who created it, and those who have carried on its tradition of service and devotion."

He rightly claimed the Society had, and has, many of the foremost Freemasons of their day. In speaking of the early members, Vrooman wrote: "To each of these pioneers we owe a debt of gratitude, both for the far-sighted inspiration they have afforded us, and for the clarity of their vision."

Vrooman repeated, as it is well to do occasionally, the primary objective of The Philalethes Society: "To create a bond of union for isolated Masonic writers and also to protect editors of Masonic publications from undeserved aggression from some dressed in a little brief authority. It might be easy to pick on one isolated individual, but the prospect of being held up to the scorn of the whole Masonic World outside his jurisdiction would (and did) make the most tyrannical pause."

The Editor covered what Willard had written in 1933: "The Philalethes Society has brought together in one compact organization those who in America and Europe have had experience in this work of Masonic education. . . . We are now bringing together the fruit of the genius of the best minds in the Craft for the service of the Craft, by making accessible the work of the best minds in it."

This is what was discussed in the fortieth year in the history of the Society. One would hope the situation had improved in the twenty years that followed. Unfortunately, Freemasonry as a whole continues to "spin its wheels." Each year Grand Lodges are spending thousands of dollars contributing to "Educational Conferences" such as the Northeast, Midwest, Southeast, Four Corners, Grand Masters, Grand Secretaries. Themes that were covered fifty years ago are covered over and over again. Leadership has been a recurring topic. Yet, for the most part, the Masonic leadership of today is too often inferior to that of a couple of decades ago.

During the past two decades there have been numerous advances in the electronic, management, and teaching environment. Freemasonry, generally, has ignored these progressive advances. Computers, for example, have taken the drudgery out of writing. No longer must the writer or author retype long manuscripts. He can "cut and paste" on the screen in front of him in minutes where it once took hours.

Because each Grand Lodge insists on total sovereignty there is no central clearing house for ideas. Each of the conferences goes its own way and the others know not what the others have done. The Philalethes Society has attempted during its long history to fill this void. Through the pages of *The Philalethes* it has reached out to the Masonic leaders who are members, and others who will listen. But too many of these leaders have never joined forces with the Society. Where they have, they and their jurisdictions have been the beneficiaries.

As Vrooman noted: "Because of the small membership of The Philalethes Society, because of its scattered activities, and lack of manpower and finances with which to do its work, it took during its first years of life the status of a small club, Masonic round table or inter-personnel group. It seemed impossible, at the time, to do much nation-wide Masonic work." Although the membership has increased, and with it the finances, much remains to be done in this its sixtieth year.

A list of the Fellows of The Philalethes Society for the first forty years was compiled by Harold V.B. Voorhis, FPS. He was number 15 and the oldest living Fellow. One hundred thirty-one had been honored with this designation. Two, George H. Imbrie and Robert I. Clegg, held the number zero because they were the prime movers of the formation of the Society.

There had been twelve Presidents of the Society: Cyrus Field Willard (twice), Robert I. Clegg, Alfred H. Moorhouse, Henry F. Evans, Walter A. Quincke, Harold H. Kinney, Lee E. Wells, Alphonse Cerza, William Moseley Brown, Elbert Bede, Charles G. Reigner, and Robert H. Gollmar.

The Society started publishing its own magazine in 1946. Through the next twenty-two years 138 issues had gone to its members. None were published in 1953 because of the upheaval in the Society caused by the deaths of its leading officers and editors.

Reigner wrote: "The Society is not primarily its magazine or its history, but the Masons who are its Fellows and Members. It emphasizes the mystic tie which binds us one to another. In these days when there are in the world so many influences and movements that are divisive in character, we do well to stress, in our words and actions, the factors that bring and keep us together as Masons."

The Executive Secretary, Carl R. Greisen, FPS, said: "It is fascinating to be associated with The Philalethes Society and its more than 1200 members. . . . The Society is friendly, its members seek more light (truth) and then impart it to those interested in seeking more light."

Andrew J. White, FPS, the Second Vice President claimed that most of the criticism of Masonry came from within. The words most often used were "the trouble with Masonry. . . ." He concluded: "I have my own theory as to 'the trouble with Masonry.' It is simply this:

"Our membership is made up predominantly of what I term 'Idlers in Respectable Places.' Other organizations, the Church, for example, suffer from the same continuing complaint. In an effort to encourage Masons to heal themselves, The Philalethes Society was conceived. For 40 years its work has continued, we believe with a beneficial impact on many, inspiring them to a truer devotion to our Order.

"To the extent that we are able to encourage men to end their idling, the trouble with Masonry will be over."

The First Vice President, William R. Denslow, FPS, wrote: " 'Life Begins After Forty!' From a modest beginning 40 years ago The Philalethes Society is undoubtedly stronger and more active today than at any time during its existence. Dedicated officers, as well as members, give unstintingly of their time. We have a comfortable financial reserve and Society activities are at an all-time high. The annual 'workshops' in February have become a high point of the ingathering for Masonic Week in the nation's capital. . . .

"[The founders] are the ones who conceived the idea of the Society, laid its cornerstone plumb, square and level and built the solid foundation on which we of the present generation labor. We salute these Masonic giants of yesteryear as we look to our leaders of the future, for in their hands life *can* begin after 40!"

"There is need to supply Masons with more reading material to elaborate on the lessons of the degrees and to keep them informed of what is happening in the world of ideas," wrote Alphonse Cerza. "The reading Mason is an informed Mason; and the informed Mason is a better Mason, is a better citizen, and a better friend.

"The Philalethes Society has been doing its part to spread Masonic light. But we can add to our beneficial work in a number of ways. First, all of us should help increase the number of our members. If this is done we will be able to increase the size of our magazine and possibly issue 'bonuses' of additional material from time to time. This can be done by talking to our friends about our Society. How about a gift subscription? How about your Lodge giving a year's subscription to each new member?"

In this thirty-two page special anniversary edition, it was announced that G. Wilbur Bell had been elected a Fellow of The Philalethes Society.

The Editor was deeply concerned about "the present unrest and lack of discipline among the Youth of the country." He felt it was time to prove not all young men were rebelling against authority. An article titled "Fifty Years of Young Men on the Go" was the result. It was written by Richard E. Harkins who outlined at length the proposed plans beginning January 1, 1969.

The planning for the DeMolay celebration was done by an impressive group of Freemasons and Senior DeMolays. These included J. Edgar Hoover, as honorary chairman, Harry S. Truman, former President of the United States, a Past Grand Master of Missouri, and long-time supporter of DeMolay and everything Masonic, Tom Clark, Gordon Cooper, Walter Cronkite (not a Freemason but a Senior DeMolay), Everett Dirksen, Dr. Norman Vincent Peale, and many others.

A memorial notice to Reginald Vanderbilt Harris, FPS, of Nova Scotia, covered his impressive Masonic career, but mentioned nothing about his membership in The Philalethes Society. He had died on August 2, 1968.

Cerza, in his "Recommended Masonic Reading," wrote : "Rarely do general historians mention items of Masonic interest." When he learned the Journal of the Illinois State Historical Society was going to commemorate the 150th anniversary of Illinois becoming a state, Cerza did something. He wrote "Freemasonry Comes to Illinois" and sent it to the journal for possible publication. It was published.

The Boston Tea Party, a new book on the subject, was reviewed by Cerza. "The claim of certain enthusiastic Masons that the Boston Tea Party was a Masonic affair by inference here is dispelled." He also mentioned the publication of *Brotherhood In Action!*, the story of the Virginia Craftsmen, and *Masonry Under Two Flags*, a previous series published in *The Philalethes*. It had been collected into a book and was available from The Masonic Service Association.

To help The Masonic Service Association kick off its fifty years of service to the Craft, the Editor ran "To Help, Aid and Assist," by Allen E. Roberts. Vrooman, in his note in this February 1968 issue, said Roberts had just completed *Freemasonry's Servant,* a history of the MSA, and the article briefly covered the highlights of that Association.

An article titled "Why is American Masonry Different?" defended Harry Carr of England for the comments he had made about the American Freemasonry he had witnessed. In this article, the writer, Henry L. Haupt of Indiana, said: "We should all know that our Masonry came from England; we should also know that all Speculative Freemasonry, no matter where you meet it in the world, is descended also from English Masonry." This observation is debatable.

The oldest existent records of operative masonry changing toward Speculative Masonry are in Scotland, not London. James Anderson was a Scotsman who may have been the instigator for the formation of the Grand Lodge of England. (Harold Voorhis, in an article in the December 1968 issue of *The Philalethes*, believes Anderson was behind the formation. For this article, "Two Theories to Look Into," Voorhis was awarded the 1968 Certificate of Literature.) Much of the early Freemasonry in America came from Scotland and Ireland through Military Lodges. Scotland and Ireland have never been enamored of the English.

Norman Dutt, FPS, noted that a group of clergymen in California had denounced Freemasonry. He also said this was nothing new. Freemasonry has been under attack since its beginning, especially as a speculative Craft. With the advances in the electronic media these attacks would become more violent in the 1980's.

The President heartily thanked Wes Cook, FPS, of Missouri, for his demonstration of what video taping can do for Freemasonry. Those who attended the 1969 Workshop witnessed what Missouri Lodge of Research was doing in this respect.

Cook interviewed Henry Wilson Coil and videotaped the session in 1968. Coil was asked what he planned on writing next. Coil said there wasn't anything left to write about, now that "Allen Roberts has written about Masonry during the Civil War." Even so, Coil wrote several more Masonic books before his death.

Conrad Hahn, FPS, wrote "Squared and Numbered in the Quarries" for the April 1969 issue of *The Philalethes*. "If Masonry is losing its influence," he said, "it will never recapture it at the Grand Lodge level. It can only recapture whatever influence it may have had (or we think it may have had) at the level of the lodge where Master Masons are made. You don't make Masons in Grand Lodge. You make Masons in a regularly constituted lodge of Master Masons."

In June 1969 a series entitled "Key to Freemasonry's Growth," advocating using the principles of management by the leadership of the Craft, began. The Mormons who were Freemasons at Nauvoo, Illinois, in the 1840s was the topic of an article by Mervin B. Hogan, MPS, in the August issue of *The Philalethes*. The President offered the sympathy of all members of the Society on the death of Mrs. John Vrooman. The third part of a series on "Continental Navy Masons," by Richard Tutt, Jr., made interesting reading.

"Books on a library shelf are useless," wrote Vrooman in the December 1969 issue of *The Philalethes*, unless taken down and read—taken and used. So it is with our work—we must make it practical, applicable to every day use, useful in making Freemasonry realistic and vivid. This is the purpose of our Masonic Workshop—to find ways and means by which the practical facts of Freemasonry can be utilized."

President Gollmar, in his last message as presiding officer of the Society, wrote: "It could be said that Philalethes has six jewels, three movable and three immovable. I would pay special tribute to the three immovable jewels: Carl R. Greisen, Executive Secretary; Ronald E. Heaton, Treasurer; and John B. Vrooman, Editor. These three men are the rocks on which the Society rests and without them no President could function. The fact is, of course, that these are the men who make the Society operate and I am grateful to them for their fine, unselfish and continued support."

Melvin L. Pfankuche, MPS, replaced Bob Stowe, FPS, as the editor of "Notes, Queries and Information on Items of Masonic Research."

William R. Denslow, FPS, Andrew J. White, Jr., FPS, and William E. Yeager were elected President, First and Second Vice Presidents for the triennium 1970-72.

Another era in the life of The Philalethes Society was about to begin.

10. PROGRESSING
(1970–1974)

"**W**e should pause to take inventory," wrote John Black Vrooman in the February 1970 issue of *The Philalethes*. "What has the past taught us, and what will the future give us." He then suggested that the officers, members and Fellows should use the past as a prologue on which to build.

Dr. Donald S. Lien, MPS, wrote about "Freemasonry in China." He said a charter had been issued for the Lodge of Amity No. 225, at Canton in 1767, and he believed there were thirty-three lodges in all prior to World War II. During that war "many of the Masons in China were persecuted. With the change in government in China, Freemasonry as we know it went out of existence on the Mainland." Many members of these Chinese Lodges moved to Formosa, or Taiwan, as it is now called.

"Times have changed," concluded Lien. "China has changed. The American people have changed. But there is an everlasting universality in Masonry. This great *Fraternity* will never change for it is founded on the never changing concepts of the Fatherhood of God and the Brotherhood of Man."

It was announced that the Masonic Book Club had been officially formed in Bloomington, Illinois, and was being headed by Alphonse Cerza, Louis Williams, and other members of the Society. Several members of the Society were asked to act as advisors. The Editor took pride in claiming Edwin E. Aldrin a member of the Craft. Aldrin, who had planted the Stars and Stripes on the moon, was a member of Montclair Lodge No. 144 of New Jersey.

The Executive Committee was asked to accept the resignation of Carl R. Greisen as Executive Secretary. It did with regret and elected Franklin J. "Andy" Anderson to the position. Anderson was named a Fellow since only a Fellow can hold this position. The Board agreed to provide a bonus book to the members at a later date. It also planned to have a representative of the Society attend each of the educational conferences throughout the country. Albert L. Woody would be asked to index *The Philalethes* to date. He agreed to do the job and completed it for publication in 1972.

The 1970 Workshop had 118 registered and an estimated 50 more present to hear Joseph A. Batchelor speak on "How To Prepare To Become An Active Master Mason." "Following this presentation, Allen E. Roberts, FPS, presented another phase of activities. Brother Roberts ran a 16mm color film in which he pointed out the principles of management—planning, goal setting, organizing, staffing, communicating, controlling. He briefly explained why a training film is necessary to cover each of the points fully." Roberts followed this by showing another film. It was *Communication Feedback* fea-

Franklin J. Anderson

turing Dr. David K. Berlo, Chairman, Department of Communication, Michigan State University. "Feedback" became a topic of discussion throughout the weekend.

The April issue of *The Philalethes* announced that Andrew J. White, Jr., the First Vice President, had died on March 3, 1970. His many achievements were recounted by Dwight L. Smith, FPS, in June.

J. Robert Watt, MPS, listed the "Vice-Presidents Who Have Been Masons." His list: Gen. George Clinton, Elbridge Gerry, Daniel K. Tompkins, Richard M. Johnson, George Millflin Dallas, William Rufus King, James C. Breckenridge, Andrew Johnson, Schuyler Colfax, Adlai E. Stevenson, Garrett A. Hobart, Theodore Roosevelt, Charles W. Fairbanks, Thomas R. Marshall, Henry A. Wallace, Harry S. Truman, Hubert H. Humphrey. Three of these, Tompkins, Dallas and Truman, had served as Grand Masters.

Mexican and Latin American Freemasonry was featured in the June 1970 issue of *The Philalethes*. The lead article, "Freemasonry In Latin America,"

119

was written by Bruce D. Hudson, MPS. "A significant difference between our Craft and Latin American Masonry is that their work is all Scottish Rite rather than York Rite (except for the York Rite bodies functioning in various jurisdictions)." He noted that the inside of the Masonic halls in those regions, because of the Catholic influence, are more ornate than are those in the United States.

Hudson, and others, claimed American Freemasons are greeted with warmth when they visit lodges across the border, but this is not the case, they said, when foreign Masons visit American lodges. They would like to receive the same treatment they offer Americans. D. Peter Laguens, MPS, Grand Secretary of the Grand Lodge of Louisiana, said Latin American Masonry had a great influence on the rise and progress of Freemasonry in Louisiana.

For several months *The Philalethes* received the names of Freemasons who fought in the the Battle of Bunker Hill. It started with three names and by the end of 1970 had listed nineteen. Twenty-one more were added early in 1971. And the search continued. The February 1971 issue of *The Philalethes* announced that the First Vice President, Robert V. Osborne, had been named a Fellow. It was also noted that Benjamin W. Ela, FPS, had died on November 17, 1970.

An ambitious project was announced in December and more fully explained in February. Mystic Tie Lodge No. 398 of Indiana, under the leadership of its Master, C.C. Faulkner, Jr., MPS, had formed "Mystic Tie Lodge Academy of Masonic Culture." The course was to run for one year with thirty-six weeks of instruction. Those who attended thirty or more sessions would receive a diploma. The "Curriculum" consisted of nine basic subjects divided into several parts. The list included: 1. The legendary and historical backgrounds of Freemasonry; 2. The story of Freemasonry in America; 3. The three degrees of Ancient Craft Masonry; 4. The spiritual aspects of Ancient Craft Masonry; 5. The lodge: cornerstone of Freemasonry; 6. The Grand Lodge of Masons in Indiana; 7. Masonic symbolism and terminology of the Craft; 8. How Freemasonry affects men; 9. What Masonry means to me.

In the February 1972 issue of *The Philalethes* Cerza pronounced the Academy a success. Thirty-six sessions had been held with an average attendance of forty-nine. Forty-eight received diplomas and were named "Fellows of Mystic Tie Lodge Academy." All claimed they had learned the difference between legends, myths and facts. Several planned on becoming Masonic researchers. Alphonse Cerza was the graduation speaker.

It is highly unusual for a Masonic teacher to be rewarded with anything but "Master's wages," but James Gale, who had headed up the Academy, was. His students, as a token of appreciation for the long hours he worked for them, presented him with two tickets for a trip to London!

Henry Wilson Coil, FPS, took issue with previous accounts of the formation of the Grand Lodge of England in 1717. "I am not aware," he wrote, "that 3 of the 4 Lodges forming the premier Grand Lodge of 1717 were predominantly operative or operative at all, and the idea that one speculative Lodge gained control of the Grand Lodge is very unlikely . . . the assemblage was of Freemasons as individuals" not as Lodges. He had other suggestions for further research.

An article titled "Virginia Craftsmen 'Invade' Canada" praised the team for carrying a Fellowcraft of Babcock Lodge No. 322 to Moncton, New Brunswick, Canada, and there opening Babcock Lodge on foreign soil. The Fellowcraft was raised to the sublime degree of Master Mason. The Grand Master of Masons in New Brunswick went out of his way to make the Craftsmen and their ladies comfortable. On the first evening he made his official visit with the lodge opened on the Fellowcraft degree so Babcock's Fellowcraft could be present. The following evening the Fellowcraft became a Master Mason.

The Executive Committee, in its meeting held on February 19, 1971, learned there were 1,243 members of the Society. Receipts for the year totaled $7,482.62; expenditures, $6,095.81. It was agreed the index when completed would be issued to the membership as a bonus book for 1972. For 1971 a booklet on the Houdon Statues by Ronald E. Heaton would be sent to the members. Franklin J. Anderson, FPS, was awarded the Certificate of Literature for 1970. Jerry Marsengill, MPS, was appointed Associate Editor of the magazine.

Well over one hundred fifty, including more than twenty-two Fellows of the Society, attended the Workshop conducted by Dr. Eugene S. Hopp, MPS, of California. The topic concerned "Physical Requirements" and whether or not they were necessary for petitioners to Freemasonry. The consensus appeared to be that the "doctrine of the perfect youth" had out-lived its usefulness, if it had ever had any.

Dwight L. Smith, FPS, of Indiana, commented: "It's a matter of curiosity to me and has been for a long time as to why Dr. Mackey, when he decided to play the role of Moses and prepare the Tablets of the Law, took only that portion of a sentence from Anderson's Constitutions that he wanted and emphasized that. . . . Here is what that paragraph actually says: 'No master should take an apprentice unless he has sufficient employment for him and unless he is a perfect youth having no maim or defect in his body that may render him incapable of learning the art of serving his Master's lord.' " Smith felt Mackey had emphasized the wrong sections of Anderson's comments.

D. Peter Laguens, MPS, of Louisiana, said: "We would rather have a man with a wooden leg than a man with a wooden head." The same statement had been made by a Grand Master in Virginia several years earlier when he was criticized for issuing a dispensation to permit a one-legged man to receive the degrees.

Laurence E. Eaton, MPS, said in April that he didn't believe George Washington was only twenty years of age when he received the Entered Apprentice degree in the Lodge at Fredericksburg in 1752. He discussed the changing of the calendar dates at length and concluded Washington was "21 years, 8 months and 23 days (old date) or 12 days (new date)." He claimed that changing the calendar date did not affect the number of years and days in the life of Washington or anyone else.

David R. Wheeler, MPS, didn't agree with Eaton. In an item in the April 1972 issue of *The Philalethes* Wheeler wrote: "As a genealogist I must take exception to his conclusion, for it is incorrect. George Washington was born 11 February 1731/2, or as they wrote it 11.XI.1731, February being the 11th month of their calendar. It was therefore incorrect to state that he was 21 on 4 November 1752. Novem in Latin means 9 therefore he was Entered 4.IX.1752, or 3 months and 7 days before his 21st birthday. His 20th birthday was 11 February 1751 (OS) and his 21st birthday was 22 February 1753." Wheeler did agree the date change "has caused many a genealogist to tear his hair."

"I can assure you that in some parts of the world there have existed and are still existing Masons meeting underground and keeping the real secrecy of Freemasonry at the price of their life." So wrote Jean O. Heineman, MPS, of France, in the *The Philalethes* for April 1971. "Do you know that Freemasonry still is banned in Spain and in Portugal where Masons are in constant danger? Do you know that Freemasonry is actually active behind a number of 'iron curtains'? Do you know what happened to your Masonic Brothers in the occupied territories of Europe during the last war? . . . Would YOU actually be prepared to pay the price of self sacrifice for your ideals, freedom, country, democracy and Freemasonry?"

In his article, "Freemasonry in Norway During World War II," Heineman continued:

> Norway was one of the countries that suffered severely during the last war from Nazi ideology and its implications in everyday's life. On the morning of April 9, 1940, we woke up surrounded by German troops, ships and planes, within the frame of a meticulously prepared invasion of a neutral country. A look at your map will show you how Germany, Denmark, Norway, Sweden, and England are located. From the German headquarters it certainly required all the strategy, planning, secrecy, organisation, intelligence and impact of decision necessary for such a venture to succeed. Though this was only one step among Hitler's military objectives: the invasion of the British Isles [was his ultimate

goal]. Norway had never been an hereditary enemy of Germany, had no reasons of being attacked, being a demilitarized area quite unprepared to any kind of armed conflicts [but its neutrality didn't stop the Nazis]. What happened?

Among the first premises to be seized were Freemasons' Hall and the Masonic temples throughout the country. One of the first decisions to be taken by the Nazi hordes was to ban Freemasonry and to confiscate all its assets. The incredible fact was that the world's strongest war machinery feared the most powerful of all weapons: spiritual arms. They believed in the savage destruction of spiritual powers, that Freemasonry symbolizes, but that actually cannot be touched, seized, destroyed.

[Freemasons, along with the other Norwegians who believed in freedom formed the Norwegian Resistance Movement.] Freemasonry had to be beheaded, often with the charge of conspiracy or, as it frequently happened, with the charge of supporting the Jewish traditions. As you know, Hitlerism's worst enemy remained the Jewish people and they claimed Freemasonry to be a 'Jewish agency in the hands of international capitalism, ruled by the Jews for the benefit of Jewish imperialism!' They opened our Masonic Temples, in the hope that their 'disclosures' would serve as propaganda for the nazi regime and legitimate their action against Freemasonry. It merely had the opposite results on the mind of the profane world. The Nazi printed the rituals, disclosed the signs, tokens, words, grips and the degrees of Freemasonry, without of course being able to get down to the heart of the True Secrets of Masonry.

During those five darkest years of our history, we were surrounded by constant dangers, meeting illegally like the first Christians hiding in the catacombs, like the Zealots and the ancient Jewish Resistance against Rome. Our towns remained in complete darkness at night for five years, soldiers and secret police patrolled our streets, youth were mobilized to work for the enemy, our radio receivers were taken from us, we had no cars and no petrol. All clubs, societies, organisations of any kind were declared illegal. Even meeting a group of men in the woods surrounding Oslo for a ski run, represented a big risk. Food supply and clothing were scarce. The slightest sign of chauvinism could mean arrestation, deportation, death. Fear and uncertainty surrounded our homes, our families, our relatives and friends, our Brothers.

[The Resistance continued to fight with few weapons.] We suffered heavy losses. Too many of our friends and Brothers were shot or caught, tortured, sentenced to death or to deportation in concentration camps. We never gave up, and kept up the morale and spirits of our brethren in those trying times, by the application of the very principles of Freemasonry, in building for the future. . . .

On May 8, 1945, after a struggle of five years, the unbelievable happened, the incredible fact came true: we were free, free from fear and darkness, free from starvation, imprisonment and atrocities. The very same day Freemasonry reappeared, recovered its belongings and started the long work of restoration of the temples, or re-organisation of the Craft as a whole. Freemasonry had survived, in spite of its 'total destruction' by the Nazis. At last, the Craft had frustrated the efforts of the Nazis in crushing freedom. But membership had suffered heavily. Norwegian Freemasonry numbered about 11,000 members, which figure was reduced to about 3,000 during the war.

The Associate Editor, Jerry Marsengill, reported on his trip to Indiana to become indoctrinated in the make-up of *The Philalethes* at the Masonic Home print shop. His article, "Through Darkest Indiana With Notebook and Pencil," appeared in the June issue.

Marsengill, in August, noted that Ethel Merman, "the widely known musical comedy star, was connected with our fraternity before she was six years old." He had read in an issue of the *Reader's Digest* that she had appeared in "her father's Masonic lodge." In 1978 Miss Merman helped the Grand Lodge of Virginia celebrate its two hundredth year in Williamsburg, the place where it was founded. At that time she was presented with a Masonic plaque in memory of her father.

In October 1971 Marsengill strongly suggested that writers should "Let Your Reader Understand You." He said the average Masonic writers "endeavor to sink their thoughts in a sea of verbiage, and lose their audience after the first paragraph." He suggested writers use a guideline which "would be to write as if you were speaking to a brother. State the central idea, tell why you think this central idea is important, and having explained the idea close as quickly as possible. . . . Stand up, Speak up, and Shut up!"

"Masonic Flags at Sea" was an article translated from the German by Albert Von Damm. These Masonic flags were described as being blue with a white square and compasses, about 14'4" by 4'10". This flag, or pennant, aided Freemasons to locate one another when in port. One captain reported seeing seven flying in Port Louis one Sunday in May in the 1850s. Another claimed that of 300 ships in Honolulu harbor, over 100 flew a Masonic flag.

An explanation of how the Masonic flag came into being appears logical, according to Von Damm. During the Coalition Wars of 1799–1802 a British vessel fired on a French ship, heavily laden and carrying the 41st Half Brigade, that had drifted into the English channel. The French captain tried in vain to strike his colors in surrender. British officers monitoring the British fire saw seventeen French officers "(Members of La Concorde Lodge) on the poop deck giving the Masonic sign of distress in unison. Firing was immediately stopped." The French were paroled. Out of gratitude, those whose lives were spared "made it their duty to organize lodges wherever they were subsequently stationed."

Vrooman, in February 1972, explained how leadership training films could help, and were helping, grow leaders in several jurisdictions. He had many kind words to say about the work of Allen E. Roberts, FPS, with these films and in the field of Masonic education.

The Virginia Craftsmen were highly praised by Marsengill who reported on the visit of the team to Riverside, Illinois, Des Moines, Iowa, and Louisville, Kentucky. In his closing paragraph he wrote: "No one who has ever witnessed this fine team in their colorful uniforms, conferring their faultless ritual, and admiring the precision of their floor work, can help feeling pride that there are men in our fraternity who will take their own vacation time and their own money and travel to distant points to exemplify Virginia ritual and to spread brotherly love. Our hats are off to the Virginia Craftsmen."

The Workshop in February 1972 found the largest attendance to date. This was surprising. A heavy snowstorm stranded many delegations on their way to Washington. Dr. William G. Peacher, FPS, chaired the panel which discussed "The Impact of Freemasonry on the Public School System." It was announced that Dr. Eugene S. Hopp, MPS, of California had been awarded the Certificate of Literature for 1971 for his article "Defining Freemasonry; Traditional Becomes Practical."

It was noted that Conrad Hahn, FPS, was to be awarded the James Royal Case Medal of Excellence by the Masonic Lodge of Research of Connecticut. James Case, FPS, was the first recipient of the medal. In all, seven Fellows of The Philalethes Society would receive it, Case, Hahn, Harold V. B. Voorhis, Dwight L. Smith, Ronald E. Heaton, Alphonse Cerza, and Allen E. Roberts.

The Editor, John Black Vrooman, FPS, received a plaque for thirty years of service to The Masonic Service Association's Hospital Visitation Program; and Ronald E. Heaton, FPS, had received a Freedoms Foundation award.

One of the most famous limericks of all time was written by Dixon Lanier Merritt, according to Harold V. B. Voorhis, FPS, writing for the *The Philalethes* for June 1972. Dixon was a made a Freemason in Owensboro Lodge No. 130, Kentucky, later affiliating with Corinthian Lodge No. 414 in Tennessee. The limerick written in 1913 reads:

> A wonderful bird is the pelican!
> His bill will hold more than his belican.
>   He can take in his beak
>   Food enough for a week,
> But I'm damned if I see how the helican.

Also in June an article written by Dr. John A. O'Brien, whom *The Philalethes* termed "President of the University of Notre Dame," analyzed various items written by Catholic theologians. He concluded these leaders believe there is nothing to restrict a Roman Catholic from becoming, or remaining, a Freemason. If Lodges adhere to the landmarks of Masonry, "That is to say: faith in a supreme being and the Bible; exclusion of any discussion in the lodge on arguments strictly political or religious; and sincere respect of the law of the state," there would be no reason for excommunication. Jesuit Father Jean Beyer of the University of Rome believed there should be no excommunication if "the Masons should reveal themselves as believers in God and defenders of their government"; and they should do this "if they want Catholic members."

O'Brien was told the Church would not come forth with "a dramatic lifting of the excommunication," but the code would be silently revised.

William J. Whalen, the author of *Freemasonry and the Catholic Church*, an anti-Masonic tome, in a letter written in November 1987, said of O'Brien: "He was a friend of mine and died some years ago. Of course, he was never the president of the University of Notre Dame as *The Philalethes* identified him, but he was wise, learned, and kindly. He was a priest of the diocese of Peoria who founded the Newman Center at the University [of] Illinois and spent his last years teaching religion at Notre Dame. He was known as a pioneer Catholic ecumenist, but he and I differed on the lodge question." There have been too few among Father O'Brien's Church who have followed his example in an endeavor to unite men of all faiths.

Benjamin Franklin was highly praised by Michel Brodsky of Belgium. Franklin held the number "106" on the register of *Les Neuf Soeurs* (Lodge of the Nine Sisters) and was offered "the apron of Helvetius" which "shows how much he was estimated." Brodsky added: "For an American what must have been a great moment for B. Franklin was the joining to the Lodge of John Paul Jones who joined in the spring 1780," and who had been "received by the King himself." The sculptor, Houdon, "made a portrait of" Jones. The Lodge was honored by the presence of "B. Franklin, the man who led Voltaire in the Lodge Rooms on the day of the initiation of the latter and it shows also that the universal spirit of Freemasonry was lively two centuries ago as it is today."

"The secrecy of Masonry is considerably overestimated by the average Mason," wrote Edward J. Franta, FPS, of North Dakota, in the October 1972 issue of *The Philalethes*. "Masonry would flourish and grow more naturally if some of the unnecessary secrecy could be avoided." He went on to recount some of the long history of Freemasonry, beginning with *The Regius Poem* of c. A.D. 1390. He wanted his readers to know that Freemasonry is "one of the most potent forces for good in the world, an institution which has outlived the history of nations, the devastations of war and disaster, and which has continually grown, because it spreads easily and naturally where men want to improve themselves through better serving their God, their country, their family and themselves."

Kenneth F. Curtis, FPS, who had served the Society as its Membership

Chairman for several years, died on September 2, 1972. A memorial notice was published in *The Philalethes* in February 1973.

Lewis C. "Wes" Cook of Missouri and Dr. Eugene S. Hopp of California were elected Fellows in December 1972. Hopp then was elected the Second Vice President; William E. Yeager became President and Robert V. Osborne First Vice President. Andy Anderson and Ronald E. Heaton were re-elected Executive Secretary and Treasurer.

Dwight L. Smith, FPS, of Indiana, in a Fellow's Masterpiece titled "Of Landmarks and Cuspidors" published in the February 1973 issue of *The Philalethes*, was concerned. He believed far too many claim landmarks are being violated whenever a change is made in a Masonic lodge. "The Grand Lodge of England," he wrote, "which should know a thing or two about the ancient landmarks, never has 'adopted' landmarks or in any way attempted to define them other than to make casual references to certain practices. To my knowledge, no Grand Lodge of Freemasons outside the United States has ever become concerned about what the landmarks are, or how many there may be." He didn't say it wasn't considered necessary to enumerate the landmarks until Albert Mackey played havoc with the subject.

Smith itemized many of the changes that had been made with the changing times and more modern conveniences. "We are wise if we can avoid the error of identifying as a landmark any practice which may have been helpful a century ago, but long since has ceased to serve us well," he continued. "Such practices are habits, and nothing more. Many of them belong in the same category as the cuspidor and the pot-bellied stove—worthy of sentiment, but no longer useful." He closed with a statement about Masonic landmarks made by Robert Freke Gould, an English historian, and which was quoted in *Key To Freemasonry's Growth* (for which Smith wrote the Foreword): "Nobody knows what they comprise or omit; they are of no earthly authority, because everything is a landmark when an opponent desires to silence you; but nothing is a landmark that stands in his own way."

English, even the version spoken by Americans, is difficult to learn, it is claimed. An item appearing under the title of "The Funniest Language You Ever Did See!" in the February issue of *The Philalethes* explains why this is so.

> We'll begin with a box, and the plural is boxes;
> But the plural of ox is oxen, not oxes.
> Then one fowl is a goose, but two are called geese,
> Yet the plural of moose should never be meese!
> You may find a lone mouse or a whole nest of mice,
> But the plural of house is houses, not hice!

If the plural of man is always called men,
Why shouldn't the plural of pan be called pen?
If I speak of a foot, and you show me your feet,
And I give you a boot—would a pair be called beet?
If one is a tooth, and a whole set are teeth,
Why should not the plural of booth be called beeth?
Then one may be that and three would be those,
Yet hat in the plural would never be hose;
And the plural of cat is cats, and not cose!
We speak of a brother, and also of brethren,
But though we say mother, we never say methren!
Then the masculine pronouns are he, his and him,
But imagine the feminine, she shis and shim!
So English, I fancy, you all will agree,
Is the funniest language you ever did see!

Stewart M. L. Pollard, MPS, told the Executive Committee that more emphasis should be placed on the international aspects of the Society. The committee agreed and named Pollard as chairman of the International Relations Committee. The membership as of December 31, 1972 was placed at 1,384. The need to form more Chapters of The Philalethes Society was stressed, but no steps were taken to implement the need. Heaton and Vrooman discussed a series of articles for *The Philalethes* throughout the bicentennial of the country. It was also suggested that a book containing the "masterpieces" of the Fellows be compiled and made available to the membership. This was never done.

On December 26, 1972 the thirty-third President of the United States, Harry S. Truman, died. His would be the only Masonic funeral ever telecast, and that almost didn't occur. The government took charge of all arrangements and it wasn't until the last moment that the officials agreed to give the Grand Master of Masons in Missouri five minutes air time. Had it not been permitted, it would have been one of the bitterest crimes ever perpetrated against Truman and Freemasonry. No man loved the Craft more than he did. His adult life was spent working for his country, God, his family, his fellow-man and Masonry. The complete story of this remarkable man will be found in *Brother Truman*. A brief obituary appeared in the February issue of *The Philalethes*.

Also in the same issue Charles S. Guthrie, MPS, wrote about "Lafayette's Visits to Kentucky Masonic Lodges in 1825." The Frenchman who became an American general in the War for American Independence made a triumphal tour of the United States in the last months of 1824 and early months of 1825. He was received by cheering throngs wherever he traveled, and Freemasons took the Marquis and his son, George Washington Lafayette, to their

*Harry S. Truman, Past Grand Master of
Masons in Missouri.*
[Painting by Greta Kempton]

hearts. He was made an honorary member of numerous Masonic lodges
throughout the country. Harold Voorhis spent a lifetime studying the life of
Lafayette and wrote extensively about him.

The Workshop for 1973 was under the leadership of Robert V. Osborne,
FPS, First Vice President. It concerned the coming bicentennial of the country. The panel discussed the varying ways in which several Grand Lodges
would be celebrating and commemorating this historical event. About 200
participated during the evening.

Among the participants was Halldor K. Halldorson, MPS, of Canada. He
suggested the Freemasons of the country obtain a railroad passenger car and
have it crisscross the country during the bicentennial. "Arrange it so that you
let your people in one end and they follow along the little corridors all the
way through. By illuminations, by screens, by pictures, by various means and
almost any articles and what have you, you could probably bring across the
message of what Freemasonry has meant in the building of the greatest society on earth, and then hopefully by the time that the people would go through
these trains and come through on the other end, they will not only have
renewed confidence in the United States of America, but they will realize

fully the part that Freemasonry has made in making it great."

Halldorson, who was to die three months later, explained how this had worked in Canada in 1967 for its centennial. It was estimated that 75% of the people of Canada passed through its train. He suggested the cost could be self-liquidating by charging a nominal fee of fifty cents. He believed a beautiful and meaningful exhibit could be set up through the cooperation of the Freemasons of the country. The idea was warmly greeted, but it came to naught.

The April 1973 issue of *The Philalethes* covered the ground breaking ceremonies on February 5 at Lexington, Massachusetts, for the new Scottish Rite Library and Museum of the Northern Masonic Jurisdiction. This would constitute a portion of the NMJ's contribution to the bicentennial.

On April 20, 1975 the "Museum of Our National Heritage" was officially opened. *The Philalethes* for June 1975 reported: "The multi-million dollar facility was built through contributions by members of the Scottish Rite of Freemasonry, Northern Masonic Jurisdiction, and presented as a gift to the American people. Admission will be free at all times."

George A. Newbury, MPS, the Sovereign Grand Commander, said: "As the story of America unfolds within these walls, it must ever be rigidly truthful, presenting those aspects of our history and our national life that we deplore as well as our successes. May we ever see it through eyes of love for this land of our birth or our adoption, unafraid of the future and highly resolved that Justice and Equity shall prevail throughout our land among all our people."

James R. Case, FPS, outlined the planned coverage of historical events that led to the founding of the United States. This ambitious program would run monthly in the pages of *The Philalethes* through 1982.

The Blue Friar for 1973 was Ralph H. Gauker of the District of Columbia. The paper he read on that occasion was printed in *The Philalethes* for April. It was entitled "Statues of Great Masons In Our Nation's Capital." He began: "There are ninety-six statues (52 marble and 44 bronze) in the United States Capitol building alone, not counting numerous others located elsewhere in the city. Of the statues in the Capitol building, 39 have definitely been established as being of Master Masons, three who received the first degree only, and at least three who are purported to have been Masons, but for whom no proof can be established.

"Of these 39 Master Masons there are seven Past Grand Masters, viz: Thomas Hart Benton . . . Iowa, 1860–1862; Lewis Cass . . . Ohio, 1810–1813, and later . . . Michigan, 1826 and re-elected in 1844; Henry Clay . . . Kentucky in 1820; Benjamin Franklin . . . Pennsylvania in 1734 . . . 1749 and again in 1760; Andrew Jackson . . . Tennessee, 1822–23; William King . . . Maine in 1820 and George L. Shoup . . . Idaho in

1889." He didn't name the other Master Masons, but covered at length the careers of Franklin, Washington and Jackson.

The forty living Fellows of The Philalethes Society were pictured in the April 1973 issue of *The Philalethes*, something that had never before occurred.

Harry S. Truman was memorialized by the Order of DeMolay during the month of April. Special memorial classes were held throughout the country. His work as an Honorary Past Grand Master of DeMolay for many years, as well as his work for Freemasonry as the leading Freemason of the country, was commemorated.

In June, the Editor reminded the members of the goals of the Society. "Primarily, The Philalethes Society was established to sponsor and foster **Masonic Research, Masonic Study and the Dissemination of Masonic Precepts** that will make for a better and more enlightened Craft. . . . We must never forget that the prime purpose of our magazine is to encourage and stimulate thought and active participation of the members in a study of some of the less-known and little-understood phases of Freemasonry; the writing, study and research by our members into unknown and unfathomed depths of Masonic thought, and above all, the stimulation of interest in and study of the greater facets of the Craft, and a better understanding, by such study, of the real meaning and message of Freemasonry."

In October it was learned that Mrs. Lucretia R. Garfield, by request, had sent a lock of James Abram Garfield's hair to be placed in a golden urn, to the Grand Lodge of Massachusetts. The urn rests beside the one made by Paul Revere to hold a lock of hair from George Washington.

In *Gesprache Mit Hitler* (Conversations With Hitler) by Hermann Rauschnigg, it is learned that Hitler knew Freemasonry "has always been harmless in Germany." However, he said: "This hierarchic structure, instead of teaching through enlightenment of the mind, achieves the fruition of fantasy through the use of symbols, rites and the magic influence of emblems of worship. Herein lies the great danger which I have taken in hand. Don't you see that our party must be something very similar, an order, an hierarchic organization of secular priesthood? This naturally means that something similar opposing us may not exist. It is either us, the Freemasons or the Church but never two side by side. The Catholic Church has made its position clear, at least in regard to the Freemasons. Now we are the strongest and, therefore, we shall eliminate both the Church and the Freemasons."

Alex Horne, who had become a new Fellow of the Society, wrote a book titled *King Solomon's Temple in the Masonic Tradition* which was distributed by Quatuor Coronati Lodge in England. Cerza noted that the first printing had been exhausted, it was in its second printing, and the book was also being translated into French.

FELLOWS OF THE PHILALETHES SOCIETY
1973

Robert V. Osborne
First Vice President

Franklin J. "Andy"
Anderson
Executive Secretary

Dr. Eugene S. Hopp
Second Vice President

William E. Yeager
President

Ronald E. Heaton
Treasurer

Living Past Presidents

Lee E. Wells (Life)
1952–53

Alphonse Cerza (Life)
1954–1957

Dr. Charles Gottshall
Reigner (Life)
1964–1966

Robert H. Golimar
1967–1969

William R. Denslow
1970–1972

Charles F. Adams

G. Wilbur Bell

Dr. James David Carter

James R. Case

Henry W. Coil (Life)

Lewis C. "Wes" Coc

George F. Draffen

Norman C. Dutt

Henry Emmerson, Jr.

Jerry R. Erikson

Edward J. Franta

Hirsch Geffen

Antonio Gonzalez

Carl R. Greisen

Conrad Hahn

Dr. Ross Hepburn

Bruce H. Hunt

Charles K. A. McGaughey

Jose Oller

William G. Peacher

Allen E. Roberts

Dr. Francis J. Scully

Dwight L. Smith

James Fairbairn Smith

Bobby Melden Stowe

Harold Van Buren Voorhis
(Life)

John Black Vrooman
(Life)

Wendell K. Walker

Wylie B. Wendt

Albert L. Woody

J. Edward Allen
(Past Fellow)

Charles S. Guthrie, MPS, spoke of the strange case of Henry Clay, a Past Grand Master of Masons in Kentucky, in the December 1973 issue of *The Philalethes*. In early 1820 Clay was Master of Lexington Lodge No. 1; on August 20 he was elected Grand Master by acclamation from the floor. In 1822 he was in the forefront of prestigious Freemasons seeking a national Grand Lodge. "This movement, which seems to have been originated by prominent Masons in Congress," wrote Guthrie, "was unsuccessful. The Grand Lodges did not wish to submit themselves to any central authority. The Grand Lodge of Kentucky was one of the majority which deemed it inexpedient to participate . . . in the movement."

Guthrie believed this defeat was the reason Clay demitted from Lexington Lodge on November 18, 1824. Yet, in 1852 when Clay died, he was buried with Masonic rites. During his lifetime, Clay attempted to be elected President of the United States on three occasions without success. Two of his losses were at the hands of Freemasons: Andrew Jackson and James K. Polk.

"Musical Society Confers Third Degree!" was the title of an article by John R. Nocas, MPS. "The Masons who had the honor of placing on record the first third degree in Masonry were members of the *Philo-Musicae et Architecturae Societas, Apollini*," wrote Nocas. This event occurred on May 12, 1725 and the record states: "Our Beloved Brothers & Directors of this Right Worshipful Societye whose names are here Underwritten (Viz.) Brother Charles Cotton Esq., Brother Papillon Ball, Were regularly passed Masters, Brother F X Geminiani, was regularly passed fellow Craft & Master. Brother James Murray Was regularly passed Fellow Craft."

"The next recorded third degree took place in March of 1729 at the Swan and Rummer Lodge of London," continued Nocas, "when six of its members were made Masters." When the Grand Lodge learned of the action of the Musical Society, Nocas said there was considerable discussion. "The new Grand Lodge was endeavoring to stop the ancient custom of making Masons outside of Lodges, but with little success until some years later."

Lionel Augustine Seemungal, MPS, of the West Indies, wrote about "The Fictitious 'Great Schism' " in the February 1974 issue of *The Philalethes*. "One of the most enduring Masonic fictions in the United States is the belief that the Ancient Grand Lodge of 1751 in London arose from a *'schism'* in the Premier Grand Lodge of 1717," wrote Seemungal. He explained how Preston, Mackey and others were incorrect in their theories. Henry Sadler, Librarian of the Grand Lodge of England, "proved that the founders of the 1751 Grand Lodge were *never* members of the 1717 Grand Lodge. Thus there was no 'schism.' Nor were the Ancients 'spurious,' 'irregular' or 'clandestine' Masons, as some have believed."

Seemungal was amused to find American Grand Lodges believing it was necessary to be descended from the 1717 Grand Lodge. "Scottish and Irish Masons think that this is very funny," he said. "Their Grand Lodges were *quite independent* foundations, purporting to derive no regularity from the 1717 English Grand Lodge. Scotland boasts of still-existing Lodges and Lodge Minute Books *far older* than any to be found in England."

"In fact, the earliest recorded initiation on the soil of *England* was in a (still existing) *Scottish* Lodge of a *Scotsman*—that of Sir Robert Moray, while on military service, in the Lodge of Edinburgh when it was in Newcastle, England in 1641." Seemungal found the American doctrine of "exclusive jurisdiction" ridiculous.

"The doctrine of 'Exclusive Jurisdiction' or 'Territorial Exclusiveness' is such a 'sacred cow' in U.S. Masonry, the 1751 Grand Lodge would be irretrievably 'damned' for breach of it. Some Grand Lodges have even erected this doctrine into a 'Landmark'. . . . Now, since a Landmark must have existed 'from time immemorial,' it is difficult to see how this doctrine can be fitted into the class. . . . The earliest expressed declaration of it was in 1796 by the Grand Lodge of New York!"

Seemungal concluded: "This theory of **'The Great Schism'** should be given a swift and unlamented burial. No corpse should be left around to putrefy from 1887 up to today—an unconscionably long period of 86 years."

The first of a long series on the American War for Independence and the Bicentennial of the Declaration of Independence began in February 1974 with James R. Case, FPS, as the leading writer.

Marsengill, in his "Chat and Comment" column, recorded that one of the most deserving Freemasons in the country had been rewarded by *his mother* Grand Lodge. He was Walter M. Callaway, Jr., MPS, of Georgia, who received the first distinguished service award ever issued by the Grand Lodge of Georgia.

Henry Wilson Coil, FPS, who had devoted his life (when he wasn't practicing law) to Freemasonry, died on January 29, 1974 at the age of 89. His encyclopedia, published in 1961, will live forever. So will his many other books. His funeral was conducted by Riverside Lodge No. 635 of California on February 1.

During the Masonic Workshop in February, Jerry Marsengill (a newly elected Fellow of The Philalethes Society) gave the Brethren much wholesome advice on " 'Riting." His first paragraph was most important: "If one intends to begin a career of Masonic writing, there are many things he must do, but there are three which are important. He must read, *read* and READ AGAIN. No one should ever undertake any writing project until he has read everything which he can find on the subject."

135

Dwight L. Smith, FPS, was awarded the 1973 Certificate of Literature for his article, "On Landmarks and Cuspidors."

Gerald R. Ford, the new Vice President of the United States, addressed the Conference of Grand Masters on the evening of February 19, 1974. "I come, as I think some of you know," he said, "from a family of Masons over not one generation but many generations. And I'm proud to be a part of Masonry in North America—some four million strong who represent the high principles and the fine ideals that give to us in America and to all of you in Mexico and Canada the realization of what's good for your people and for our people.

"Every place I go, wherever I run into those of us who are brethren, I find that you are the leaders. You do not necessarily always agree about political philosophy or partisan ideas, but you have an interest in and a dedication to the things that are good for our country and for your country as each of us sees it." *The Philalethes* account covered other things he said about learning of his selection as Vice President. He then concluded:

> But let me say that having come from a family which has a long tradition of Masonry, I'm proud to have an opportunity just to say a few words tonight. I don't think anybody would be more proud than my father if he were here. I can recall very distinctly when my three brothers and I were given the great honor of joining Masonry at one time. It meant so much to my dad. He was active in degrees; he was active from beginning to end. And I learned from him, as I have learned from others, the superb contributions that all of you and the others who are our brethren among the four million in North America have made to each of our governments and to our people.
>
> We should be proud of our organization, proud of our respective countries. And as we leave Washington and go back to our various communities or respective states, we should hold our heads high and be proud of what this means to each of us and what it means to our communities and our country.
>
> That's my feeling toward Masonry and what it has meant to me, what it has meant to my family.
>
> Masonry exists in those countries which are free. And it is important that we maintain that freedom so that organizations such as Masonry can exist and flourish, because what we do can have an impact on our respective countries and the world at large. Freedom is a priceless heritage for each of you and all of our fellow citizens. And our contribution can be immeasurable in protecting that freedom worldwide.
>
> I conclude by saying I'm grateful to be a part, as all of you are, of this great organization and what it stood for and what it will project in the days and months and years ahead.

In October 1974 *The Philalethes* reported: "In one of the most dramatic episodes of American history, Gerald R. Ford, Jr., was sworn in as the thirty-

eighth President of the United States, immediately following the unprecedented resignation from that office of Richard M. Nixon [August 8, 1974].

"Still another unprecedented fact was that [Brother] Ford had neither been
elected to the office of either Vice President, nor President, but was named
Vice President on the resignation of the former holder [Spiro Agnew] of that
office, and later nominated and confirmed as President by the House of
Representatives and the United States Senate by an overwhelming voice
vote." Ford was (and is) a member of Malta Lodge No. 465 of Grand Rapids,
Michigan.

On February 17, 1975 Ford's plaque was unveiled at the George Washington National Masonic Memorial and placed among those of the other Presidents who had been Freemasons. In his comments on this occasion he said:

> Let us today rededicate ourselves to new efforts as Masons and as Americans.
> Let us demonstrate our confidence in our beloved Nation, and a future that will
> flow from the glory of the past.
>
> When I think of the things right about America, I think of this Order with its
> sense of duty to country, its esteem for brotherhood and traditional values, its
> spiritual high principles and its humble acceptance of God as the Supreme
> Being.
>
> Today we honor our first President, who was also our first Masonic President.
> In a letter in 1798, to the Grand Lodge of Maryland, Washington used some
> words which are now especially appropriate.
>
> Washington told the Order that he "conceived it to be the indispensable duty of
> every American to come forward in support of the government of his choice and
> to give all the aid in his power towards maintaining that independence, which we
> have so dearly purchased."

"Is Islam Forbidding Freemasonry?" asked Albert E.K. Von Damm in an
article translated from *Die Bruderschaft* and published in the April 1974
issue of *The Philalethes*. He outlined the strength and interest in Freemasonry in the middle eastern countries. But in June 1973 the Islamic World
Congress asked the Islamic world to condemn "British originated Speculative
Freemasonry." Von Damm noted that Freemasonry was fairly strong and
active in Egypt, Morocco, Tunisia, Algeria, Syria, Lebanon, Arabia, Iran
(formerly Persia) and Turkey.

"At the present time," wrote Von Damm, "in the Islamic Orient, lodges
are working in Persia, Jordan and Pakistan as well as in the Saudi-Arabian
centers of the European and American Oil Companies. To a large extent the
latter is also true of Persia in spite of the great efforts of our Persian brothers
to establish their own image. Freemasonry, on the whole, in spite of contrary
reports, has never been permitted in the heart of Islam-Saudi Arabia." He
suggested the Masons in the Islamic countries be encouraged to "resurrect

the old Islamic freemasonry based on the Koran." Otherwise, he warned, the opportunity would be lost "to prevent masonic light from being completely extinguished. If the ban comes, except for the small island of Israel where 3,000 Brothers, Jews, Moslems and Christians work, the entire Islamic world will be without the sound of the masonic gavel."

The President of the Society, William E. Yeager, FPS, died on April 8, 1974. He was an exceptional leader in Freemasonry and his community. He served the Grand Lodge of Pennsylvania as Grand Master in 1950–51. Before that, and long after, he was a leading proponent of Masonic education. He proved to be one of the ablest Presidents of The Philalethes Society. Not even his work as president of the Community Consumer Discount Company could interfere with his work with and for young people and Freemasonry.

Robert V. Osborne was named President of The Philalethes Society to succeed Yeager. Dr. Eugene S. Hopp became the First Vice President and Dwight L. Smith, FPS, of Indiana was chosen the Second Vice President.

A new era began. With it the Society continued to put into action its plans for the celebration of the bicentennial of the United States.

11. BICENTENNIAL (1974–1976)

The bicentennial series of articles continued and the search went on for Masonic historians in areas where historical events occurred during the war.

One of these was found in the person of Norris G. Abbott, Jr., not a member of the Society, but well-known in Masonic circles in Rhode Island. He wrote about "The Gaspee Affair." It has not been commonly known, but the destruction of the British warship *Gaspee* was the "first blow for freedom" from English rule. It pre-dated the "Boston Tea Party" and by three years the battles of Lexington and Concord.

Rhode Island had determined it alone had the right to "lay taxes and imports upon the inhabitants of this colony." It defied the navigational acts and the Townshend Acts of 1767. Consequently the British stepped up their enforcement powers and sent more armed vessels into Narraganset Bay and along the coast from Maine to Delaware. Among these was the sloop *Gaspee* whose captain didn't hesitate to board and search all vessels entering or leaving Rhode Island ports.

"On June 9, 1772," wrote Abbott, "the sloop *Hannah,* commanded by Captain Benjamin Lindsey, having cleared customs in Newport, set out upon the Bay for Providence. As might be expected, the *Gaspee* soon took off after her and fired a warning shot across her bow. Captain Lindsey had no intention of stopping to be searched. He crowded on all sail and the race was on. For several miles it was touch and go but when the *Hannah* cleared Namquit Point (now Gaspee Point) about seven miles below Providence, and headed westward, [Lieutenant William] Dudingston, in close chase, changed his course to take a more direct route and ran aground [off] the Point, where his ship stuck fast.

"The *Hannah* proceeded on her way to Providence and spread the word. Shortly thereafter there was the sound of a drum in the streets and the voice of the Town Crier was heard calling: 'The Gaspee is run aground off Namquit Point and cannot float before three o'clock tomorrow morning. Those people who feel disposed to go and destroy that troublesome vessel are invited to repair to Mr. James Sabin's house this evening.' There was plenty of enthusiasm and by nine o'clock a large company had gathered in Sabin's Tavern to cast bullets in the kitchen and to listen to the plans for the attack as outlined by John Brown, one of the most enterprising and wealthy merchants in New England."

Captain Abraham Whipple led the attacking Rhode Islanders in their eight longboats. The attack was successful. Dudingston, the first to fire a gun, was

139

wounded, but a doctor in the boarding party dressed his wounds. The crew was ordered to take their possessions and then landed on the shore. The *Gaspee* was set on fire. The attackers watched as the powder exploded and nothing was left of the ship but charred wreckage. Large rewards were offered for any of "the perpetrators of the said villainy." No one could be found who could identify any of the "villains."

Unlike the "Mohawk Indians" of "Boston Tea Party Fame," no disguises were employed, "yet not an individual could be found who knew anything about the affair. In later years it has been confirmed that among the participants were John Brown, Abraham Whipple, Silas Talbot, John Mawney and Ephriam Bowen, all members of St. John's Lodge [No. 1] of Providence."

Abraham Whipple was the brother of William Whipple, one of the Freemasons who signed the Declaration of Independence. In his own right, Abraham was an outstanding sea captain. In 1759–60 he commanded the *Gamecock* and captured twenty-eight French vessels in a single cruise. He fired the first gun of the War for American Independence on the water when he captured the *Rose*, a British vessel. In July 1779 he maneuvered through a convoy and captured eight English merchantmen, a prize of over a million dollars. In 1780 he was finally captured by the British and held prisoner until the end of the war. In 1790 he joined the Ohio Company and settled in Marietta, Ohio, the final home of American Union Lodge.

The August 1974 issue of *The Philalethes* had an article about the so-called "Boston Massacre" which had no Masonic significance. Ronald E. Heaton, FPS, covered "The First Continental Congress." Heaton asked: "What of Masonry and Masons in this first organized effort which eventually led to the independence of the Colonies? Of the fifty-three signers of the Articles of Association, we learn that ten were members of the Fraternity."

The ten Freemasons Heaton named were Peyton Randolph of Virginia, the first President of the Congress; Edward Biddle of Pennsylvania; Richard Caswell of North Carolina; John Dickinson of Pennsylvania; Joseph Hewes and William Hooper, both of North Carolina; Charles Humphreys of Pennsylvania; Robert Treat Paine of Massachusetts; John Sullivan of New Hampshire; and George Washington of Virginia.

The late Jacob Hugo Tatsch, FPS, who died in 1937, was brought to "life" to recount his tale of "Freemasons and the Boston Tea Party" for *The Philalethes* in October 1974. In his article he readily admitted: "It is to be regretted that no authentic record of the names of the persons who composed the Boston Tea Party in 1773 has come down to us. Although St. Andrews Lodge of Boston couldn't meet because not enough members were present, no reason for this is recorded." The so-called "T" in its minutes of Thursday, December 16, the night Boston Harbor was turned into a giant tea pot, was a penman's flourish in the form of a scroll with absolutely no significance.

Harold V. B. Voorhis and J. Hugo Tatsch

Tatsch did say: "That [Joseph] Warren was present as a leader in the affair, does not admit of any serious doubt; nor is there any question that his personal friends Samuel Adams [not a Mason] John Hancock, Joseph Webb, Paul Revere, Thomas Melville, Adam Collson, Henry Puckett, . . . and other patriots of the day, were cognizant of it,—and some of whom at least are known to have participated in its final consummation."

Tatsch said he had looked in vain for a rallying song sung at the Green Dragon Tavern, but all he could recall was this:

> Rally, Mohawks—bring out your axes!
> And tell King George we'll pay no taxes
>   On his foreign tea!
> His threats are vain—and vain to think
> To force our girls and wives to drink
>   His vile Bohea!
> Then rally boys, and hasten on
> To meet our Chiefs at the Green Dragon.
> Our Warren's there, and bold Revere,
> With hands to do and words to cheer
>   For Liberty and Laws!
> Our country's "Braves" and firm defenders,
> Shall ne'er be left by true North-Enders,
>   Fighting Freedom's cause!
> Then rally boys, and hasten on
> To meet our Chiefs at the Green Dragon.

"Broadly speaking," Tatsch continued, "it was the virility of the patriotic clubs of the period which gave strength to the public movements and the Masons who were members and leaders of the groups were of 'Ancient' derivation, as compared to the brethren whose allegiance was with the 'Moderns' and among whom many were loyalists. While not germane to the present subject, it should be observed that the American Revolution was not so popular a movement as is generally supposed after reading school book histories."

The Philalethes for February 1975 recorded that Allen E. Roberts, FPS, had received a silver award from the International Film and TV Festival of New York. His *The Saga of the Holy Royal Arch of Freemasonry* had been judged one of the best documentaries produced in 1974. Earlier Roberts had been presented with a commemorative chalice by the General Grand Chapter of Royal Arch Masons. In September he and James Fairbairn Smith, FPS, one of the script advisors for the film, received a Silver Medal of the General Grand Chapter for distinguished service.

The Saga tells the story of Freemasonry and shows how Royal Arch Masonry is an important part of the whole structure. A cast from the Royal Order of Scotland re-enacted the first recorded conferral of the Royal Arch degree in the Lodge at Fredericksburg in 1753 in a replica of the Lodge room in which George Washington received his degrees. Colorado Masons brought to life "The Lodge Room Over Simpkins' Store," a familiar poem by Brother Lawrence N. Greenleaf. A scene depicting a Mason helping a Brother during the American Civil War shows why Freemasonry remained a house undivided during that conflict. Jerry Rasor of Ohio, the narrator, Edward M. Selby, MPS, the General Grand High Priest who fulfilled his mission to have such a film, Smith and the writer-producer were highly commended by the General Grand Chapter.

"Westward Ho!" was the theme for one of the most interesting Workshops in the twenty-one years it had been a feature in Washington. DeMoville P. Jones, MPS, of Kentucky was the chairman. He was assisted by N. Tracy Walker, MPS, of Illinois, Gordon R. Merrick, MPS, of Colorado, and Dr. Eugene S. Hopp, FPS, of California. Each of them discussed the Masonic movement toward the west, actually as far west as Hawaii. More than 200 Freemasons were in attendance.

Walter M. Callaway, Jr., of Georgia was elected a Fellow of The Philalethes Society. The following Sunday, he became the newest, and one of the most deserving, members of the Society of Blue Friars. John R. Nocas, MPS, of California was awarded the Certificate of Literature for 1974 for his article "Josephus: The Great Jewish Historian."

A search was announced in the April 1975 issue of *The Philalethes* for articles that could be turned into motion picture scripts. These were to show why the youth of the day needed what Freemasonry had to offer. Although prizes and awards were offered, nothing was ever submitted.

Marsengill wrote a guest editorial for the June 1975 issue of *The Phila-lethes*. "Article after article crosses our desk which necessitates our writing numerous letters to the various authors in order to check some small point in something they quote," he wrote. "Many of these articles display a woeful lack of acquaintance with literature." He went on to urge all writers to become readers.

The Associate Editor also noted: "Vrooman has not completely retired but has turned a large share of the editing over to me. This is especially gratifying at this time since I can say what I want to in this column without him sticking his fingers into it." He then went on to commend the Editor, John Black Vrooman, for his thirty-three years as a Field Agent for The Masonic Service Association.

The Grand Master of Masons in Israel, Zvi Levin, wrote to Jerry Marsengill asking for the help of the Freemasons of the United States so Israel could continue to count on the friendship of the people of America. "We both know that we don't mix in politics," said Levin, "but our situation here is quite dangerous and I find it our duty as Masons to do whatever we can. I wrote, as Grand Master, to President Ford, as a Freemason, believing in the Masonic tenets. I had the honour of an answer but very diplomatic."

Marsengill reminded his readers that genocide takes place because good men refuse to get involved. "Freemasons played a large part in the founding of Israel. Had it not been for M.W. Brother Harry S. Truman, and had he not been a man of firm fiber and strong integrity, Israel would have never become a reality."

Norman C. Dutt, FPS, wrote about the trials, frustrations, and triumphs of George Washington as Commander-in-Chief of American armed forces, in the continuing series on "The Bicentennial of the American Revolution." In this same August 1975 issue of *The Philalethes* the *Masonic Square* of England, a new Masonic publication, was commended. It would become one of the more prestigious Masonic magazines.

A memorial notice for Dr. Francis Joseph Scully, FPS, discussed his work as a Masonic researcher, among other things. He died on March 10, 1975. Religious services were conducted in the St. Mary of the Springs Catholic Church in Hot Springs, Arkansas. The Grand Lodge of Arkansas conducted his burial service in Calvary Catholic Cemetery. An unusual episode for a Past Grand Master of Masons.

Alphonse Cerza believed it was time to do some evaluating of particular political and other systems then prevalent. He did this in the October 1975 issue of *The Philalethes*. "A comparison of Bolshevism [another term for communism] and Freemasonry is in order at this time. In 1917 when the

Bolsheviks took over Russia they outlawed the Craft and there has been Masonic darkness in that great country ever since. Wherever Bolshevism becomes supreme it destroys the Craft and all other groups that are not under its complete control. And, above all, the basic concepts of Bolshevism are incompatible with the fundamentals of Freemasonry.

"Freemasonry is based on a belief in God; Bolshevism is an atheistic concept with religion considered as 'the opium of the people.' Freemasonry is based on love; Bolshevism is based on class hatred. Freemasonry glorifies the worth of the person; Bolshevism places all the emphasis on the Party and the State. Freemasonry believes in complete freedom so each individual may develop his skills and enjoy complete freedom of choice in every area of human endeavor, restricted solely when his acts interfere with the equal rights of others; Bolshevism believes in slavish obedience to the State and stifles individual freedom.

"Let every Mason ponder on the differences. Let every Mason recognize the vital difference between Communist doctrine on the academic plane and how it is put to work in actual practice in the lives of the people."

Another view of Russia and Freemasonry was recorded by Albert Von Damm in the February 1976 issue of *The Philalethes*. "Peter the Great, the father of modern Russia, became the sole ruler in 1696," he wrote. He "opened doors to the west" and with this opening Freemasons entered. England appointed Provincial Grand Masters in Russia in 1731 and 1740. "About 1765 a masonic system of Russian origin was founded in St. Petersburg. . . . It was a peculiar combination of symbolic masonry with Templar grades upon which semi-Catholic Church ceremonies were superimposed. It was imbued with vague mystical teachings interspersed with Kabbalistic and Alchemical notions. The Rite consisted of seven degrees. Meetings of Adepts (the higher degrees) were held either in Churches of in Chapels especially consecrated for the purpose."

Von Damm continued: "From 1731 to 1770 there was really no authoritative masonic organization playing a serious part in the awakening Empire. After 1770 Freemasonry became a fashionable pastime for the nobility. . . . The next Emperor, Peter III, was a protector of the Craft and probably a mason. He was forced from the throne in less than a year by a strong-willed wife who was supported by a palace revolution. She ascended the throne as Catherine II, or Catherine the Great, a strict disciplinarian possessed of a skeptical mind." But Freemasonry grew.

Although there were varying systems practiced, the growth continued. Then there were schisms that caused the Grand Lodge to split. Their differences couldn't be reconciled, so "on August 1, 1822, Tsar Alexander decreed closing of all masonic lodges in Russia. They were not officially reopened for the balance of the century." Freemasonry went underground.

"In 1908 both the Grand Orient and the Grand Lodge of France opened a lodge under their respective jurisdictions in both Moscow and St. Petersburg," Von Damm continued. "They were discovered by the government the following year and suspended work. In 1911, however, several members of these suspended lodges decided to renew their activities, their chief aim being political and *not* masonic."

It would appear from Von Damm and other accounts that for all practical purposes, Freemasonry had been abolished in Russia before the Soviet regime conquered the country.

General Herman Nickerson, Jr., MPS, who had been a Marine for thirty-five years, wrote about "Marines in the American Revolution." Included in the same issue was an article about "American Navies In Our War For Independence" which had been written by the late Richard Tutt, Jr.

Gerald D. Foss of New Hampshire was elected a Fellow in October 1975.

Giacomo Casanova was a Freemason. Of this Allen Cabaniss, MPS, reminded the readers of *The Philalethes* of October 1975 in his article "Casanova and Freemasonry." In his *Memoirs* Casanova wrote: "At Lyons a respectable person . . . obtained for me the favor of being initiated into the sublime rudiments of Freemasonry. When I reached Paris, I was a simple Apprentice; but several months afterwards I became a Fellow and Master." This was about 1750.

"Born in Venice in 1725," wrote Cabaniss, "he became at the age of fifteen a churchman in Minor Orders. In 1742 he received, according to his own statement, the degree of doctor of laws at Padua. Already his amorous promiscuity had begun, as well as his habitual wandering from place to place. Always bright and inquisitive, gifted with a retentive memory, he was a favorite in any company for his sparkling and witty conversation."

In what is apparently and understatement, Cabaniss added: "It is entirely possible that Casanova was not the only person of his kind to be drawn to Masonry. As a matter of fact the doughty old Benjamin Franklin can be mentioned along with him." Cabaniss could have added, at least, Robert Burns. He did mention Laurence Dermott who wrote his *Ahiman Rezon* in 1756. In this book Dermott included "at least six passages in verse, three songs and three 'epilogues,' that have a distinctly rakish Casanova ring." These can be found in the 1972 Masonic Book Club replica of *Ahiman Rezon*.

"A Mason's Daughter fair and young," told her young man:

> None shall untie my Virgin Zone,
> But one to whome the Secret's known,
>   Of fam'd Free-Masonry;
> In which the Great and Good combine,

> To raise with generous Design,
>   Man to Felicity.
>
> The Lodge excludes the Fop and Fool,
> The plodding Knave and Party-Tool,
>   That Liberty wou'd fell;
> The Noble, Faithful, and the Brave,
> No golden Charms can e'er deceive,
>   In Slavery to dwell.

He left, applied for the degrees, returned and married the daughter, and "Connubial Joys their Days have blest."

In another song the ladies are told that Masons can "keep us in Transport all night." In another a Mason sings: "Then always happy me; Likewise a gentle She I crave, Until I'm summon'd to my Grave, Adieu my Lodge and she." And a toast: "To each charming Fair and faithful She, That loves the Craft of Masonry."

"Arnold's March and the Canadian Campaign" was written by Ralph J. Pollard, MPS, of Maine, for the December issue of *The Philalethes* prior to his death in July 1975. Pollard gave credit to the military expertise of Benedict Arnold, a Freemason, that was fully deserved.

One of the fine Masonic poets of the day was Walter K. Belt, MPS, of Oregon. He claimed he wasn't a poet: "It would be more accurate to call me a rhymer, or a versifier, but, I hope, something more than a poetaster." In his article, "How I Write Masonic Verses," for the December 1975 issue of *The Philalethes*, he made another confession: "I am a traditionalist who believes that a poem must have Rhythm, Rhyme, or Reason, and, preferably, all three. I consider these the indispensable three Rs of versification; and, if a piece of writing does not have at least one of them, I do not consider it a poem, regardless of any 'poems' you may see in the printed media today."

Belt considered *The Complete Rhyming Dictionary and Poet's Craft Book* by Clement Wood "one of the most important working tools of a would-be poet," even though it was published in 1936. A good dictionary, a thesaurus, a word guide and such reference books were also important to him. "I have been rhyming for more than sixty years," he wrote, "so I should be well-practiced. Someone has said that genius is 10% inspiration and 90% perspiration. I do not claim to be a genius, and my percentages would be different. I would claim that my formula is 1% inspiration (I hope that a few of my verses are inspired), probably 10% perspiration (I tend to be lazy), and the other 89% cogitation (including time with my reference books)."

To give an example of how he worked, Belt chose *Ecclesiastes XII*. After a couple of trials he came up with this:

Ecclesiastes XII

Remember thy Creator now, oh, man,
  While still your strength and health endure,
And work by your great Master's lofty plan,
  And keep your actions ever pure.
For all too soon must come that evil day,
  And all those dreaded years draw nigh,
When pleasures of this life have passed away,
  And gone the sun and moon on high.
When teeth are few, and eyesight rather dim,
  Hands shake, and sturdy legs are bowed,
For all of life is but an interim—
  We near the ending of the road.
The thread of life, the silver cord, for you
  Will soon be loosed. So ends your climb.
Thus, Brother, if you have good deeds to do,
  Let them be done. Now is the time!

For those who desire to try their hand at writing poetry, Belt suggested they get their working tools together and get ready to build the poem. Here's how:

If you think of an incident, real or imaginary, you can make it into a narrative poem.

Most Masonic poems, however, are hortatory, that is—encouraging to good deeds. All of the Masonic ritual is devoted to that end, so you can call to mind any of the tenets of Masonry or any parts of the ritual—it does not matter much where—and think about it for a minute or two. In my case, I take any of these bits of Masonic wisdom, mull it over in my mind until a word or a phrase develops, write it down, and see what other thoughts I can come up with along the same line. Then I write them down, too, till I have words and scraps of phrases all over the page. I try to string these together, in a definite pattern, with a definite beat, referring to the Poet's Craft Book as necessary to get started, and fill my pattern in with rhymed words, finding them in the Rhyming Dictionary if I can't find them in my mind. Clement Wood says anybody can do it.

In February 1976 Dr. Eugene F. Hopp, FPS, of California took over the helm of The Philalethes Society as President. Dwight L. Smith, FPS, of Indiana became the First Vice President; Conrad Hahn, FPS, of Maryland, Second Vice President. Anderson and Heaton retained their offices.

James R. Case continued the bicentennial series with an article about "American Union Lodge, Feb.–Aug. 1776." It's interesting to note that John Rowe, a professed Loyalist, authorized the formation of this Lodge, with Joel

Clark as Master, with permission to meet "wherever your Body shall remove on the Continent of American, provided its where no Grand Master is appointed." Strangely, Richard Gridley, the Deputy Grand Master, who issued the warrant for the Lodge, never sat in one of its meetings. John Rowe, the Grand Master, did, and this was on March 20, 1776 at Waterman's Tavern, Roxbury, Massachusetts. Colonel Joseph Webb, who succeeded Joseph Warren as Grand Master of the "Antients," was also a visitor to American Union Lodge. The Commander-in-Chief, George Washington, was closely associated with the Lodge throughout the war.

The Lodge would meet periodically throughout the war, and its warrant would be taken to Fort Harmar, across from what is now Marietta, Ohio. In 1790 it would be revived and eventually become American Union Lodge No. 1 on the roster of the Grand Lodge of Ohio.

"The Discover of the Regius Poem" was the title of an interesting article by Alphonse Cerza for the February 1976 issue of *The Philalethes*. James Orchard Halliwell was born in 1820, and "before he was nineteen years of age," wrote Cerza, "was elected a Fellow of the Society of Antiquarians and a Fellow of the Royal Society." While in the British Museum in 1839 Halliwell found a book in the King's Library listed as "A Poem of Moral Duties." He described this to his colleagues of the Society.

"The next year," Cerza continued, "he published a brochure entitled 'The Early History of Freemasonry in England,' with a new printing in 1844, using the discovered book as the basis of publication. . . . The book had been presented originally to the British Museum by George II and was placed in the King's Library which had been started by Henry VII. The discovered book is now known as the Halliwell Manuscript (after its discoverer) and is also known as the *Regius Poem*. The book is of interest to Masons because it is the oldest known Masonic book in existence today. It is believed to have been written about the year 1390."

Cerza records an interesting and important footnote. Sir Thomas Phillips, a "super-book collector," arranged for the marriage of his daughter, Henrietta, to Halliwell. Prior to the marriage Phillips became "disenchanted for some reason never discovered and he opposed the marriage." The youngsters were married, anyhow. In his will Phillips disinherited his daughter "unless her husband adopted her maiden name; he wanted the name of Phillips to be perpetuated. The same day that Halliwell found out about this he directed his lawyer to take steps to have the name Phillips added to his name. Thenceforth he became known as James Orchard Halliwell-Phillips. This has caused some confusion in Masonic books as he is described under both names without the reason being given." Incidentally, the youngsters became wealthy because Halliwell added Phillips to his name.

The Workshop for 1976 was different. Eugene H. Kelchner, MPS, "presented a delightful and interesting program of transparencies and taped music of the Colonial period, depicting the background development and importance of the events of the Revolutionary War." Kelchner was highly praised by the officers of the Society and those present, which was attested to when he received an unusual standing ovation. And the attendance was the largest recorded to that time.

The Executive Committee (now called the Board), after a heated and lengthy discussion, agreed that the Society would offer Life Memberships. The rate set was $100. This money was to be invested and only the interest used for the general fund. The joining fee was increased from $3.00 to $5.00. Alex Horne was awarded the Certificate of Literature for 1975 for his article "Prince Edwin, 926, A.D., Our First Speculative Mason." The membership stood at 1,556. The cash balance was $6,835.89.

Albert Woody, FPS, insisted in the February issue of *The Philalethes* that the Associate Editor was wrong. He used a period after the "S" in Harry Truman. Marsengill apologized (he shouldn't have). William R. Denslow in April wrote: "It is true that when a man's middle initial stands for nothing except an initial . . . that no period should be used. Following this line of thought, Truman's initial should not have a period. However this rule is overthrown when it comes to how the man used it himself. *Truman used a period after the S.*" Denslow found this true in the hundreds of letters he and especially his dad received from Truman.

Actually, the "S" did mean something. Truman's grandfathers were Solomon Young (maternal) and Anderson Shippe Truman (paternal). Only smiles greeted the inquiry: "Whose name does the 'S' represent?" That Truman's parents added the initial for a reason can't be questioned.

(Note: I also found this true in the thousands of letters, notes, memos, and so on that I handled in gathering first-hand material for my book, *Brother Truman.* But it appears in everything in which his full name is typed. *Occasionally* the period *was* left out. Occasionally I don't use it after my middle initial!)

The Executive Secretary, Franklin J. "Andy" Anderson, FPS, retired as associate editor and business manager of *The Royal Arch Mason* in Fulton, Missouri. He moved to Columbia, Maryland, in August 1976 to be with his family.

A member of the Society in South Carolina wanted to know the meaning of "7(1/6-5(2/3-3." He said he found these "illustrated several times in the AHIMAN REZON of the Grand Lodge of South Carolina." In August 1976 Lewis J. Birt, MPS, Dr. S. Brent Morris, MPS, and fifteen others, provided the answer. Morris put it this way: "If you will recall your lectures explaining the minimum number of Masons necessary to open various types of lodge, some understanding is available. An Entered Apprentice Lodge is opened by Seven Masons, one MM and 6 EA. A FC Lodge is opened by 5 Masons, 2 MM and 3 FC. A Master Masons Lodge is opened by three MM."

C. B. Knox, MPS, of Caribou, Maine, told Marsengill: "If you are mystified by them, then you'd better turn in your recently acquired trappings as Grand Master of the Grand Council of Iowa, return to your mother lodge and work through the chairs—or at least listen attentively to the Master Mason degree lectures a few more times. Any Master Mason should know [what] they mean." To which Marsengill added: "Reckon he sure told us whose boar ate the cabbage, didn't he?" Actually, Marsengill, an expert Masonic lecturer, knew the answer but believed the question would be an excellent vehicle to promote discussion. He was correct.

Two more important episodes in the bicentennial series appeared in the October 1976 issue of *The Philalethes*. General Herman Nickerson, MPS, wrote about "Marines In the American Revolution" (his part I appeared in August); and Richard Tutt, Jr., MPS, spoke about "Benedict Arnold's Navy on Lake Champlain."

Stewart M. L. Pollard, MPS, struck a blow for international participation in The Philalethes Society. "Since its founding in 1928, The Philalethes Society has claimed to be 'international' in scope and activity. Yet, in actual practice, we have been quite provincial. The vast majority of our membership is composed of American Masons. Our officers have all been American Masons and our research efforts have quite naturally been largely oriented toward American Freemasonry. True, we do have *some* members in other parts of the World—'Freemasons who seek more Light and who have more Light to impart.' "

As Chairman of the International Activities Committee, Pollard was presenting a case for his cause. He failed to mention that the Society had sought worthy members from foreign climes since its inception. Over the years, as the appendix relating to Fellows of The Philalethes Society will attest, a large percentage of "foreign" Freemasons have been honored for their Masonic dedication.

From the beginning of The Philalethes Society, Freemasons of every country in the world were urged to participate. Things didn't work out the way they were expected to. A letter from Walter A. Quincke to a Brother in Sweden written on May 12, 1951 tells part of the story:

> Brother Cyrus Field Willard, when founding our Society, had 40 Fellows, all of whom were editors of well-known Craft papers here and abroad, whose function it was to promote the Society through the medium of their respective papers.

John Black Vrooman

In addition, Corresponding Members were appointed in foreign countries whose function it was to send Masonic news from their respective jurisdictions.

Corresponding Members did not pay dues because of their obligation to send Masonic news, which was a sort of barter agreement. This plan proved a grand headache even during Willard's time, because the number of Corresponding Members increased at such a rate that it became top-heavy. After radio and wire-service was more fully developed, the Masonic news sent by these brethren was considered old by the time it reached us and for that reason could not be used.

Along about our reorganization in 1945, it was decided to eliminate this sort of membership, because we saw that hordes of foreign brothers, although worthy and well-qualified, wanted to become members of our Society under that classification. If you will recall your own case, and as you said in your letter, your own membership card was obtained free of charge. Under the old Corresponding Membership status, you failed in fulfilling your end of the bargain, that of sending Masonic news of your jurisdiction which we in turn could use in *The Phila-lethes*. It was therefore necessary not only to eliminate the Corresponding Membership status, but to ask you to pay annual dues if you cared to maintain your membership in The Philalethes Society and receive our official literature as published.

I think you have materially gained by paying, and we have been most generous in supplying you with odds and ends of Craft material.

With warmest personal regards, believe us

The Philalethes Society
by WALTER A. QUINCKE

"VROOMAN RETIRES AS EDITOR; MARSENGILL NAMED TO POST" read the headline under a picture of John Black Vrooman with his ever present pipe on the cover of the December 1976 issue of *The Phila-lethes*. It caused mixed emotions among many of the long-time members of the Society. Hundreds had grown up Masonically during the twenty-two years Vrooman had edited the magazine. Since 1931, when he first joined the Society, he had worked for it in many capacities. He could have easily been its President on numerous occasions, but he preferred to work behind the scenes.

Vrooman became an integral part of the "little Masonic Bodies" that met in Washington each year. He presided over many of them and then became the spiritual overseer of several. To the younger Freemasons who first met him in awe, he became "Mr. Mason." Although he demanded something approaching perfection in those writing for *The Philalethes*, he patiently developed those writers who showed potential.

The era of *Editor* John Black Vrooman had come to an end, but he would remain an inspiration to oldster and youngster alike as The Philalethes Society moved into its fifth decade.

12. HALF CENTURY
(1976–1978)

Conrad Hahn, FPS, Second Vice President, was selected by the Executive Committee to begin planning for the celebration of fifty years of service by The Philalethes Society. In the December 1976 issue of *The Philalethes* he asked for help. He wanted every member to have a part in the commemoration.

As Chairman of the Workshop for February Hahn had assigned tasks to several members. Dr. Eugene S. Hopp, the President, would take a look at where the Society is today. "Then a thorough look will be taken at our magazine, *The Philalethes*, today and tomorrow, in a 'give-and-take' led by Brother Allen E. Roberts, FPS, of Highland Springs, Virginia." Allan D. Parsons would take a look at the membership and Chapters. James R. Case, FPS, "will lead the concluding discussion on 'Plans for the 50th Anniversary in 1978.' "

John Black Vrooman said: "It is with a sense of loss that I bow out as editor and turn this important job over to one who is so capable and efficient. What has been done in the past is the result of united cooperation and good will; of effort for the good to the Society and the whole Masonic fraternity. . . . I urge you to give this continued cooperation to Jerry Marsengill, FPS, who is taking over this job."

Vrooman concluded: "Jerry Marsengill is capable and willing—now let each of us do our part to make his job easier and more fruitful. FORWARD WITH INSPIRATION FOR OUR BELOVED SOCIETY!"

The new Editor laid down some ground rules for potential writers for *The Philalethes*. He wanted well-researched articles of a Masonic nature, 1,500 to 2,000 words in length. They should be checked and double checked for accuracy; the wishful thinking was to be left for other publications. He would accept Masonic articles of a controversial nature provided they were factual and the writer wasn't trying to grind his own axe. Letters, complimentary or abusive, would be welcome. The writer should write as he talks because he wanted the potential reader to become an actual reader. Readers are turned off by the use of "a bunch of big words with a high 'fog index.' The 'fog index' is measured by the number of words over one syllable you have." And "don't use a bunch of footnotes. If it is necessary to give someone or some source credit, do it in the article."

These ground rules are the same in 1988 as they were in 1976. Footnotes and bibliographies, some of great length, will be found occasionally.

Marsengill was concerned about how the media had handled what they called a "race" problem that wasn't one at all. He set the record straight:

> The papers have been having a field day with the story that a Black Girl was denied admission to the Rainbow Assembly at Indianola, Iowa, [wrote Marsengill in the February 1977 issue of *The Philalethes*]. The story, which I got from the girl, her parents, the Masonic officials involved, and the Rainbow Girls, goes like this.
>
> Twelve-year-old Michelle wasn't trying to start a controversy. She just wanted to be a Rainbow Girl. Two of the members of the Indianola Assembly had asked her to join. She accepted. When her petition was presented, rather than letting the girls vote on it, the Advisors held it up for action by the state. The Grand Master of Masons, W. Ross McCulla, ruled that if the Rainbow Assembly discriminated because of race, the Order of Rainbow could not meet in Masonic lodge rooms in Iowa. Michelle was willing to withdraw her petition. The other girls wouldn't let her. They believed what they had been taught about brotherhood and wanted to see it put into practice. This was just a case of one little girl wanting to join an organization composed of other girls. After all the hassle they accepted her—just as they had intended to do all along. They were backed by all Masonic authorities in the state of Iowa. These Rainbow Girls have put into practice something the adults should have learned. Rainbows are composed of all colors.
>
> FLASH:
> As we go to press we have just learned that the International Order of Rainbow has changed its discriminatory policies. Iowa Rainbow will be affiliated with the International Order again.
>
> Hope this gives everyone the picture on what happened in Iowa. This was strictly a local matter.

Donald L. Bowman, Ph.D, MPS, wrote "Modified Peter Principle for Masonic Organizations." In his article he said: "It makes sense that good and proper management of Masonic bodies must begin at the Symbolic Lodge level. All too often such Lodges do not incorporate sound principles of Lodge administration. As such, the so-called administrative (or management) abilities—really the lack of such abilities—are compounded to the degree that we end up with a progression of ineptness perpetrated from the very bottom of Symbolic Lodge operations. Hence, we can now incorporate what Lawrence J. Peter calls 'the Level of Incompetence.' "

Bowman modified "the Peter Principle" for Freemasonry: "In a hierarchy, each officer tends to rise to his level of incompetence. Every office tends to be occupied by an officer incompetent to execute its duties."

Personally, Bowman believed nothing could be done about improving this situation, but felt an endeavor should be made to do something. "I'm afraid leadership is becoming a lost art," he continued. "Most hierarchies are now-adays so cumbered with rules and traditions that even high officers do not have to lead anyone anywhere. . . . They simply follow precedents, obey regulations, and move at the head of the crowd. Such officers lead only in the sense that the carved wooden figurehead leads the ship."

Bowman cautioned: "Beware of the officer who walks on water and never makes a mistake."

A letter "To the Masons of Arkansas" was reproduced. It was written to thank them for answering a plea of an orphan named Minnie. She had wanted to know in 1884 if there were any "funs" available to "edacate Massons offens." Minnie concluded her letter of November 16, 1889 by thanking the generous Masons for assisting Mr. Vann Hoose "who took me out of the cotton fields and brought me to his home in Fayette where I have been in school for four years."

Well over two hundred, the largest attendance to date, attended the Work-shop on February 18, 1977 with Conrad Hahn as the Chairman. Dr. Hopp covered "What the Society is, Has Been, Is Now, and the Future." Allen Roberts "spoke on the Magazine, Its Contents, Format, Purpose and Use." Allan D. Parsons talked about membership; James Case answered many questions and suggestions about how the Society should celebrate its fiftieth year celebration. Each of the speakers answered dozens of questions on the facets of Freemasonry in general.

Cerza noted the price of books had "sky-rocketed so that paper-backs are selling today for the price of hard bound books five years ago." He said it was unusual to find a cloth bound book for under ten dollars. Later he would raise this price to $15, and before his death in 1987 another five dollars. In the April issue of *The Philalethes* Cerza was highly praised for receiving the "James Royal Case Medal of Excellence" from the Masonic Lodge of Re-search of Connecticut.

Each issue of *The Philalethes* continued to carry pertinent articles about the War for Independence. The June 1977 issue was no exception. Alex Horne, FPS, wrote "Financing a Revolution: The Epic of Haym Salomon, Master Mason"; Norman C. Dutt, FPS, continued the story of "John Paul Jones." In August, "Burgoyne's Invasion" by Wilmer E. Bresee, MPS, was featured.

An interesting article with far-reaching information was written by Al-phonse Cerza, FPS, a professor of law, for the August 1977 issue of *The Philalethes*. It was titled "What Are Our Rights: Can an Association Restrict Its Members from Joining Another Group?" He cited the rule of law as found in Volume 7 of *Corpus Juris Secundum*, a law encyclopedia, page 33: "The articles of association, constitution, or by-laws of an unincorporated associa-tion are designed to define the privileges and duties of its members, and if not contrary to public policy may be of whatever character the members care to adopt." On page 60 this book states: "As a general rule, a member may be expelled for violation of a law of the association, providing for expulsion even if unreasonable."

Cerza mentions two cases involving Masonic groups concerning the question asked in the title. In the first example Royal Arch Masons in California were prohibited from joining certain groups conferring the order of knighthood. A fellow did join one of the outlawed groups and was promptly expelled. He went to court. The trial court agreed with the Royal Arch; so did the Supreme Court of California, which said: "Individuals who associate themselves in a voluntary fraternal organization may prescribe conditions upon which membership in the association may be acquired, or upon which it may continue, and may also prescribe rules of conduct for themselves during their membership, with penalties for their violation, and the tribunal and mode in which offenses shall be determined and the penalty enforced. These rules constitute their agreement, and, unless they contravene some law of the land, are regarded in the same light as the terms of any other contract."

In the other example, the Grand Chapter of the Order of the Eastern Star of Maryland told its members not to join the White Shrine of Jerusalem. A lady was expelled by the Eastern Star for ignoring this edict. She appealed to the court. Its opinion: "The internal policy of the order in regard to qualifications for membership should not be questioned by this Court, unless some principle or public policy is involved. It does not appear that any such principle is contravened by the provision now being considered."

The answer to Cerza's title question? Yes, an association can restrict its members from joining other groups.

Prince Hall, Life and Legacy by Dr. Charles H. Wesley, was recommended by Cerza because "it frankly corrects specifically the many factual errors in the [William H.] Grimshaw book." Cerza suggested the question of "regularity" of Prince Hall Masonry be left up to the Grand Lodges. "This has no place in scholarly research and discussion," he concluded.

Dwight L. Smith, FPS, for the December 1977 issue of *The Philalethes*, told the story of how he prepared to write the history of Freemasonry in Indiana He determined "it would be intimately related to the history of our country in general and to the State of Indiana in particular. This approach I now feel is a 'must' for an interesting and informative Grand Lodge history, yet it is seldom, if ever, used." He also said "there was no pussyfooting over the fact that the first Grand Master of Masons in Indiana had fought a duel" and other Grand Lodge officers had not been exemplary in character. "It would be a history in which individual Grand Masters would figure only to

Conrad Hahn

the extent that they had a part in making events happen or in handling certain situations."

Smith's book, *Goodly Heritage,* received rave reviews in the daily media as well as within Masonic circles when it was published in 1968.

Conrad Hahn, the Second Vice President of the Society, had been looking forward to the celebration of the fiftieth anniversary of The Philalethes Society. His plans were interrupted by the grim reaper. Without any warning he died on December 15, 1977. He was among the most highly decorated and exceptionally well respected Freemasons in the country. His memorial service was conducted by his adopted lodge in Bethesda, Maryland.

Nine days earlier, on December 6, another Masonic stalwart, Walter M. Callaway, Jr., FPS, of Georgia, died. The opening paragraph of his memorial in the April issue of *The Philalethes* said: "Now and then a man comes along who will truly go on foot and out of his way to serve his fellowman. Such a man was Walter M. Callaway, Jr. He loved deeply—his family, his God, his Fraternity called Freemasonry, all of his fellowmen, the Confederate States of America, and the United States of America."

The February 1978 issue of *The Philalethes* contained an item from the Knoxville, Iowa, *Express* about something which horrifies all editors, writers and publishers:

> The typographical error is a slippery thing and sly.
> You can hunt till you are dizzy, but it somehow will get by.
> Till the forms are off the presses it is strange how still it keeps;
> It shrinks down into a corner and it never stirs or peeps.
>
> That typographical error, too small for human eyes,
> Till the ink is on the paper, when it grows to mountain size.
> The boss he stares with horror, then he grabs his hair and groans;
> The copy reader drops his head upon his hands and moans—
> The remainder of the issue may be clean as clean can be,
> But that typographical error is the only thing you see.

As it had annually for almost fifty years, the Executive Committee met to discuss the affairs of the Society. It elected four new Fellows: Forrest D. Haggard, Robert L. Dillard, Stewart M.L. Pollard, and Louis L. Williams. The recent death of Conrad Hahn caused the meeting to be unusually brief. The committee preferred to wait until after the results of the Workshop were in before completing the agenda for the year. It was determined, however, to hold a "Golden Anniversary Celebration of The Philalethes Society" in Chicago on August 12, 1978.

The attendance for the 1978 Workshop was unprecedented and so were the papers presented. John Black Vrooman discussed the early days of the Society. Stewart M.L. Pollard, the newly appointed Executive Secretary of The Masonic Service Association, covered "Where The Philalethes Society is Now." "How are we seen by others?" he asked. "To some we are seen as an elite group of intellectuals. To others we are a bunch of crackpots. To some, we're confused with philatelists. But, to the majority of the Craft, we are an unknown quantity. They never heard of The Philalethes Society and know nothing about it. Parenthetically, this can be attributed to our own lack of endeavor, or our individual complacency.

"And how are we seen by our own membership? Here there is an even wider disparity of opinion! We are researchers; students; teachers; compilers; Masonic good-will ambassadors; educators; watchdogs; and a hundred more descriptive adjectives.

"Basically, we still are what we set out to be fifty years ago—an international organization composed of members of the Masonic fraternity who are seeking Masonic light, and who have light to impart." He closed by saying: "Let us strive for TRUTH! The state of the Society—it is healthy and meaningful—And, Brethren, that's the TRUTH!"

Dwight L. Smith talked about the future. "Had our plans materialized," he said, "I would be sharing the platform with a dear friend and one of the truly great Freemasons of our day. In discussing our assignment through correspondence, Connie Hahn observed that we had some 'gardens to spade,' and that if I would work half of them, he would dig the others." He suggested the Freemason's goal should be to improve himself and "that's enough of a job for one lifetime."

Smith strongly suggested: "We must raise our sights as a Society because to do otherwise would mean to lower our sights or to remain at dead center. I submit that to do either of those alternatives would be to render The Philalethes Society useless as an effective force in Freemasonry."

He agreed the Society had done "an heroic job in its early years"; it has filled a need "during the years it was approaching middle age. But in moving into the second half-century we need to think in terms of a Society that will fill a greater need, become a more effective force, establish a more impressive reputation as a vehicle, or agency, for dispensing Masonic light."

Smith suggested the term "Workshop" is degrading and a better selection should be made. "Why couldn't we return to something basic in Freemasonry and meet about the dinner tables? Let every man buy his own meal ticket. And instead of having papers on shoptalk matters, or discussions such as this on the menial housekeeping chores necessary to keep an organization alive, why not establish an annual *Philalethes Society Lecture* by distinguished Freemasons, Brethren whose very presence would lift the Society's reputation to new heights. Such lectures could eventually become assignments of such prestige as to be greatly coveted and forever prized. . .

"I am suggesting—pleading, if you please—for the restoration of Masonic fellowship and conviviality, that vital ingredient which does more than anything else to make the pursuit of Light not something to be endured, but something to be anticipated and enjoyed. I am pleading for a return to the Annual Feast, almost forgotten but still a part of our heritage; not a feast exclusively for our physical nourishment (although that is of far more importance in Freemasonry than Americans like to admit), but also for mental nourishment, and intellectual nourishment, and spiritual nourishment." Changes would be made by Smith when he took over as President of the Society.

On February 22, 1978, Freedoms Foundation of Valley Forge presented The George Washington Honor Medal for nonprofit publications to *The Philalethes*. Its editor, Jerry Marsengill, also received a medal for his work on the magazine.

"George Rogers Clark: Gideon of the West" was another article in the continuing bicentennial series. This article had been written by Dwight L. Smith for the August 1978 issue of *The Philalethes*. It recorded many of the exploits of Clark, the Mason and outstanding warrior. Smith would help Vincennes Lodge No. 1 celebrate Clark's victory in freeing Vincennes. The event took place on July 1 and 2, 1979, with the Virginia Craftsmen playing an important role. Several members of The Philalethes Society were there.

"The Gutenberg Bible" was the subject of an article by Harold V.B. Voorhis in the August 1978 issue of *The Philalethes*. He wanted to set the record straight about this "so-called Gutenberg Bible." In 1398 Johannes Gensfleisch zur Laden was born in Mainz, Germany. "For some reason not known," wrote Voorhis, "he used another name, which was that of his mother": Gutenberg. He died in Mainz on February 3, 1438. The printer's financial and other difficulties were outlined by Voorhis. He then wrote about Gutenberg's work.

> The famous bibles, bearing his name, were the first books printed by use of movable type and came from his press 1450–56. The language was Latin, the type face being "black letter" or Gothic. There are 324 pages in a complete bible, printed on both sides, approximately 15 x 11 inches. Those on paper are still in excellent condition. His first copies were not to his liking so he reset the type in 42 lines per column, two columns per page. Estimates of the number of copies printed are 165 on paper and 35 on vellum. There are 47 copies known (complete or in part).
>
> Gutenberg's Bible was made from the text of a copy of the Jerome Latin Vulgate Bible, the original then being something over a thousand years old.

According to Voorhis, a bronze monument by Albert Bertel Thorwald was erected to the memory of Gutenberg in Mainz in 1857.

Several fifty-year anniversary celebrations were held throughout the country during 1978. The Chicago Chapter of The Philalethes Society held its Golden Anniversary Celebration of The Philalethes Society on August 12. It featured N. Tracy Walker, MPS, Jerry Marsengill, FPS, and Stanley Maxwell, a Past Grand Master of Masons in Massachusetts. Each of those attending received a "Certificate of Participation."

"A Golden Anniversary Luncheon" was held on September 15 in Guthrieville, Pennsylvania, by Chester County and Valley Forge Chapters of The Philalethes Society. Alphonse Cerza was the speaker for the historic occasion.

Northern Indiana Chapter celebrated its formation on September 9. Three speakers from the Society were featured: Dwight L. Smith, First Vice President; Alphonse Cerza spoke on "Masonic Literature and the Masonic Book Club"; and Allen E. Roberts, "The Masonic Educator." The affair was under the leadership of Paul E. Rudbeck, MPS.

The October 1978 issue of *The Philalethes* recapped much of the history of the Society. It recorded the recipients of the Certificate of Literature since its inception in 1956 (for 1955); plus all who had served as officers and those who had been elected Fellows. It also outlined the Workshops held since 1955, their topics, and those who had participated.

In the same issue George Draffen of Newington, FPS, commented on Cerza's article on exclusive Grand Lodge jurisdiction. It's entitled "Multiple Jurisdiction" and reads:

> In his most interesting article entitled *"Exclusive Jurisdiction"* which appeared in the April 1978 issue of *The Philalethes* the author, **Alphonse Cerza,** states "The doctrine of exclusive jurisdiction has worked well in the United States of America and has contributed to the orderly and harmonious working of the Craft in spite of the many states composing the United States of America." That is a statement with which I could not possibly quarrel, but if it is intended to imply that "multiple jurisdiction" would not necessarily have led to the same happy state of affairs then I am in disagreement.
>
> As Alphonse Cerza says, The Grand Lodges of England, Ireland, and Scotland do not recognize the doctrine of exclusive jurisdiction and one might ask if the Grand Lodge of Massachusetts does so in entirety for that Grand Lodge shares territory, very happily I may say, with the Grand Lodge of Peru (which it recognizes) and the Grand Lodge of Scotland. In Peru there are lodges under the Grand Lodge of Peru, the Grand Lodge of Scotland, and the Grand Lodge of Massachusetts—and no difficulties arise.
>
> From the earliest times, when the Grand Lodges in the British Isles began to warrant lodges overseas in other countries and in the colonies and dominions of the British Crown there was no question of exclusive jurisdiction. The whole world was "open territory" and England, Scotland and Ireland warranted Lodges to meet almost wherever English was spoken. When, with the passing of time, Grand Lodges were set up in many parts of the Commonwealth, the British Grand Lodges, in recognizing these new Grand Lodges, always refused to compel any Lodges which did not wish to join the new Grand Lodge to do so. The

British Grand Lodges did not issue any new warrants for lodges in the territory of the new Grand Lodges. Many of their lodges preferred to remain under England, Scotland or Ireland as the case may be. It is as a result of this that today one finds Lodges under *four* Grand Lodges meeting in New Zealand; under *four* Grand Lodges in India; under *five* Grand Lodges in South Africa. . . .

Under certain circumstances the doctrine of exclusive jurisdiction may well be convenient but I cannot agree with Alphonse Cerza that it is essential for the peace, harmony and good government of the Craft. There is one curious point in that all the United States Grand Lodges, strong upholders of the doctrine of exclusive jurisdiction, recognized the TWO Grand Lodges in Czecho-Slovakia, one Czech-speaking, and the other German-speaking. Here it is clear that under certain circumstances it may well be that the doctrine of exclusive jurisdiction is not applicable nor desirable.

This "doctrine" has long been contentious and Draffen covered the subject in an interesting fashion. He could have added Freemasonry has the same problem with "the landmarks of Masonry." Until 1858 when Albert Mackey decided to tell the Masonic world what these "landmarks" were, no Grand Lodge in the world had endeavored to compile a list. Since then, numerous lists have been cataloged. Robert Freke Gould, the English Masonic historian, correctly claimed: "Nobody knows what they comprise. . . ," as mentioned earlier.

"It is a mistake, of course," wrote Cerza in December 1978, "to point to our past history and to the men who have belonged to the Craft in the years gone by and to take the position that we will now rest on our past laurels. Such an attitude would be self-defeating and a serious mistake. But it can be a great advantage to study our history to help us solve our present day problems and to point to the great men who have been members and to follow their example."

Dr. Forrest Haggard, FPS, in an article entitled "Religious Renewal: Its Impact on Freemasonry," related many of the problems he had as a Freemason and a clergyman. While he was Grand Master of Masons in Kansas he was also World President of the Churches of Christ.

Haggard conducted a "non-Christian" worship service for an appendant body. He did this because he rightly considered Freemasonry nondenominational with members "who encompass a multiplicity of religious viewpoints and faiths." He said his action "produced a crisis." He noted some of the letters he received: "You have betrayed your calling as a minister of the gospel"; "You are destroying the unity of Freemasonry"; "When I joined the Masons thirty years ago, I was told that I was becoming a member of a Christian Rite of Masonry"; "Masonry is basically Christian"; "In today's return to the true faith, I could no longer defend my position as a Christian if you persist in such a 'Universal Religious Service.' "

To which Haggard replied:

"Historically, factually, currently; Freemasonry is, for the majority part, Universal in nature. That battle was fought long ago." "I am well aware of the areas (particular and general) where Freemasonry is only open to those of the 'Christian faith.' " "I feel the force of your personal emotions, but I will not deviate from my stance, unless you can prove me wrong. Nor will I allow any personal intimidation (theologically speaking) for as World President of the Churches of Christ (Christian Church/Disciples of Christ) I have received all the flak that it is possible for any clergyman to have received about being a Christian and a Freemason." "York Rite Masonry is not 'basically Christian' and the burden of proof is upon you, not upon me. I await your reply."

It is difficult today, with the constant changing of the guard and the lifting up on the "honor of being a Grand Master" and the huge amount of time spent in restructuring, personal travel, for any but a few to spend time in a real study of changing patterns of our culture, or shifting population trends; or economic, social, and cultural role changes or advances in science and technology; much less in the more important and more difficult areas of our purposes and platform in Freemasonry *as* Freemasons. But such is the key to our existence.

Before he became Grand Master Haggard determined to learn why the ritual explanation of the "Blazing Star" in Kansas contained Christian terminology. He found the Christian wording had been added after the original ritual had been written. Under the "universality" clause in Freemasonry, he ordered it changed when he was elected Grand Master. Two-thirds of the delegates upheld his decision. One Brother condemned him for deleting the Christian references and claimed: "King Solomon wrote those words with his own hand and, by God, you have no authority to change them!"

Haggard closed his article by stating:

We are brothers in a venture where we hold a particularly high responsibility. There is a storehouse of treasures given to us, not of gold and silver and jewels, but of moral, intellectual, and social virtues. All members of the Craft may partake of that storehouse, but we must return the same treasure to the storehouse or it will be depleted; we must share our treasures or they will evaporate. Our personal Craftsmanship is vitally necessary for the continual growth, maintenance, and beauty of our BUILDING. If the **Building of Freemasonry is maintained, and used, as well as adorned, then it will not only withstand the outside storm, it will perform its intended function.**

Haggard continued his work for Christianity as a clergyman and he continued to work for Freemasonry. The Philalethes Society recognized his heroism in fighting the opponents of the Craft, and opposing the professed

"Christians" who were anti-Masonic. During the Assembly, Feast and Workshop of 1988 he was awarded the Society's Distinguished Service Medal.

The fiftieth anniversary year of The Philalethes Society came to an end, but its influence would be felt. Members of the Society had spread the word about what the organization had done and was doing. Almost 400 new members were added to the roster. The total membership stood at 2,338, indicating a continuing growth. Issues of *The Philalethes* contained more pages of excellent Masonic information.

The founders of the Society would have been proud of what they had launched. Freemasonry in general had become the beneficiary of their foresight.

13. MODERNIZING
(1979-1983)

A new decade began with a continuation of the excellent bicentennial series of articles about the trials and tribulations of the founding of the United States of America. James R. Case, who had started the series, continued his contributions in the February 1979 issue of *The Philalethes*. His article on "American Union Lodge" was the thirty-ninth in the series. In it he reported on its activities from February to September 1779. He corrected many of the errors found in previous accounts and books about this Military Lodge.

New officers were elected and installed to begin the second half-century in the life of the Society. Dwight L. Smith became the President, Robert L. Dillard and Bruce H. Hunt, First and Second Vice Presidents. Franklin J. "Andy" Anderson remained as Executive Secretary, and Ronald E. Heaton as Treasurer. Jerry Marsengill continued as Editor.

The Workshop for 1979, selected by the President, consisted of members of the Texas Lodge of Research. They were Dr. George H.T. French, MPS, Plez A. Transou, MPS, and Thomas J. Burnett, MPS. The theme was "Masonology = A Challenge." Of this Dwight Smith said: "It will be the same dish as that served on previous occasions, but in one vital area it will be different. This year we're going to pay particular attention to what the purpose of our Society says we should be doing." He noted that there would be changes in the format the following year.

Over 250 were present for the Workshop, among them were six Masons from the Grand Lodge of China.

In his comments on "Masonology" during the Workshop, Dr. George H.T. French said: "Unfortunately, too few brothers think beyond the ritual. They do not try to find out the whence, where, who, what or how of it. Notwithstanding the fact that we are taught that Freemasonry's purposes are to diffuse light, to banish ignorance, and to make its members wiser and happier. Masonic education should be the aim of a real Masonic leader. Every brother needs education in the mission and purpose of Freemasonry."

"The Masonic system is complicated," said Plez Transou during the Workshop in speaking of Brotherhood. "Its appeal is varied. If we had to sum up in a single word, that word might be 'brotherhood.' Our Fraternity is a brotherhood. The Greek word *phrater* means brother. 'Fraternity' is a Latin form of the Anglo-Saxon word *brotherhood.* The doctrine of brotherhood is the essential ingredient of our Order."

T.J. "Jeff" Burnett, Jr., spoke about "The Music of Masonry." He began: "If masonry is a science, its music is measured, precise. If masonry is an art, its music is harmonic, concordant. If masonry is a way of life, its music must be the dream of fulfilled hope and the hope of mankind's ultimate destiny. Part of this evolution has been man's desire to give expression in a way that ordinary speech cannot. Once inspired, he sang. Once he sang, he dreamed. Once he dreamed, he discovered his brother and Brotherhood was recreated."

Louis C. King, MPS, received the Certificate of Literature for 1978 for his article "Building a Cathedral." The Treasurer reported $1063.64 in the general fund; $10,300 in the Life Membership Fund. The Executive Committee decided that *The Philalethes* would contain sixteen pages, except for April and February when it would have twenty-four. Any deviation from this would require the approval of the President and Treasurer.

Charles Guthrie, MPS, ended his article about "Rob Morris and the Conservators in Kentucky," by stating: "Despite the conservator uproar, Morris today is recognized as perhaps the most outstanding Mason ever to be a member of a Kentucky lodge." As this sentence suggests, the road to acclaim had been difficult.

According to Guthrie, "the great diversity of ritual which he encountered as he visited lodges throughout the United States" caused Morris to eventually form a movement he called the "Conservators." This became a secret movement to force lodges and Grand Lodges to adopt Morris's ritual as set out in his *Mnemonics*. An overwhelming majority of Masons regarded this as a violation of their obligations. The movement was outlawed by many Grand Lodges. In 1865 even Morris's Grand Lodge of Kentucky ordered all copies of the Morris work turned into its Grand Secretary. Although Guthrie defended Morris, few others have ventured to do so, at least as far as his Conservator movement is concerned. However, Morris did return to the good graces of the Masonic hierarchy in 1884 when he was made "Poet-Laureate of Freemasonry." He died at LaGrange, Kentucky in 1888.

In the same February 1979 issue of *The Philalethes*, Laurence E. Eaton, MPS, had an article titled "Newman vs Pulling, or Who Hung the Lanterns?" According to Eaton, Paul Revere said: "I agreed that if the British went out by water we should show two lanthorns in the North Church steeple and if by land, one as a signal." It had to be the North Church, then known as Christ Church on Salem Street, said Eaton, because the other church didn't have a steeple. The lantern must have been hung by John Pulling, Jr., because he was a Freemason and trusted by Revere and others. Newman wasn't a Mason. And Newman, when arrested the following morning, implicated Pulling. About 1884 "the Massachusetts Historical Society carefully investigated and found for Pulling and that W. B. Clark of Boston reached the same conclusion after extensive research," said Eaton.

C. W. Coons, MPS, in his column, "From Time Immemorial," strongly suggested the preparation room should become as important today as it was in the time of the operative masons. At that time candidates were closely examined to make certain they were not women posing as men, slaves, or castrated. Flat chested women had been known to pass for men, and slaves had been often marked on the souls of their feet. Trust was important to the operative guilds, and this, he argued, ought to be true today.

Cerza highly recommended Harold V. B. Voorhis' revised *Facts for Freemasons* which was available from Macoy Publishing and Masonic Supply Co. of Richmond, Virginia. "The book presents Masonic information in a question and answer format in twenty-five chapters. The subjects covered are Masonic history, customs, symbolism, philosophy, the appendant bodies, biographical sketches of famous Masons, and a definition of Masonic words and phrases. One chapter is devoted to the subject of Prince Hall and the organization that bears his name."

Dwight L. Smith, the President, announced in the October 1979 issue of *The Philalethes*: "The word 'Workshop' will be abandoned and the format will be altered to emphasize how the pursuit of Masonic light . . . can be made a happy, interesting, challenging experience; not something to be endured, but something to be anticipated and enjoyed.

"We are indebted to our editor, Brother Jerry Marsengill, for the name to be assigned to our meeting. Instead of workshop, or seminar, or any of those much overworked terms with deadly dull connotation, Brother Jerry said: 'Why not go back to the most important date in all Masonic history and call it the Annual Assembly and Feast!'"

"Brilliant!" was Smith's response. "Absolutely perfect!" And Smith continued:

And so, Annual Assembly and Feast it will be. If precedent is needed, that portion of Anderson's *Constitutions of 1738* which describes the meeting of the four old Lodges in London on the Feast of St. John the Baptist, 1717, should suffice.

We read that the old Lodges came together at the Goose and Gridiron alehouse to "form a Center of Union and Harmony" and to "hold the Annual Assembly and Feast."

Our meeting will be about the dinner tables. The occasion will, I trust, evoke a smile now and then, so that our Society can begin to get away (for all time, I hope) from what Haywood terms "cheerlessness, repetition, monotony, dullness."

Smith added there would be music, singing, and the drinking of toasts. The theme would be "The Ideal Lodge," and papers would be presented and discussed. "A second revival, akin, perhaps, to 1717? It could be. Let The Philalethes Society lead the way."

Along the same vein William Stemper, MPS, wrote about "Lost Leaders." He suggested: "At the local level, the form for Masonic renewal is simple. No Master, or other presiding officer, should be elected or installed without a planned and well-executed effort to revive the 'ancient' custom of Masonic and social discourse around the 'festive board.' It is not enough to carry on 'Masonic education' via magazine subscription, books, pamphlets, etc. Masonic education must be the essence and core of a lodge's life. It should be an indispensable element of each regular Masonic communication. . . .

"At the national level, the necessary form for Masonic renewal is closer cooperation and communication among and between Grand Lodges and the various appendant, allied, and concordant bodies." He advocated the "formation of a centralized institute or research center designed to stimulate ideas about the nature of social and fraternal organisms." This, basically, is what The Masonic Service Association was formed in 1918 to do. But it ran into insurmountable problems shortly thereafter with the leadership of several Grand Lodges.

"The Ceremonies in Operative Masonry" was the theme used by Alex Horne, FPS, for an article in the December issue of *The Philalethes*. By quoting from the "Old Charges" or *Manuscript Constitutions,* he proved that the operative masons were not "purely trade organizations." Nearly all of these early documents contain some form of ceremony and obligation that each craftsmen had to assume.

Alphonse Cerza continued to report on the many books published by Iowa Research Lodge No. 2. This Lodge maintained its record of sending complimentary copies to each of its members. The latest books were *Knight Masons, a History* and *Attentive Ears, Instructive Tongues, and Faithful Breasts.*

The February 1980 issue of *The Philalethes* announced that S. Brent Morris, MPS, had been appointed Assistant Executive Secretary because of the continuing illness of Andy Anderson. It was evident on the evening of February 15, when the Society met for its first Annual Assembly and Feast that Anderson was seriously ill. He died early the following day. Morris was named a Fellow of The Philalethes Society and appointed its Executive Secretary.

John Mauk Hilliard, MPS, replaced Ronald E. Heaton as Treasurer. Keith Arrington was elected a Fellow of The Philalethes Society. Charles S. Guthrie, MPS, was awarded the Certificate of Literature for 1979 for his "Rob Morris and the Conservators in Kentucky."

Dwight L. Smith, the President, had requested the Reverend William H. Stemper, MPS, and some of his colleagues of the Goose and Gridiron club, many of whose members were Freemasons, to build a program of toasts and responses around the theme of "The Ideal Lodge." Others who proposed toasts included John Mauk Hilliard, MPS, Peter Martin, Jeff Gill and William H. Werle. Each emphasized that the Ideal Lodge doesn't forget the festive board, the feast around which the beginnings of the Grand Lodge system was commenced.

A suggestion was made to Alphonse Cerza that the Masonic Book Club should establish a correspondence course, which would include questions on Masonic philosophy, symbolism and history. In an item entitled "Craftsmen of the Round Table" published in the February 1980 issue of *The Philalethes*, Cerza suggested this would be a good project for the Chapters of The Philalethes Society. He said *The Builders* by Joseph Fort Newton would be a good place to start. The Cincinnati Masonic Study School had prepared questions based on the book, and these could be found in *The Builder Magazine*, Volume XI. *The Builder* had been out of print for years, but the Society later had the whole series placed on microfiche.

James R. Case continued his series on American Union Lodge during the Revolutionary period.

In the August 1980 issue of *The Philalethes* Alphonse Cerza considered the woes of "Getting That Book Published." He began: "For a time publishers of Masonic books were an endangered species; now they are almost extinct. A Masonic author with a masterpiece in his hands is frustrated with the thought that a dozen publishers are not beating a path to his door to issue the book to an anxiously awaiting crowd of readers." Where there were dozens a few decades ago in America, only Macoy Publishing and Masonic Supply Company remained.

Cerza and Charles Reigner discussed why general publishers aren't interested in handling Masonic books. They found those few that had published them had lost money, and the word spread throughout the publishing business. Cerza also mentioned: "Today a good paper back costs as much as a cloth bound book just five years ago [a claim Cerza had rightly made several times], and the situation in the last two years has gotten so bad that most general publishers have reduced the number of books they are issuing." He suggested Masonic authors look to research lodges for possible salvation.

Cerza continued his account of the publishing of Masonic books in the April 1981 issue of *The Philalethes*. "We have been hearing in recent months that book publishers have reduced their staff of employees and decided to issue less books in the year 1981," he wrote. Too many readers, he claimed, are borrowing from libraries. This makes it difficult for Freemasons because few libraries carry legitimate Masonic books. "With the small market for

Masonic books it will not be too long before the price of publishing books relating to the Craft may become prohibitive. Few persons will want to take the risk of publishing a Masonic book and not being able to recover the actual cost of producing them." He suggested cooperative publishing may be one of the answers.

This is one of the reasons Anchor Communications was formed in 1981. By taking much less profit than ordinary publishers, and by printing good books for several Research Lodges, excellent Masonic books were, and are, made available at a reasonable cost. Iowa Research Lodge No. 2, Missouri Lodge of Research, The Philalethes Society, and even the Macoy Publishing Company have taken advantage of this concept.

Alphonse Cerza was congratulated on his acceptance as a full member of Quatuor Coronati Lodge No. 2076 of London, England. This is often termed "The Premier Research Lodge." Alex Horne, FPS, had been elected to full membership earlier. Dwight L. Smith was also elected at the same time as Cerza. And it's interesting to note that Wallace E. McLeod of Toronto, Canada (who would later become a Fellow of the Society), in 1982 would become the only North American ever to be elected Master of this Lodge.

John Black Vrooman celebrated fifty years of membership in The Philalethes Society in 1981. In the February 1981 issue of *The Philalethes* he looked back on those years he had served the Society. He was pleased with the results, but felt he could still be of further service to the Craft in general.

The same issue contained the fiftieth article in the on-going bicentennial series. It was "The Green Pasture" by Norman C. Dutt, FPS, and featured Nathanael Greene who may have been a Freemason.

The history of the emblem of The Philalethes Society was explained by Alphonse Cerza. He had lived with the original and the subsequent changes. The original emblem had appeared on the May 1952 issue of the magazine, the last issue before the Society became inactive because of the death of its leaders. When publishing was revived in October 1954 the same emblem was used, and it was criticized. A new emblem was designed and over the months changes made. In October 1955 the new emblem adorned the covers of *The Philalethes*. The official emblem remains the same, but in October 1980 it was simplified for the magazine.

"This is a chance to turn the clock back some 250 years and meet, as did our brethren in the coffeehouses and taverns of England," read an article to attract the members to attend the second annual Assembly and Feast of The Philalethes Society. "This year the prestigious *Philalethes Lecture* will be given by Allen Earl Roberts . . . [author] of many . . . Masonic books." The subject selected, "Leadership: Often Sought; Seldom Attained," followed the theme of "The Ideal Lodge" of the previous year. It was published in the April issue of *The Philalethes*.

Original Seal, 1928–1955

Proposed Seal in 1954

Official Seal, Adopted in
1955

The Seal as used in the
Society's Magazine

John Mauk Hilliard and Charles Snow Guthrie were elected Fellows of The Philalethes Society. Hilliard was awarded the Certificate of Literature for 1980 for his article "The Lodge as Primary Community." Seldom had an article appearing in *The Philalethes* provoked as much abuse and praise. It covered several issues, and the praise became much more prominent than the abuse.

It was announced that dues would be increased from $7.00 to $10.00 per year beginning January 1, 1982; Life Membership would increase from $100 to $150 at the same time. It was also suggested that the term of office run for one year rather than for three as it had been since the reorganization in 1955.

The Executive Secretary, S. Brent Morris, FPS, told the members he wasn't crazy, nor was he malicious. He had been converting the old record-keeping system to a more modern format—the computer. The error rate had been about 10%, but this was expected to decrease considerably as the system improved. The dues card had been eliminated to save money, and this disturbed many members. With the new accounting system those delinquent in their payments could be dropped quickly, saving the Society about $1,400 a year. Brent closed his account by saying: "One thing that I have learned from a year in this job is that I will never, never again complain about the mistakes of a Secretary. I may not be perfect, but I mean well."

"Retreat to Victory—Philalethes Style," in the August 1981 issue of *The Philalethes*, was an unusual report. The Southwest Chapter of The Philalethes Society met on Memorial Day weekend at the Lazy Hills Guest Ranch, near Kerrville, Texas. John E. Jack Kelly, the Chapter Secretary, who would become Grand Master of Masons in Texas in 1987, was the moderator for a round table discussion that encompassed a wide range of Masonic subjects. Families were not left behind. They participated in several of the functions.

"Discussions were lively, frank, controversial, highly informative," claimed the report. "Where disagreement existed, participants disagreed agreeably. At the end, the group was unanimous in its opinion that the word 'retreat' has now taken on a new connotation. This one, at least, was a victory for Freemasonry."

Otis V. Jones, Jr., MPS, writing for the February 1982 issue of *The Philalethes* suggested "Take Care of Your Speakers." He was concerned. He compared the fine treatment organizations, other than Masonic, give their speakers. "I have been surprised and exasperated, even left wondering how Masonry has done as well as it usually does with speakers and distinguished guests," he wrote. "It is surprising how little is done even when the visitor or guest speaker is a Grand Lodge officer." He strongly recommended Masonic speakers be treated courteously and at least their expenses should be reimbursed.

Robert L. Dillard was elected President; Bruce H. Hunt and Stewart M.L. Pollard First and Second Vice Presidents. S. Brent Morris and John Mauk Hilliard remained Executive Secretary and Treasurer. The Philalethes Lecturer for 1982 was William P. Vaughan, MPS, of Texas. He spoke on material from his recently published book, *The Anti-Masonic Party.*

"We regret to see *The Altar Light*," wrote Jerry Marsengill at the end of the April 1982 issue of *The Philalethes*, "the latest casualty of the postage rates and high printing costs, become defunct. There is, however, a brighter side to the death of *The Altar Light. The Philalethes* magazine has been fortunate enough to obtain the services of Al Roberts to write his column, 'Through Masonic Windows,' for *The Philalethes*. This will become a regular feature of the magazine and, for those who have been subscribers to *The Altar Light,* this should be a popular one. Watch for it in each issue." The Editor's prediction proved correct.

Jerry Marsengill wrote "How To Make An Anti-Masonic Film" for the June 1982 issue of *The Philalethes*; it proved to be a popular item for Masonic editors. This is how Marsengill would go about it:

Allen Roberts spends a great deal of his time producing promotional films for various Masonic organizations. He has done a great deal of good with these films and many of the Masonic bodies in the United States are gaining in membership and interest because of them.

Probably no one would ever want to make an anti-Masonic film. Certainly, the anti-Masonic literature of Edmund Ronayne and Ezra Cook has never hit the best seller lists. An anti-Masonic film would probably not have much more of an audience.

If I were called upon to produce an anti-Masonic film, I would get the cameras, lights and other equipment and rush to my lodge's monthly stated communication. I would wait until the opening ritual was completed, then I would begin to film.

Watching the Secretary talk to the knot on his necktie and drone through the minutes, reading every word of the last stated and all intervening communications, would begin a memorable film.

The new business, most probably whether to pay the light, heat and water bills, which have already been paid, would make another highlight of the production.

If an argument on some important point, such as whether to have a ladies night, could be started, we could see lodgedom triumphant in all its glory.

The youngest Master Mason, in the northeast corner of the lodge, could propose such an innovation and the oldest Past Master could give the mating call of the Past Masters: "We've never done it that way," or "We didn't do it that way in MY year," or even "These kids are going to ruin the lodge."

Then I would take the camera and "pan" the lodge. I would get a shot of two of the brethren, bored to distraction, visiting on the sidelines, and a good shot of the older brothers taking this opportunity to catch a short nap.

I am a Past Master. I am a Secretary. If I am bored by the mechanics of the stated communication and the incredible amount of time which is wasted on totally unnecessary business, is it any wonder that our younger members, who are not presently holding office, seldom, if ever, attend lodge meetings?

William Shakespeare has always been an interesting person for Masonic writers. J. Fairbairn Smith, FPS, a long-time Masonic historian, asked "Did Shakespeare Create Masonic Ritual?" in the August 1982 issue of *The Phila-lethes*. ". . . [F]or considerably more than two hundred years a large number of the world's leading Masonic authorities have, with reason, maintained that Sir William also wrote the Ritual of the Craft. It must be admitted that many portions of his literary creations are more than just merely Masonically oriented."

Smith noted that "Shakespeare lived in the century that preceded the revival of Freemasonry and the beginnings of the modern Craft in England in 1717. Reading his plays and noting the Masonic allusions and passages that almost seem to stand out of the ritual and lectures, one can only come to the conclusion that Shakespeare was either a Mason or that Masons drew upon him for their material." Most Masonic scholars believe the latter premise is more accurate. It wasn't until long after the formation of the Grand Lodge of England that Masonic ritual was considered important.

A "negative response" to Smith's article was presented in the December 1982 issue of *The Philalethes* by Leslie L. Walker Jr., MPS, of Texas. "First of all," wrote Walker, "Brother Smith refers to Shakespeare as 'Sir William.' No record exists of William Shakespeare having been knighted." He also noted: "There seems to be very general agreement among Masonic historians that the Third Degree was formulated some time after the beginning of the era of modern Masonry, in 1717. This fact should be borne in mind, for it has relevance to the further consideration of Brother Smith's arguments."

Referring to Smith's quotations from *The Tempest*, Walker said: "If by reading 'The Tempest' some Mason is able to find hidden truth, by that much has he profited. We should not, however, on the basis of words and phrases lifted out of context, jump to the conclusion that the play has meaning which only Masons can comprehend."

Walker concluded that Shakespeare *may* have been a Mason, "but the proof of it will not be found in the ritual, nor will the proof of his authorship of the ritual be found in his plays."

In October 1982, John Black Vrooman suggested that Freemasonry should stop "lamenting the lack of leadership, lack of attendance, lack of interest and activity by members of the Craft." He wanted the leadership to consider all the **doers** in the Fraternity. He said there will always be drones in the organization, any organization, but emphasis should be placed on the many who are workers.

The interesting story of "The National Masonic Research Society" of Anamosa, Iowa, was told by Alphonse Cerza. This Society was the brain-child of George L. Schoonover, who would become Grand Master of Masons in Iowa, in 1918. He had found that many Freemasons were seeking more information and knowledge of the Craft than was contained in the ritual alone. So Schoonover proposed the subject to his Grand Lodge in 1914, suggesting that such a society must be supported by Masons from all over the country. The Grand Lodge of Iowa agreed.

Schoonover, using his own funds, erected a modern two-story building in Anamosa to serve as headquarters for the new society. Cerza, quoting from the *Grand Lodge Bulletin* of Iowa, described the large reception room in the headquarters building located on "spacious grounds on the side of a hill. Brother Schoonover occupied one office among many on the first floor. Books and magazines were all over the fire proof building which had several parlors. On the walls were three appropriately painted pictures by a young artist named Grant Wood, who was to achieve national fame in the years ahead. One room had an organ suitable for supplying music at the receptions held there from time to time.

"The office was equipped with the latest equipment and labor saving devices. A separate building existed in the rear for the storage of material. . . . 'The place is surely a beehive of industry, with a large working force, each having his or her special work to look after.' "

His "employees" consisted mainly of volunteers. Joseph Fort Newton, a year before he wrote *The Builders*, became the Editor of *The Builder,* the excellent publication of the Society. The first issue of the monthly journal was published in January 1915. The best Masonic writers and students had been, and would be, solicited to provide authentic material for publication. Originally the dues were $2.50 a year but were shortly increased to $3.00. For this the subscribers received, in addition to the magazine, booklets and study material. Later the Society entered the book publishing business. The growth was tremendous, according to Cerza. Keith Arrington later said subscriptions reached fourteen thousand.

Newton was called to be minister of the City Temple in London, England, in 1916. Arrington said Newton expected to return in a couple of months, so he remained the editor until 1917. Harry Leroy Haywood followed Newton as Editor of the magazine, or did he? Arrington also said "so little emphasis was placed upon names, it was difficult to tell who was acting as editor. Library notes indicate that from 1917 to 1920 there was no official editor," but there were associate editors. If Haywood wasn't officially editor, he was one of the associates, being named editor in 1921, remaining in this position until 1925 when he went to New York to edit the *Masonic Outlook*. Robert J. Meekren of Canada then became the Executive Editor of *The Builder*.

The Society moved its headquarters to Cedar Rapids in 1923. "The move was made necessary because more room was needed and the new location had larger offices" and so on. But "there were intimations that the move was made necessary because Schoonover's relationship with the Society had cooled." Several other moves, including its final move to St. Louis, were made before the death of the Society. The final issue appeared in May 1930.

Cerza concluded: "Many years ago I had a talk with H.L. Haywood about the matter and he stated that the Society could have been saved with a little cooperation among the officers, but this could not be brought about because of petty squabbles that existed. I have no way of checking this out and he may have said this because he felt a bit unfriendly towards the officers for refusing him permission to reproduce his history articles in book form." It would appear that Haywood was correct, but the full story of the in-fighting has never been recorded.

Keith Arrington, FPS, continued the story of this Research Society in an article in his continuing series on "Iowa's Masonic Magazines." In the June 1984 issue of *The Philalethes* he wrote about "The Builder," that Society's official publication. Arrington recorded Joseph Fort Newton's Foreword to the first issue of *The Builder:*

> Some things need to be set down plainly, by way of preface, in behalf of a frank and full understanding. Let it be said once and for all that this movement has back of it no motive of personal aggrandizement, much less of pecuniary profit. Instead of trying to make money out of Masonry, the founders of this Society are putting time, money and energy into it, thinking little and caring less of any returns other than to find the truth and tell it. They have no axe to grind, no vanity to vent, no fad to air. Were it possible, they would prefer to remain unnamed, and be known only by their work—like the old cathedral builders, whose labors live but whose names are lost. Their solitary aim is to diffuse Masonic light and understanding, and thus to extend the influence and power of this, the greatest order of men upon the earth. . . .
>
> Time was, not so long ago, when it required courage for a man to be a Mason. Feeling against the Order was intense, often fanatical and its innocent secrets were imagined by the ignorant or malicious to hide some dark design. How different it is now, when the Order is everywhere held in honor, and justly so, for the benignity of its spirit and the nobility of its principles. No wonder its temple gates are thronged with alert young men, eager to enter its ancient fellowship. But these young men must know what Masonry is, whence it came, what it cost in the sacrifice of brave men, and what it is trying to do in the world. Otherwise, they cannot realize in what a benign tradition they stand, much less be able to

find a reason for their faith. Every argument in favor of any kind of education has equal force in behalf of the education of young Masons in the truths of Masonry. So and only so can they ever hope to know what the ritual really means, and what high and haunting beauties lie hidden in the simplest emblems.

Arrington said that Newton, even after he had been called to England, continued to support *The Builder*. He sent several sketches for publication.

Throughout the sixteen year life of the Research Society its contributors read like a Who's Who in Freemasonry. Much of what they wrote then is as wise and timely today as it was when published.

In later years *The Philalethes* would follow the sentiments expressed in *The Builder*: "Each of its contributors writes under his own name, and is responsible for his opinions. Believing that a unity of spirit is better than a uniformity of opinion, the Research Society, as such, does not champion any one school of Masonic thought as over or against another; but offers to all alike a medium for fellowship and instruction, leaving each to stand or fall by its own merits."

Arrington recorded that articles often had to be withheld because of the volume of letters requesting answers to pressing Masonic questions. This the editor considered healthy. Many of the queries were frequently "as instructive as the original article."

The Philalethes Society would take up some of the slack from the demise of the National Masonic Research Society, but as is readily apparent, it has never approached the number of Freemasons reached by the group from Anamosa. Arrington, a professional librarian and researcher, praised the publication highly. "*The Builder,*" he said, "ranks among the finest scholarly Masonic periodicals ever to be published and still serves as a valuable mine of Masonic information." To keep this information alive, the Executive Board of The Philalethes Society, in 1987, authorized every issue of the magazine to be recorded on film, and the michrofiche made available to anyone desiring a set.

The Executive Secretary, S. Brent Morris, reminded the members of The Philalethes Society that those who didn't pay their dues within two months would be dropped from the mailing list. He also told them no dues cards would be mailed because of the cost of such mailings. The cost of handling foreign checks was staggering, and small checks for payment of dues made this cost intolerable. He asked that all checks be drawn on a U.S. bank and in U.S. funds.

The Editor, Jerry Marsengill, took his pen in his hand for the December 1982 issue of *The Philalethes*, something he rarely did. That is, his pen was usually used to correct the glaring errors he would find in the submissions. He was disturbed. "Every time I pick up a Masonic magazine," he wrote, "I discover some new theory about the origin or some particular facet of Freemasonry. Most of these are completely fanciful, and endeavor to trace Freemasonry to the Egyptians, the Rosicrucians, the Babylonians or the Greek mysteries. Any vague similarity in Freemasonry of other fraternal organizations with one of the ancient mysteries is seized upon and given as irrefutable proof that Masonry, as we know it, must have descended from one or another of these sects."

Articles appearing in *The Philalethes* were not immune to this disease, he noted and named some. "Any theory should be formed by gathering the known facts," he cautioned, "fitting them into a hypothesis, testing that hypothesis in all possible ways and, all which can not be entirely proved, discarded, and not propound a theory which may, or may not, be true. To develop a theory without first testing every facet of the theory is nothing less than negligent. No wonder qualified historians scoff at our pretensions to scholarship."

Marsengill concluded: "We need theoretical studies of the origin of Freemasonry but these should not be undertaken without a qualified researcher, thoroughly grounded in his particular discipline, who will state his theories in language which conforms to the known facts and which can be tried and proven. By such a method of research we can 'bring credit rather than disgrace' to the Masonic order."

In an author's note he said: "Yes, I know some scientists shoot from the hip and make up theories and then twist the facts to fit them. I also know that a large number of our religious leaders do the same thing. I don't advocate that these men should be drawn and quartered for their methods of research. Impalement will be sufficient."

The Philalethes congratulated the Virginia Crafstmen, a Masonic traveling degree team, on its twentieth anniversary. Several members of The Philalethes Society were present to help the Craftsmen celebrate. Among them was Stewart M.L. Pollard, FPS, the Second Vice President. Covered in a separate article was the work done by the Craftsmen in Connecticut for the 250th anniversary celebration of the birth of George Washington. Again many members of The Philalethes Society participated.

Those planning to attend the Annual Assembly and Feast were urged to make their reservations early. The Lecturer would be Richard H. Sands, MPS, of Michigan who planned to speak on "The Northwest Ordinance." But he wouldn't make it; neither would dozens of others!

14. SERVICE
(1983–1986)

*T*he Annual Assembly and Feast was scheduled for Friday, February 11, 1983. It took place, but over three-fourths of the seats were empty. One of the severest blizzards ever to strike Washington started Thursday afternoon and raged throughout the night and the following day. The nation's capital was at a stand-still.

The officers of the Society had all arrived at the Hotel Washington before the snow started falling, so the business meeting took place as scheduled. The election of the officers was certified. Bruce H. Hunt became the President. Stewart M.L. Pollard was elected First Vice President and Allen E. Roberts became the Second Vice President. However, Pollard, because of his duties as Executive Secretary of The Masonic Service Association, found it necessary to resign. Roberts was named First Vice President and John R. Nocas Second Vice President. Morris and Hilliard remained as Executive Secretary and Treasurer.

The Constitution and Bylaws were consolidated and brought up-to-date (see Appendix A). Included in the Bylaws was a section pertaining to the formation and operation of Chapters of the Society. For the first time Chapters were recognized as an important activity of The Philalethes Society. Those few in existence were given one year in which to comply with the adopted regulations. John R. Nocas, Mervin B. Hogan and George H.T. French were elected Fellows.

The blizzard forced the airline to strand Richard Sands, the Lecturer for the Assembly and Feast, about half way on his journey to Washington. S. Brent Morris capably replaced him as the Lecturer. His talk was printed in the April 1983 issue of *The Philalethes*.

The snow, which continued throughout Friday, forced almost everyone to stay inside the hotel. The meetings on Saturday were depleted drastically. The stories of the hardship suffered by many of those who finally made it to the hotel were horrifying. It was a weekend that would be remembered.

The chief proponent, founder and supporter of many of the "little Masonic Bodies" that met in the District of Columbia each February was Harold Van Buren Voorhis, FPS. He was well known for his distinctive dress, but mainly for his cryptic speech and knowledge of Freemasonry. His death on May 23, 1983 left a void that could never be filled. Fortunately he left a precious legacy in the form of the written word, and a host of disciples. The inspiring words of wisdom that he penned, unlike the human body, would never die.

In fact, Voorhis conducted his own funeral! He did it by means of an audio tape. The full transcript appeared in the February 1985 issue of *The Phila-lethes*. He began: "My friends, although I will have passed from earthly life when you hear my voice, please express no surprise because, if you will recall, you have heard voices of deceased persons many times—on phonograph records in song, and from wire or tape recordings of addresses and interviews. The present instance is probably mildly shocking to you because you are at my funeral and did not expect anything like this, that is, hearing the voice of the deceased.

"Actually, in a sense, I am conducting my own funeral. Usually relatives are burdened with such affairs, but I have taken enough time to arrange my own service—the way I want it, rather than have others arrange it to conform to some religious and/or commercial custom. If you have come to spend a few minutes here out of respect to my memory, I appreciate that. You may even gaze upon my countenance and know that I am grateful for that respect."

Voorhis set forth some of his "pet peeves," many of them he had expressed over the years. He didn't think much of fraternal funerals for members who seldom, if ever, attended their association meetings. Most eulogies are nothing more than "window dressing" provided by clergymen who knew nothing about the deceased. Families are secluded and later "there is wonderment as to who many" of those who signed the registers are. He deplored the "unkept cemeteries" which were "disgraces to a so-called Christian neighborhood." He thought this might be so because only the soul is worth saving, "so they must conclude that as the soul is no longer in the body that there is no further use in bothering about it."

There was no ordained clergyman to conduct Voorhis' service. "I did my own praying before my soul departed from the earth, just as I was taught by my parents, two God-loving people. . . . If my own prayers are not answered, it is my own fault." He deplored the "hodgepodge of systems which have developed to foster the Christian and other faiths, none of which seem to have produced any worthwhile over-all results."

The service at the grave was also in Voorhis's voice on tape. He covered the history of the Bible. He claimed it had been compiled by men who "incidentally, never had any sort of ecclesiastical authority." He also claimed that the King James version was rejected by the Catholic hierarchy.

Ironically, a short item that was printed in *The Philalethes* right after the conclusion of Voorhis' funeral service said that Alphonse Cerza had been elected a full member of Quatuor Coronati Lodge No. 2076, London, England. This was something Voorhis had rightly believed he deserved for many years.

The October 1983 issue of *The Philalethes* ran articles 69, 70 and 71 of the continuing bicentennial series on the founding of the United States. Alphonse Cerza wrote "New York City Evacuated"; James R. Case covered two: "The Big Parade of 1783" and "New York City Masonry: 1776–1783." The final article in the series (number 74) was published in the December 1983 issue. In the issue Alphonse Cerza thanked the committee that had worked diligently to present Freemasonry's side of the founding of the United States. The committee consisted of those Masonic historians of the Revolutionary War, James R. Case and Ronald E. Heaton.

The Editor, Jerry Marsengill, reported on his visit to Italy as one of the speakers for the 250th anniversary of Freemasonry in Italy for the Grand Orient. He said he was particularly impressed with the courtesy of the Italian people. He did report a peculiar experience, however. "When I arrived at the Palazzo [dei Congressi]," he wrote, "I found it was being picketed by the Communists. I was stopped and one of the young men began to give me a long speech in Italian. Since I didn't understand a single word, he called another young Communist over. The second one spoke excellent English and gave me a long talk on what was wrong with Masonry in general and Italian Masonry in particular. He ended by asking me if I would want the Masons to take over the government of the United States. Since I was a stranger in the country, I played it cool and didn't tell him that I couldn't think of anything better for the government.

"He advised me that I shouldn't go into the palazzo. I thanked him and went on in to see guards, armed with submachine guns, around the perimeter. I had seen these carabini at DaVinci International in Rome with the submachine guns and the guard dogs, but hadn't any idea that they would be guarding a Masonic meeting.

"About 1500 people were on hand for the conference which was conducted in five languages: Italian, English, French, German and Spanish, with simultaneous translations into all languages."

Marsengill said one of the highlights of his participation was the opportunity to talk for nearly two hours with Cyril Batham of England. He claimed it was a Masonic experience he would never forget. Of this visitation, John Vrooman said: "It seems to me that the selection of Jerry Marsengill, FPS, editor of *The Philalethes* and *The Royal Arch* magazines, to represent American Freemasonry at the 250th anniversary of Freemasonry in Italy, was not only a real tribute to him, but also a splendid boost for The Philalethes Society, long known as our International Research Society."

The President of The Philalethes Society, Bruce H. Hunt, was privileged to be at Pearl Harbor, Honolulu, Hawaii, on July 9, 1983, with the General Grand Council of Cryptic Masons. The government, after years of discus-

Jerry Marsengill in Italy

sions, permitted the Cryptic Masons to present a plaque in the *USS Arizona* Memorial Museum honoring those men who had died during the attack by the Japanese on December 7, 1941.

The plaque, the only Masonic memento in the Memorial, measured approximately twelve inches square, and it weighed close to twelve pounds. During a special Masonic ceremony the presentation of the plaque was made by Hunt, the Acting General Grand Master.

John Black Vrooman, during the annual communication of the Grand Lodge of Missouri in September 1983, received the first "Harry S. Truman medal for distinguished service." His more than fifty years of service to the Craft had been recognized by his own peers.

General Grand Council plaque

Harry Carr, no stranger to American Freemasons, died on October 20, 1983. He had long been a student of Freemasonry, and for years edited the Transactions of Quatuor Coronati Lodge No. 2076, London, England. In recent years he had made several lecture tours in the United States. *Harry Carr's World of Freemasonry*, a book published after his death, covered much of what he had discovered concerning the Craft during his years of research.

The February 1984 issue of *The Philalethes* concluded the three part series about "The Rise and Development of Freemasonry in Australia" by E.R. Castle, MPS. Keith Arrington, FPS, wrote his second article on "Iowa's Masonic Magazines." He received the 1983 Certificate of Literature for his first article in this series. A series on "Masonic Leadership" was started by Allen E. Roberts. John R. Nocas, FPS, told about James Anderson and his "Masonic Best Sellers."

During the meeting of the Executive Board on February 10, 1984, Bruce H. Hunt asked that he not be considered as President for another year. His duties as General Grand Recorder for the General Grand Council of Cryptic Masons was taking more and more of his time. Consequently, Allen E. Roberts was elected President, John R. Nocas, First Vice President, and Jerry Marsengill, Second Vice President. The latter would also continue as Editor of *The Philalethes*. Morris and Hilliard continued as Executive Secretary and Treasurer.

Richard H. Sands was elected a Fellow of The Philalethes Society, and this was announced at the time he presented his Lecture during the Assembly and Feast. Wallace McLeod, MPS, became the new Blue Friar.

The President had asked the members of the Society for their help. There had been severe criticism of the discontinuance of the annual Workshop when the Assembly and Feast started in 1980. He wanted to know how many wanted to continue the later and how many wanted the former. In April 1984 the results were in: the membership wanted both! This, he promised them, would be the case.

Burton Kessler, MPS, had suggested in an article that The Philalethes Society should speak for Freemasons. The President consulted Dwight L. Smith, a former President whose name had been mentioned by Kessler. Smith had said the Society's prime mission is to provide "responsible authentic Masonic research and information" for all Freemasons. Roberts said: "I'll underline that. I'll also agree with Burton that the Society should 'seek and offer Light in Masonry . . . by discovering, displaying and honoring leadership quality, by continuing to provide information to those who seek more Masonic knowledge.' "

Smith and Roberts both agreed that no one person, or group, can speak for Freemasons or Freemasonry. Roberts added: "There are perhaps no two Freemasons in the world who have 'needled' our Masonic leadership more than Dwight and I. However, and this is important, we've done it as *individuals*—not as representatives of any organization. This is as it should be. No one else should take our lumps."

The revised Bylaws of The Philalethes Society which appeared in the June 1984 issue of *The Philalethes* was received well by the membership. Placing the Chapters on a fully legitimate basis met with hearty approval. Before 1984 came to a close all the active Chapters had complied with the "grandfather" clause to receive their charters.

A "Masonic Host and Information Center" was opened in Los Angeles by the Grand Lodge of California. It was California's contribution for the assistance of visitors for the 1984 Olympic Games. Among its many conveniences, it housed a short-wave radio unit to "enable guests to send messages to their home towns around the world."

"Harry S. Truman, Mason" was the title of an article by C. Warren Ohrvall, MPS, Archivist for the Truman Library and Museum in Independence, Missouri. It appeared in the August 1984 issue of *The Philalethes*. He told how Truman had become a Freemason seventy-five years earlier and Freemasonry would celebrate the 100th anniversary of the thirty-third President's birth on May 8, 1984. Ohrvall spoke of Truman's life-long love for the Craft, and how, even as an active Senator, Vice President and President, he took the time to work for Freemasonry. In 1940 he was elected Grand Master of Masons in Missouri, an office he often said was the most important honor he ever received. In 1950, while President of the United States, he served as Master of Missouri Lodge of Research. The full Masonic story of Truman will be found in *Brother Truman: The Masonic Life and Philosophy of Harry S. Truman.*

A little-known story was told in the October issue of *The Philalethes* by Thomas Rigas, MPS. His article was entitled "Lafayette's Burial Place: The Flag That Never Came Down." Rigas wrote: "The American flag has flown over the tomb of Bro. and Marquis de Lafayette every day for about 150 years. During the Nazi occupation of France in World War II, it was the only American Flag to wave in occupied Europe."

Two white-robed nuns, said Rigas, have "recited prayers in the cemetery convent . . . 24 hours around the clock in honor of the victims of the Reign of Terror in 1794. General Lafayette died in 1834, and at the time the state of Virginia shipped to France the earth in which he was to be buried so that Bro. Lafayette might lie eternally under American soil."

According to Rigas, the prayer recited by the Sisters of the Order of the Sacred Heart and Perpetual Adoration, is: *"Bestow upon them, O Lord, eternal tranquillity. And grant Your forgiveness unto all those who did not know how to forgive."* This prayer is reported to have been made by Adrienne, Lafayette's wife, who died on Christmas Eve, 1807. Her family had been put to death by the guillotine during the uprising. It was she who had built a chapel on the site where the family and other victims had been buried in a common grave. It is there that she and her husband rest eternally.

Wallace McLeod asked why many Lodges are named for St. Alban. In the course of his article, *Why St. Alban?*, in the October 1984 issue of *The Philalethes* he answered the question. The story of Alban's steadfast devotion to Christianity, as related at length by McLeod, is a blood-curdling tale of martyrdom. Alban, who was murdered in 303–305 because he would not renounce his religion, was the first to die for the new persuasion. He was the first Christian martyr of England. McLeod concluded his article by saying:

Those of you who belong to these lodges, and to others of the same name, hold high your heads with pride. Not only do you commemorate a man who preferred to suffer death rather than betray the sacred trust reposed in him, you also bear testimony to a Masonic tradition that goes back more than 600 years. St. Alban has had a demonstrable connection with the Craft since 1350, though latterly it is not much remembered. The name should constantly remind you that you are part of a continuous chain of good men, thousands of them, going back through the impenetrable mists of time. The vast majority are no longer with us, for they have been summoned to the Grand Lodge Above, but they have left their deeds behind, as monuments for us to emulate. And we may perhaps imagine that though dead they still speak to us through these monuments; and maybe even (who knows?) from on high they look down with interest on the deeds of us, their successors. It is pleasant to think so anyway. If we bear that picture in mind, perhaps we may, without irreverence, apply to ourselves the words of the apostle:

Wherefore seeing we also are compassed about with so great a cloud of witnesses, let us lay aside every weight, and the sin which doth so easily beset us, and let us run with patience the race that is set before us.

Hundreds of articles and dozens of books have been written about William Morgan, the individual who, in 1826, was responsible for the birth of the anti-Masonry that almost destroyed Freemasonry in the United States. Little has been told about his wife. John E. Thompson in an extremely well documented article entitled "The Mormon Baptism of William Morgan" tells something of her story.

"Lucinda Morgan herself was barely twenty-five years of age at the time [of Morgan's disappearance]," Thompson wrote, "and if contemporary reports be believed, a petite blue-eyed blond pleasing to the eye." She had two small children, and the anti-Masons made this a trigger in their hate campaign. She, along with unscrupulous politicians, "identified" the actual body of one Timothy Munroe, a Canadian, as "being good enough" to be that of Morgan until after the election. Lucinda became a leading figure in the anti-Masonic movement.

Then, according to Thompson, Lucinda decided to remarry in 1830. This upset the leading politicians of the anti-Masonic movement. They were going to lose their best drawing card to attract anti votes in the 1832 election. She ignored their pleas and married George W. Harris, a Batavia silversmith, twenty-one years older than she was. Harris had housed the Morgans over his shop when they first arrived in Batavia.

"Shortly after their marriage," said Thompson, "the Harrises seem to have disappeared. We do not really know what happened." But in 1834 they were living in Terre Haute, Indiana. There they became Mormons. In 1837 they were living among Mormons in Caldwell County, Missouri. It was in the home of the Harrises that plural marriages and "nasty" affairs were discussed.

"In 1842, Sarah Pratt was sought by Joseph [Smith] as a plural wife," wrote Thompson. She happened to discuss this matter with Lucinda. Sarah later said she had confidence in Lucinda. "When Joseph made his dastardly attempt on me, I went to Mrs. Harris to unbosom my grief to her," said Sarah. "To my utter astonishment, she said laughing heartily: 'How foolish you are! Why I am his mistress since four years.' " According to Thompson's research, George Harris, at least from 1838, had risen high in Mormon circles. And it was in 1841 that Morgan "became one of the first persons to receive by proxy the new Mormon rite of Baptism for the Dead."

Thompson found that Lucinda ended her years in Memphis, Tennessee. She apparently joined the Catholic Sisters of Charity and worked with the Leah Asylum of Memphis. She later died in obscurity.

Lewis J. Birt, MPS, wrote about "Unusual Events in a Lodge of Research" for the February 1985 issue of *The Philalethes*. He found "that the powers and restrictions imposed on Research Lodges will vary according to the provisions placed by the founders in their Charters or Warrants. All of which hinges on the wisdom and forethought of those who founded the Lodges of Research." Most of these Lodges do not confer degrees; however, the one in Arkansas may do so.

Two Research Lodges, Birt found, did reluctantly accept initiates. One was Sidney Lodge of Research No. 290, Australia. The other was a Research Lodge in a Southern state for which Birt did not have a name. He also found that most Research Lodges are interested in the philosophical and educational aspects of Freemasonry rather than the ritualistic portions.

A Canadian member of the Society, Wallace McLeod, a Professor of Classics at the University of Toronto, created something of a tumult in February. In his article, "Loyalist Masons," he wrote: "For the past ten years the people of the United States of America have been privileged to indulge in an orgy of self-congratulation, with hundreds of publications commemorating the American Revolution. Freemasons, as is right, have shared in this emotional outpouring. . . . *The Philalethes* has run more than one series on the people and events of two hundred years ago. It has doubtless been a wonderful experience for those five million Masons who happen to be American citizens. For the rest of us, all this literature has been not quite so fascinating."

McLeod correctly said: "Some of our patriotic posturings are based not on simple facts, but on a subjective interpretation of historical events. War at the best of times is hideous." He quoted from the "Charges of a Free-Mason" what many others have quoted to "prove" the Patriots violated their Masonic oaths. "A Mason . . . is never to be concern'd in Plots or Conspiracies against the Peace and Welfare of the Nation." A truism. But when the Continental Congress broke away from the tyranny of the British Crown, a new country was born—even though a handful of Patriots had to fight to make it a reality. Actually, no Masonic oaths were broken, not even by those Tories who fled to Canada. McLeod discussed the Reverend John Beardsley of New York, who took his family to Nova Scotia. Later he became "Founder of Freemasonry in the Province of New Brunswick."

During the meeting of the Executive Board in February 1985, because of the press of business, S. Brent Morris and John Mauk Hilliard resigned as Executive Secretary and Treasurer. The Board elected Edward R. Schmidt,

MPS, as Secretary to assist the President until such time as another Executive Secretary could be selected. Thomas E. Weir, MPS, agreed to accept the position of Treasurer. A month later he resigned and Henry G. Law, MPS, of Delaware, was chosen.

The dues structure had been thoroughly analyzed and it was determined the Society had been operating on "a shoe string." The dues were raised to $15, and Life Membership to $200, effective January 1, 1986. To enhance the image of the Society, it was decided to print a four-color brochure to act as a petition for membership, and to explain what The Philalethes Society is.

Four Chapters received charters, one of them in Canada. The Chapters were recorded as: Virginia, at Richmond; Wm. M. Taylor, Houston, Texas; Western Reserve, at Cleveland, Ohio; Chester County, Pennsylvania; Southwest, at San Antonio, Texas; Tennessee Valley, Alabama; Kentucky; Indiana; High Desert, at Apple Valley, California; Lowell Thomas, at New York City; Lux Quaro, at London, Ontario, Canada; and San Diego, for the county, at San Diego, California. Toronto (Canada) was operating under a dispensation which was continued.

Wallace McLeod was awarded the Certificate of Literature for 1984. The Philalethes Lecturer was Donald H. Smith, MPS. His excellent presentation, "A Foundation for Century Twenty-one," would be printed in the April issue of *The Philalethes*.

Smith spoke about the past, the present and the future, not only of Freemasonry but of the world. He outlined the several stages in the history of the country and mentioned the changes that had evolved in the Craft because of each stage. "It is the ability to change our public image that has brought us through our most trying times," he said. He praised the work of those Freemasons who participated in their communities.

"We need to unify masonic bodies insofar as possible to reduce administrative costs and at the same time to increase communication with our members," Smith believed. "We need to use computers and word processors to insure continuity.

"In the successful movement toward the twenty-first century, we need a national public relations campaign, both internal and external to let people of this great nation know what Masons do for them and with them. Wouldn't it be wonderful if every Mason knew what Masons do for him and for others? And wouldn't it be even better if half the people of our country knew the same thing? Yes, it will cost money, but even more it will require cooperation beyond any we have ever demonstrated."

We need "Masonry With a Smile" wrote George H. T. French, FPS, in the April 1985 issue of *The Philalethes*. "Our Speculative Freemasonry started out in meetings where food, libations, toasts, games and raucous singing alternated with informative Masonic catechistical Lectures. Why have we banned that cohesive conviviality? May we not learn with smiles instead of with sighs?" French added: "Our Craft grew by addition, deletion, correction, gradually over several centuries. In other words, it grew by change. And it is still changing and growing."

The Executive Board had accepted an invitation to hold a semi-annual meeting in Houston, Texas, in October. It would have been the first such meeting ever held, but it was abruptly canceled. Someone in the area determined it shouldn't take place.

Robin Carr, MPS, paid "A Tribute to Robert Burns: Masonic Poet" in the August 1985 issue of *The Philalethes*. "Not only did Burns love the bottle, he loved language, even the off-color, and satisfied his craving for bawdy in two ways," wrote Carr. "First, he collected the raunchy, rollicking songs and ballads of the Scottish countryside, and with the help of Sir Walter Scott, a Brother Mason, strived to preserve their essence while cleaning them up for polite society." Carr included several of Burn's poem with Masonic connotations.

"Freemasonry offered Burns much," said Carr. "It allowed a ploughboy poet to transcend, but not to leave, his social class. It enabled him to gain the confidence, respect and ear of Ministers, teachers, lawyers, the gentry and the literateurs who controlled the day's society. Yet, Burns gave much. He was always an active Mason, who wrote songs and verse used only on Lodge occasions. He served in elected stations in various Lodges and was chosen Poet-Laureate of Cannongate-Kilwinning Lodge No. One in Edinburgh." Burns had become a Mason in Lodge St. David No. 174, Tarbolton, Scotland, on July 4, 1781.

In an article entitled "The Power of Positive Hating," Jerry Marsengill explains why far too many religious denominations hate Freemasonry—they don't want to share man's time, money or talent. He was disturbed because too many Masonic leaders remain passive to the unwarranted attacks on the Craft. "If we believe in the essential good of that which we are doing," Marsengill wrote, "we should have the stamina to stand up and be counted as Freemasons. If the fraternity is good, we should defend it. If it is bad, we should leave it. We should not alter our principles or our attitudes to fit any particular public sentiment. If we change Freemasonry today because some church does not like the penalties or the secrecy, what will we be required to do tomorrow? When a Joseph Fort Newton or a Norman Vincent Peale can be an active productive member of the fraternity and still be a noted and loved minister, why should we allow ourselves to be pushed around by some preachers whose concept of Christianity has gone far afield from that which the founder of that religion taught?"

In the October 1985 issue of *The Philalethes*, the President, in his dual capacity of Executive Secretary, reminded the members that the records were in the process of being revised. The computer program had been changed. During the course of these changes it had been learned that many had been receiving the magazine and owed several years' dues. They would be dropped as of October 31.

Louis L. Williams, FPS, asked: "Christopher Wren, Mason or No?" This was a continuation of an article he wrote for the August issue. "Let's first look at the setting and environment," he suggested. "He was born in 1632, almost a century before the Grand Lodge was organized in 1717. He died in 1723, 91 years of age. He was an organizer of the Royal Society for the Advancement of Science while still a professor at Oxford, and its President in 1681–83. He was a close friend of the leading citizens of England, and this included Dr. Desaguliers, also a fellow of the Royal Society, one of the organizers of the Grand Lodge, and its third Grand Master in 1719. He was a friend of John Aubrey, of Dr. Robert Plot, of Elias Ashmole [the first to leave a written record of becoming a Mason], and he was unquestionably well known to, if not a friend of Dr. James Anderson, one of the organizers of the Grand Lodge, and the author of its *Constitutions* of 1723 and 1738. Why, then, do we not have a better record of Wren's membership in the Craft, if he were indeed a member?"

Williams added: "Young Wren wrote the earliest biography of his father's life, called *Parentalia,* published by the grandson, Stephen Wren. It is completely silent on Sir Christopher's Masonic membership, if it ever existed. But, then, it is also silent on hundreds of other details we should like to know about, and was described by a later biographer, one James Elmes, as 'a miserable compilation, a bungling performance.'

"And so it goes. But despite the fact that young Christopher, the son, said nothing about his father's Masonic affiliations, he does quote his father at length on his father's dissertation of how operative masonry came into being, and how the great European Cathedrals were built by transient groups of operative masons."

John Aubrey wrote a note on the back of a folio which read: "1691. Mdm, this day May the 18th being after Rogation Sunday. Monday is a great convention at St. Paul's church of the Fraternity of the Accepted Free Masons: where Sr Christopher Wren is to be adopted a Brother and Sr. Henry Goodric . . . of ye Tower, & divers others . . . There have been kings, that haue been of this Sodalitie." Williams said this entry had been hidden and not found until 1844. He also noted that Robert F. Gould gave no credence to this account; neither did Henry Wilson Coil, FPS. But, "It is the well considered belief of the author that notwithstanding the very well constructed and logical arguments of Gould, Coil and others, that we have over-reacted to the evidence, and have failed in the logical inferences that may be drawn from it in view of the current conditions of the times, and the almost complete absence of any Masonic record."

Williams concludes: "I can well believe that Wren was a knowledgeable operative mason, and an initiated Speculative Mason, who thereafter had little or no time to devote to active participation in any recorded work of the Craft."

The Masonic world was saddened on learning of the death of John Black Vrooman on November 3, 1985. His memorial was written by Allen E. Roberts for the February 1986 issue of *The Philalethes*.

IN MEMORIAM
JOHN BLACK VROOMAN, FPS-LIFE
March 4, 1899–November 3, 1985

"Who's that big fellow with the giant-sized pipe?" I asked William Moseley Brown during my first visit to the meetings of the Allied Masonic Bodies in 1957. Bill laughed: "Come with me and I'll introduce you to one of the finest Masons in the world."

Less than a half hour later I knew that Bill had told the truth. No finer, more dedicated, and enthusiastic Freemason ever lived. Vrooman was a quiet man, vocally, letting his pen do the speaking for him. He had kept The Philalethes Society alive during some mighty dark periods. His articles, editorials, and editing of work submitted for *The Philalethes* kept the Society in the forefront in the literary circles of Freemasonry.

John could have devoted his life to more lucrative causes than Freemasonry, but it was this he loved with a passion few men have. He was educated at Oxford, England, and graduated from Wabash College, Crawford, Indiana, in 1921. He attended every reunion at that college until a year ago when his health failed. He was a teacher, an instructor in French, a reporter, and an editor. From 1954 until 1976 he edited *The Philalethes*. For over twenty years he edited *The Freemason* of the Grand Lodge of Missouri. For Kansas he edited the *Masonic Digest*. He was librarian for the Scottish Rite bodies and editor of its publication.

Every year John joined Dottie and me in our room in the hotel and we learned about his heartaches, his joys, his triumphs, and his enormous love of his fellowman. His greatest joy was his work for The Masonic Service Association where he became the servant of America's hospitalized veterans. Early in 1941 he wrote to Carl Claudy asking for the job. Claudy wrote back: "No, John, the pay is too small, the work too difficult, and the hours too long—you would not be interested." Said John: "That made me more enthusiastic and more eager to participate." He became one of the first Field Agents for the MSA at its Rolla, Missouri, Service Center for our Armed Forces. And again he became a teacher and trained countless other Field Agents. Forty years later he retired.

John Became a Master Mason on May 9, 1921, in Montgomery Lodge No. 59, Crawfordsville, Indiana. Later he affiliated with, and became the Master (and *earned* the title of "Worshipful") of Equality Lodge No. 497 of Newburg, Missouri. He joined the Royal Arch, Council of Royal and Select Masters, the Commandery, the Scottish Rite, National Sojourners, and was a Hero of '76. He also belonged to the Order of the Eastern Star. He held the KYCH and received several awards, including medals from Vermont, the Cryptic Masons, and the Virginia Craftsmen. He was the first recipient of the Harry S. Truman medal of the Grand Lodge of Missouri. He was an original member of the Masonic Brotherhood of the Blue Forget-Me-Not, and a member of the Society of Blue Friars. He enjoyed his memberships in all the Allied Masonic Bodies meeting in the District of Columbia, and served as an officer of most of them. Several Research Lodges throughout the country elected him to Honorary Membership.

John Vrooman is survived by a son, countless numbers of friends and an untold number of beneficiaries of his kindness over more than eight decades. Thousands of words can be written about this thoughtful man, but none can better sum up his philosophy than what he wrote in *A Third of a Century as an M.S.A. Field Agent*.

"Being a Field Agent," said John, "has made me realize, with the force of a conviction, that Masonry *is* brotherhood in action, and that when our Brethren know the needs we try to meet, they are eager to help, aid, and assist in answering the cries of the distressed humanity."

John Black Vrooman spent his life "answering the cries of distressed humanity." This unusual man gave the credit for his benevolence to Freemasonry and the lessons he had absorbed within the Craft. He served his fellowman, not for gold, but through love.

The President had received a couple of complaints about articles appearing in *The Philalethes*. In the December 1985 issue he said he wanted to set the record straight. "Our Editor, Jerry Marsengill, one of the best informed Freemasons in the country, is the sole judge of what appears in our pages. All of us are invited to make suggestions, but he makes the final determination. The Society may not necessarily agree with a writer of an article, but it's only by 'listening' to all points of view that we can make an intelligent judgement. This Society was formed in 1928 by a group of Masonic writers for protection against would-be censors—and the world is full of them. There are few 'perfect' Masons; there are plenty of 'warts' in Freemasonry, and our critics are quick to point them out. It's only by knowing what the undesirable elements are that we can do some necessary weeding. So, censorship, by whatever name it may be called, will not be practiced here.

"A 'house organ'—a publication for a business, Masonic jurisdiction, Masonic organization or association—is charged to make that particular organ follow an editorial policy that makes its parent look fabulous. Its editor won't last long if he doesn't. It also means he can't be honest. Naturally, we want to make Freemasonry throughout the world, because our members will be found in all free countries, look good, and I think we succeed. At the same time we want to be honest. To accomplish this honesty there must be times when being truthful will cause some pain. But through pain comes growth."

In the February 1986 issue of *The Philalethes* the President wrote: "The past four years have been exciting to say the least. I'm supposed to still be waiting to be elected to this office! But unforeseen circumstances caused the resignation of one of the Vice Presidents. That moved me up the ladder too quickly. Bruce Hunt also moved up quickly and had to leave after one year. And there I was—your President. I had hoped to have a couple of years to prepare for the responsibilities associated with the office. I didn't get them, but I attempted to continue building on a solid foundation."

The out-going President promised to continue working for the Society as he had during the past thirty years. The Executive Board saw to that. It elected him Executive Secretary. John R. Nocas became the President; Jerry Marsengill, First Vice President and Editor; John Mauk Hilliard, Second Vice President; and Henry G. Law remained the Treasurer.

The Executive Board adopted a Grant Program in an attempt to encourage Masonic writers, authors, researchers and Masonic film producers and script writers. The Board also asked Allen Roberts to produce a "how to" manual directed toward Masonic educational workshops, seminars and programs. The Board ordered four leadership training films produced by Imagination Unlimited to be purchased for the use of the Chapters desiring to hold leadership seminars. The Board thanked Albert Woody, FPS, of Washington for compiling an index of *The Philalethes* to date.

The Board established a Philalethes Society Distinguished Service Medal, and at the Assembly and Feast the first were awarded. They went to Alphonse Cerza, Ronald E. Heaton, Allen E. Roberts, and Jerald "Jerry" Marsengill. The Certificate of Literature for 1985 went to Louis L. Williams for his series on Christopher Wren.

The Philalethes Lecturer was Wallace E. McLeod, who was informed as he was introduced that he had been elected a Fellow of The Philalethes Society. His topic, "The Effect of Victorian Obscenity Laws on Masonic Historians," would be printed in the June to October issues of *The Philalethes*.

As another era came to an end The Philalethes Society had continued to build on the solid foundation laid down by its founders. The membership had continued to increase. More Masonic leaders had begun to recognize the value of the Society. The financial position had improved to such an extent the leadership of the Society could seek more and better ways to be of service to the Craft in general.

15. Toward the Future
(1986–1988)

"*T*he Philalethes Workshop is Back" read the title of a brief article in the February 1986 issue of *The Philalethes*. The Workshops had been missed, and the Society had been criticized by many of its members and others attending the Allied Masonic meetings. They wanted the popular, informal, but informative yearly gatherings resumed. The Workshop had become a "missing link" among the students of the Allied Bodies.

The Workshop followed the Assembly and Feast, and it wasn't necessary to attend the former to participate in the latter. The subject was "Communication" and featured the Masonic Leadership film *Breaking Barriers to Communication.*

In the film, the late Conrad Hahn covered the barriers to meaningful communication and how to break them. The discussion at the conclusion was lively; the handouts given to each of those in attendance were appreciated. The enthusiasm made it mandatory to continue holding a workshop following the Assembly and Feast.

The Editor, Jerry Marsengill, was concerned about "checkbook charity." He was disturbed by comments he had heard: "Freemasonry is not a charitable organization, its only purpose is to build character!" Marsengill said: "This may, or may not, be true. If it is true, what better way to build character than by being of service to one's fellow man? In the *Vision of Sir Launfal*, James Russell Lowell states: "He gives nothing but worthless gold who gives from a sense of duty. . . ." Much later, in the conclusion of the poem when Sir Launfal has given his last crust to a leper, Lowell states:

"Then the voice which was softer than silence said,
Lo, it is I, be not afraid;
In many climes without avail
Thou has spent thy life for the Holy Grail.
Behold, it is here. This cup which thou
Didst fill at the streamlet for me but now;
This crust is my body broken for thee.
This water his blood which was shed on the tree.
The holy supper is kept indeed,
When we share ourselves to another's need.
Not what we give, but what we share."

For *the gift without the giver is bare.*
Who gives himself with his gifts feeds three,
Himself, his hungry neighbor and me. . . ."

Over the years millions of words have been written about Anderson's *Constitutions of the Freemasons* of 1723, and *The Constitutions of the Right Worshipful Fraternity of the Free and accepted Masons* of 1738. Many of those words written about these *Constitutions* have been fanciful and meaningless. Although it's seldom mentioned, Anderson had to base much of what he wrote on *Old Gothic Constitutions*, some of which were discovered long after Anderson had left this earthly scene. *The Regius Poem*, for instance, wasn't found to be a valuable Masonic document until 1838, although it had been presented to the British Museum by George II in 1757.

The Masonic Book Club of Bloomington, Illinois, reprinted and published the *Constitutions* of 1738 in 1978. In 1985 this Book Club published *The Old Gothic Constitutions*. Wallace E. McLeod, MPS, interpreted them for the book. The column, "Through Masonic Windows," devoted more space to a review of this book than it had any previous volume. It was done for several reasons, but mainly because "if we had followed the direction of our intelligent forefathers, we wouldn't have the leadership problems in Freemasonry we have; and we need to be reminded from time to time of the intelligence and dedication of those in whose footsteps we now tread."

The article said that few men would have the time, patience, or knowledge to interpret the *Old Gothic Constitutions*. It took someone with the education and background in Freemasonry such as McLeod had to do the job. Within his "Introduction" he proved that Dr. James Anderson had followed, for the most part, the reasoning found in the old documents. He vindicated the few who have defended Anderson.

McLeod had this to say: "We see that Anderson did take seriously his mandate to digest the Old Gothic Constitutions 'in a new and better method.' He includes a traditional history and a set of regulations, just like the Old Charges, although after his fashion he updates it by wilfully interpolating new notions. The precise choice of wording indicated that he consulted at least three versions of the text: the Cooke Manuscript; . . . the Bolt-Coleraine Manuscript; . . . and of which a congener was apparently available to Samuel Prichard in 1730; . . . the Heade Manuscript."

About Anderson's *Constitutions of 1738* McLeod wrote: "This is the second edition of Anderson's *Constitutions*. It is a considerably larger work, incorporating much new material. Even when he repeats material from the edition of 1723, he invariably changes the wording. In this new edition he makes even greater use of the Old Charges than he did in the earlier text."

Throughout his "Introduction" McLeod compares the various texts side by side.

In his column, Roberts commented: "It's interesting to note that Anderson didn't manufacture an important point too seldom adhered to in our modern Craft. The Old Charges read: 'And that they should Ordain the wisest of them to be the Master of their Lord and Master's work.' Anderson wrote: 'The most expert of the Fellow Craftsmen shall be chosen or appointed by the Master, or Overseer of the Lord's Work; who is to be call'd Master by those that work under him.' "

It would appear, from McLeod's critique, that the important points found in Anderson's *Constitutions* were not a work of fiction or imagination. They were the regulations followed by the craftsmen for decades prior to 1723.

A report of the Executive Board meeting was printed in the April 1986 issue of *The Philalethes*.

The life of one of the most vehement anti-Masons in history, Thaddeus Stevens of Pennsylvania, was covered by C. Clark Julius, MPS. According to Julius's account, Stevens led an unsavory life, one that made him an excellent choice as a leader of anti-Masonry. And it was the disappearance of William Morgan in 1826 that launched Stevens's political career.

For centuries Freemasonry has been attacked by well-meaning, but more often unscrupulous, characters. These attacks have come from dictators who fear the freedom of man encouraged by the teachings of Freemasonry, and from religious bigots. With the coming of the electronic age and particularly television, the attacks increased. The satellite dish opened the airwaves to numerous off-shoot religious and other factions. Each of these factions, needing conflict to draw viewers and their money, used Freemasonry, among other things, as a whipping boy.

John Ankerberg, who said he was a "Baptist" and a "born again Christian," enlisted the aid of a fellow from Maryland who claimed to be a "former Worshipful Master." Together they went on the air to purportedly reveal the ritual of the Craft. They attempted to portray Freemasonry as un-Christian because "self means nothing." It's only "through the shed blood of Jesus Christ" that a man can reach heaven. Ankerberg quoted Albert Pike to "prove" that a Mason doesn't know what the ritual means; he is only expected to "imagine he understands it."

The April 1986 issue of *The Philalethes* covered Ankerberg's cable and satellite shows and the remarks of the Maryland "Past Master." Their whole concept appeared to be that Freemasons who profess to be Christians aren't; the only way they could be is if they believed only as Ankerberg, the "Past Master," and their adherents did. Good works mean nothing to God, according to them. A man has to be "born again" by being "washed in the blood of Jesus Christ."

In the same issue appeared a review of "The Catholic Bishops' Report on Freemasonry," by Allen E. Roberts. The "Report" covered many facets; an important part concerned Freemasonry. Most of of what this covered had been written by William J. Whalen, a Professor at Purdue University in Indiana, who was revising his *Christianity and American Freemasonry* when the report was made public. Whalen had made a thorough study of Freemasonry and undoubtedly knew more about the Craft than did 95% of the Craft. He had to know that much of the documentation he furnished was erroneous. In this report, and in his book, he quoted extensively from Albert Pike's *Morals and Dogma*, as well as many anti-Masonic tomes. The legitimate books about Freemasonry were ignored.

Among other things Whalen claimed a Bishop couldn't conduct an investigation into Freemasonry "in view of the fact that members of the lodge, like members of the IRA, the mafia and other secret organizations, were sworn to secrecy." To which Roberts replied: "Wow! If he really studied Freemasonry he would know better than make a statement like this. He certainly knows that Masonry is NOT a SECRET Organization. Its members are known, and most take pride in letting the world know they are members of the Craft. Their meeting places are marked, their proceedings are published. In no way can Masonry be compared with the dastardly IRA and Mafia whose members, meeting places, and proceedings are unknown to the outside world."

Whalen admitted Roberts was correct! In the preface to his revised book Whalen wrote: "If there is one secret in Masonry, it is that there are no secrets." Yet, to help the Catholic Bishops reinforce their shaky position, he had deliberately told a falsehood about secrecy.

"Some Masons see the church of Rome as the church of the Inquisition, the Crusades, the prop for discredited monarchies," wrote Whalen. "No one benefits from such caricatures." To which Roberts replied: "This is a goodly part of the history of the church of Rome. Should this be dismissed and ignored while the church of Rome condemns an organization that has never had blood on its hands?"

Point by point the Catholic Bishops' report was answered, and Roberts ended his review by saying: "Let me point out, please, that I'm not attempting to 'whitewash' Freemasonry. Although the *system* is as close to perfection as it can get, it's made up of human beings. Human beings will never be perfect."

Among the misleading comments in the Bishops' report was: "Either the oaths mean what they say, or they do not. . . . If they mean what they say, the candidate is entering into a pact consenting to his own murder by barbarous torture and mutilation should he break it. . . . If they do not mean what they say, then he (the candidate) is swearing schoolboy nonsense on the Bible, which verges on blasphemy." This caused one Grand Master, a mem-

197

ber of The Philalethes Society, to issue an edict taking the penalties out of the ritual in his state. Several Freemasons were disturbed. Among them was John Mauk Hilliard, FPS. His concern was expressed in "To Violate a Vow, To Betray a Trust" which appeared in the October issue of *The Philalethes*.

"Those religious bodies who take issue with the Craft do so because they regard it as being a *religion*, and hold to this concept in spite of the fact that Freemasonry tells its adherents only that they *should* believe in a Supreme Being or Power in the Universe beyond man," wrote Hilliard. He went on to strongly condemn the Masonic leadership that bowed to the demands of the critics to do away with the old-time jargon of the penalties. He suggested that if these were to be modified at all, it should be done by simply adding "symbolic" or "symbolically." He also hoped "the more conservative Grand Lodges will resist being stampeded on this issue by the great urban Grand Lodges."

Several writers took exception to Hilliard's article, and some of their rebuttals were printed in subsequent issues of *The Philalethes*. Many others supported what he had to say.

L. L. Walker, Jr., MPS, in a lengthy article in the same October issue entitled "Of Oaths, Vows & Obligations," covered the history of these subjects. He said: "While oaths and affirmations are primarily identified with the law of the state, vows are associated with the church and with religion. We see that the three terms—oath, affirmation and vow—have in common the characteristic of solemnity. As acts, they are set apart from the common things of life. In the widest possible sense, each is an asseveration; that is, each affirms or averts positively and does so in a solemn manner. The distinction seems to lie in the fact that an oath or affirmation is an act of verification which Deity is adjured to witness, while a vow is an act of consecration to which the Deity is a party."

Walker closed his article by quoting "from Dorothy Ann Lipson's excellent work, *Freemasonry In Federalist Connecticut, 1789-1835.*" Lipson in turn had quoted from Amasa Walker of Massachusetts: "The opposition to these oaths is the sure foundation of anti-masonry. If a basic article of social morality required men to keep their oaths, Anti-masons were faced with the immediate contradiction of persuading Masons to disavow their oaths. If Masons could be convinced that oaths are neither morally, legally, or religiously binding it would be the most effectual measure we can possibly take to destroy the institution."

And Lipson concluded: "The Antimasons failed in their efforts to destroy because, giving high value to their own principles, they failed to realize that the kind of man who becomes a Mason is the kind of man who feels the obligation to do 'according to all that proceeds from out of his mouth.' "

The Philalethes continued to be the only Masonic publication answering the religious bigots and their attacks on the Craft. Another article in the October issue entitled " . . . How Long?" by F. Thomas Starkweather, MPS, was carried. He named many of the so-called religious organizations opposed to Freemasonry. He felt the time to ignore these attacks had long passed. "So, let's take the offensive!" he wrote. "Let's prepare the Brethren to confront our assailants and better them. Let's furnish fact sheets to every Grand Lodge to be forwarded to every member in their jurisdiction. Allow them to expand on one side—the Masonic side." He included the names of many prominent Americans who are and were members of Freemasonry that others could use as ammunition.

Starkweather's article was highly praised in some circles, and permission was granted several publications to reprint it. It also drew condemnation. He received so many comments, pro and con, that he was compelled to answer his critics. He did so in the June issue of *The Philalethes*.

Tom Mote, MPS, in the February 1987 issue of *The Philalethes* was one who didn't agree with Starkweather's suggestion that Freemasonry should go on the offensive. In his lengthy article, " . . . How Long? A Rebuttal," Mote, in his well-reasoned essay, covered a long period in the history of religion and Masonry.

"I urge you to remember the principle of 'cognitive dissonance,' " wrote Mote, "and then to expand the admonition against arguing religion with preachers to one of refusing to argue religion with anyone. As a psychologist who specializes in statistics, I assure you that your probability of winning such an argument is much lower than that of your winning a football pool or the daily double at the track." Earlier Mote had strongly suggested: "Don't mess with the guy with the microphone!" He later rightly added that you better not mess with one who controls "the camera or who can in any way edit the results!"

Mote, and many others, note that Coil, Mackey and Pike, Masonic writers, said, or suggested, that Freemasonry is a religion. These are among the most quoted by the foes of Freemasonry. Yet, Forrest Haggard, Joseph Fort Newton, Norman Vincent Peale, Thomas Roy, all Doctors of Divinity and members of the Craft, say that Freemasonry is *not* a religion. They are never quoted by the anti-Masons.

The Reverend Dr. Lloyd Worley, in a letter to the Editor, asked for permission to comment on Mote's thesis. Worley, in the April 1987 issue of *The Philalethes*, tore asunder the Bishops' (more accurately, Whalen's) statement about the penalties.

Now that's an astonishing criterion, because it shows a complete lack of understanding of what Freemasonry is all about. Educated Freemasons everywhere say that Freemasonry uses allegory and symbol, and the parable constitutes the very fabric of our Fraternity. In other words, what the Roman Catholic Bishops are saying is that allegories, symbols, or parables mean *exactly what they say.* But that, frankly, is *stupid,* because allegories, symbols, and parables mean *more* than what they say. For example, will the Roman Catholic Bishops say this:

"Either Jesus meant what he said, or he did not."

I would hope not, because if they want to hold Jesus to the same criterion they use on the Masons, then at Mark 9:47, or Matthew 5:29, or Matthew 18:9 the Christian is bound to self-mutilation if his eye (somehow) offends. And, under the same criterion, Jesus also recommends that the Christian cut off his hands and his feet if they offend (Matthew 5:30; Mark 9:43; Mark 9:45). Well, what's going on? Let me offer a slight rephrase of their Eminences' accusation:

Either Jesus meant what he said, or he did not. If Jesus means what he says, the Christian is entering into a pact with his Lord by consenting to his own barbarous torture and mutilation should he break the moral code. . . . If Jesus does not mean what he says, then the Christian is agreeing to schoolboy nonsense in the Bible which verges on blasphemy!

Now, that doesn't sound very good, does it? And it doesn't sound very good because it is wrong; Jesus does not want his followers to mutilate themselves because that would be completely out of character with what we know of Jesus. Therefore, it is safe to think (as biblical scholars do) that Jesus' language was hyperbolic for the purpose of *strongly and powerfully impressing* upon his followers the importance of moral conduct.

Well, friends, *that is exactly what the so-called "penalties" of the Masonic obligations are for!* They don't mean merely what they say, they mean *much more* than what they say. That is, the *purpose* of the so-called "penalties" is to cause the man who is taking the Obligation to be powerfully impressed with what he is doing, to cause that man to ponder on and discuss what he has done—and all must agree that the so-called penalties have certainly achieved their desired purposes of impression and discussion.

* * * * * *

Of course, there are Freemasons who are as blind as the Bishops. Those Grand Lodges (or, in some cases, Grand Masters) who are busy altering the fabric of Freemasonry to suit the anti-masons are making extremely serious errors from which they may not be able to recover. It does no good to say, "Well, we started getting rid of our 'penalties' before all the fuss about the penalties," because the ignorant have been fussing about so-called penalties for two centuries, and *no* Grand Lodge or Grand Officer was thinking about removing the so-called penalties until only recently. . . .

And what would I recommend to a Grand Lodge that is thinking about removing the so-called penalties? I would say DON'T. You have no real reason to do it, other than to please the Roman Catholic Bishops and others who have a fear or a lack of understanding of the power of language. To the Grand Lodge or Grand Master who has already done the deed, I would say **Restore What Has Been Removed As Soon As Possible.**

It was noted with pleasure that the United Grand Lodge of England "had decided to bring Freemasonry into the 20th century." This Grand Lodge had long "turned the other cheek" and ignored its critics. This had encouraged its enemies. Attacks, even from unlikely places, had become more and more prominent. Churches that had never found Freemasonry disturbing were encouraged to do so. Even individuals in Scotland Yard were telling their officers to stay out, or get out, of Masonry. The British bullies were having everything their own way. The Masonic leadership in England finally decided to answer the critics. Freemasons' Hall was opened to the public.

Anti-Masonry reached into the United States Senate and was reported in "Through Masonic Windows" from October 1987 through April 1988. President Reagan nominated Judge David B. Sentelle for the United States Court of Appeals. During the confirmation hearings (called "inquisitions" by some) the question of his Masonic membership was raised. Certain "Civil Rights" groups strongly objected to any Freemason being selected for anything they could oppose. Certain Senators readily jumped on their bandwagon. Months later, after the Freemasons in the Senate had vigorously abhorred the actions of some of their colleagues, Judge Sentelle's nomination was approved.

Shortly following his confirmation, Judge Sentelle made a "humorous, educational and poignantly revealing" talk in Cherrydale Lodge in Arlington, Virginia. The Judge named some of his chief inquisitors: "Senator [Patrick J.] Leahy of Vermont characterized the Masonic Fraternity as an organization that routinely discriminates against blacks and women."

When asked if he would resign from Freemasonry, Judge Sentelle said NO. So, Senator Paul Simon of Illinois had a hold placed on Sentelle's nomination in an attempt to kill it. Senator Strom Thurmond of South Carolina, a Freemason, protested strongly, and so did other Masons in the Senate. The nomination was finally cleared for debate. Then Senator Kennedy of Massachusetts, in his usual manner, held the nomination hostage. The Knights of Columbus opposed the actions of the political anti-Masons in the Senate; so did Prince Hall Masons.

Judge Sentelle said: "If I were to give up my membership in Excelsior Lodge No. 260, my membership in the Scottish Rite and in Oasis Temple of the Shrine it would be like saying that I had been doing something wrong in all the years I had been a judge; I would have been repudiating the principles that led my father, my grandfathers, my uncles and my brother into this Fraternity."

Cherrydale Lodge requested a dispensation from the Grand Master of Masons in Virginia, Donald M. Robey, MPS, for permission to elect Judge Sentelle to Honorary Membership. Robey readily agreed with the lodge. He said that any man who believed as strongly as Sentelle deserved any honor that could be awarded him.

In December 1986 Jerry R. Korstad, MPS, had an article published in *The Philalethes* entitled "Freemasonry and Religion." In his essay he said: "Freemasonry is the very support of all religion. The problem arises with religions which must condemn all so called non-believers of their particular belief or theology. They preach hate, war against the devils, and non-believers, etc. This is not confined to Christianity. How they can justify their religious beliefs by preaching hate and condemning those they do not believe with, and still call themselves godly people has always mystified me." He added many quotations from other writers to support his thesis.

Harold Voorhis, in his dissertation that he delivered by means of a tape recording at his funeral, spoke of the Bible not being divinely inspired. Korstad supported this argument. He said "the King James Bible is a rigid idol, all the more deceptive for being translated into the most melodious English and for being an anthology of ancient literature that contains sublime wisdom along with barbaric histories and the war songs of tribes on the rampage." He added: "Now, the King James Bible did not, as one might gather from listening to fundamentalists, descend with an angel from heaven A.D. 1611, when it was first published. It was an elegant, but often inaccurate, translation of Hebrew and Greek documents composed between 900 B.C. and A.D. 120. . . . Several books that had formerly been read in the churches, such as the *Shepherd of Hermas* and the marvelous *Gospel of Saint Thomas*, were then excluded.

"The point is that the books translated in the King James Bible were declared canonical and divinely inspired by the authority (A) of the Synod of Jamnia and (B) of the Catholic Church, meetings in Carthage more than 300 years after the time of Jesus. It is thus the fundamentalist Protestants get the authority of their Bible from Jews who had rejected Jesus and from Catholics whom they abominate as the Scarlet Woman mentioned in Revelation."

In the same issue The Reverend William H. Stemper, MPS, wrote about "Understanding and Planning for Masonic Criticism." He noted that because of the political climate of the day, many politicians are staying away from "exclusive" organizations such as Freemasonry. "At one time," Stemper wrote, "a Masonic affiliation was *sine-qua-non* for election to political office in the United States. . . . Today, even conservative-minded politicians deem Freemasonry too inefficient and its membership too aged to be a political asset." He suggested the larger Masonic-affiliated bodies, along with "the more progressive Grand Lodges," consult and "plan for the future of the Fraternity."

Stemper concluded: "Three basic elements should be included in such a planning process: (1) development of models of successful lodge and appendant body functioning; (2) establishment of liaison between Masonic leaders and the leaders of other major segments of the nation's life; and (3) the development of a cooperative approach to public relations. . . . The right progressive steps will make a difference in whether or not the Fraternity survives as a vital brotherhood into the next century."

The Executive Secretary reported in the February 1987 issue of *The Philalethes* that 1986 had been a good year for the Society. The membership had increased; there were more Life Members; and for the first time ever the magazine had been published with twenty-four pages in each of the six issues. This reflected the improved financial condition of the Society. He noted that an awarded-winning magician and Past Master, Walter J. "Jerry" Harmon, had been awarded a grant to write a book about Freemasonry and the art of magic.

In keeping with the editorial policy of the Society's magazine, the Editor, in February, ran an article by Mr. Harmon R. Taylor entitled "Mixing Oil With Water." Other Masonic editors had refused to handle what they considered to be "a hot potato." Taylor had once been a New York Mason, Master of a Lodge, and one of some forty Grand Chaplains of the Grand Lodge of New York. He was also pastor of a United Methodist Church. His article was loaded with half-truths and outright distortions, but adhered completely to the line propagated by anti-Masons for more than a century. Marsengill was highly praised in many quarters for letting the Craft know what its enemies were saying. He was condemned by a small segment.

In the same issue a series on the Constitutional Convention of 1787 by Allen E. Roberts began. And the Editor noted that the long-time reviewer of books for *The Philalethes* had found it necessary to curtail his activities. Alphonse Cerza's health had deteriorated.

One of the main topics of discussion during the meeting of the Executive Board on February 20, 1987 was the question of who should speak officially for the Society. Over the years there had been individuals, some of them appointed to various positions, who posed as official spokesmen for The Philalethes Society. It was determined the only official spokesmen would be the President and the Executive Secretary.

The Editor, Jerry Marsengill, was commended for the continued excellence of *The Philalethes*. It was emphasized that there would continue to be no censorship, but discretion in what is published would, as always, be exercised. The Board, as usual, didn't agree with the sentiments of some of the writers, but it did support their right to express their opinions.

Henry G. Law of Delaware, the Treasurer, Christopher Haffner of Hong Kong, and Johannes Marinus van Beusekom of Guatemala, were elected Fellows of The Philalethes Society. S. Brent Morris, FPS, Executive Secretary-Emeritus, and William F. Koeckart of Ohio were chosen to receive the Society's Distinguished Service Medal.

The Board agreed to continue the Grant Program. Dr. Forrest D. Haggard was offered a grant if he would agree to write a sequel to his book *The Clergy and the Craft*. It also agreed to hold a semi-annual meeting in Cleveland, Ohio, on September 26, 1987.

A hospitality room was opened by the Society on Friday evening following the Assembly, Feast and Workshop. It was hosted by Dottie Roberts, wife of the Executive Secretary. This proved so successful the Board decided to continue this practice.

The Assembly and Feast was an outstanding success. Again there were late-comers who had to be turned away. Forrest D. Haggard, spoke on Freemasonry and religion, discussing the attacks being made against the Craft. Certificates were presented to the new Fellows. The Certificate of Literature was awarded to Leslie L. Walker, Jr., of Texas.

The Workshop featured planning for tomorrow and the future. The discussion was based on the Leadership Training Film *Planning Unlocks the Door.* The discussion was led by Allen E. Roberts.

The Reverend Dr. Lloyd Worley, MPS, in a copyrighted article entitled "The Truth About Freemasonry" responded "with truth to the anti-Masonic lies" in the April 1987 issue of *The Philalethes*. He stated that Freemasonry is not a religion. He believed that in the case of those few who claim "the lodge is my church" have been failed by the church, not by the Craft. Those who claim the lodge has "Christless prayers" overlook one of the most important prayers of all—The Lord's Prayer, said Worley. This "exactly fits their definition of a 'Christless prayer.' However, I am not surprised," wrote Worley, "that they haven't noticed this because the ability to think straight is not a strong point of anti-masons."

"The number of symbols associated with Masonry astonishes even the most experienced Mason," wrote Lieutenant Colonel David G. Boyd, MPS, while stationed in West Germany. In his article, *Das Vergissmeinnicht,* in the April 1987 issue of *The Philalethes*, he mentioned one that's different. "It is, first of all, very new—not much more than fifty years old. It is not even a tool, and it appears in no ritual, yet—tested by persecution—it symbolizes something we all can understand: Masonry itself. There is no more poignant symbol in Masonry, no symbol with so much meaning, nor one so little celebrated in Masonic literature. It is a little blue flower—the forget-me-not—which draws its significance from courage in the face of tyranny."

Boyd covered the years of Nazism in Germany and that regime's persecution of Freemasons and Jews. In the early days the attacks on the Craft were overlooked. They were considered "so clearly ridiculous that they took the same sort of action most American Grand Lodges now take in the face of attacks on the institution: it ignored them, expecting them to fade away." But they didn't end, not even after Freemasonry had been successfully abolished in Germany.

"Not all Masons, however, abandoned Freemasonry during the liquidation of the Grand Lodges," wrote Boyd. "Many collected the symbols and regalia of their lodges and hid them." One of these was a Master's jewel dating back to 1785. It was cut into small pieces and hidden. (After the war it was soldered together and is highly prized today.) "It was during this period that the forget-me-not became a Masonic symbol. . . . In Bayreuth in early 1934, the *Grossloge zur Sonne* (Grand Lodge of the Sun) decided a more subtle symbol [other than the square and compasses] was required, and elected to wear the forget-me-not, an unobtrusive little blue flower."

Boyd noted that The Masonic Brotherhood of the Blue Forget-Me-Not in America honors those Freemasons who devote their lives and talents in the fields of Masonic education and writing. He concluded his article by saying:

> To those who understand its origins, the forget-me-not is a powerful symbol, worthy of reverence among Masons everywhere. It represents the best features of Masonry—dedication to the Fraternity and its ideals in the face of oppression, courage, and a fellowship so committed that—even in the face of real danger— Masons wanted some way to identify themselves to others. Even its very name suits the task it was called for in those dark days—the protection of the very memory of our institution. [Boyd then added "An Ode to the Forget Me Not" by J. J. Watson]:

> When to the flowers so beautiful, the Father gave a name,
> There was a little blue eyed one, all timidly it came.
> And standing at the Father's feet, and gazing in His face,
> It said with low soft spoken voice, and yet with timed grace,
> "Dear Lord, the name thou gavest me, alas, I have forgot."
> The Father looked so kindly on him and said: "Forget-Me-Not."

Several Chapters of The Philalethes Society had been holding interesting and sometimes unusual meetings. One of them, Virginia Chapter, reported in the June issue of *The Philalethes* it had held a "Leadership Seminar." The two-day seminar had been opened to any Master Mason interested at no cost to the participant. The Chapter paid the cost of the meals; Babcock Lodge furnished the meeting place; Anchor Communications provided the hand-outs; Allen Roberts furnished the equipment and films and led the instruction. The Grand Master, Donald M. Robey, MPS, not only gave his blessing for the seminar, he was one of the participants.

"Amadeus and Freemasonry" was the topic of an article by Robin L. Carr, MPS, also in the June issue. Carr noted that the motion picture *Amadeus* won the Academy Award as the best picture of 1985. Although Mozart was a Freemason, supported by and financed by Freemasons, and the stage play from which the film script was taken makes this clear, nothing in the film mentions this fact. Carr basically ignored the screen play but covered the stage script at length. He covers the remarks of Peter Shaffer, the author of the book and the screen play. Many little-known facts are brought out in the article. A condensed version of the Philalethes Lecture given by Dr. Forrest D. Haggard entitled "Freemasonry in a Time of Crisis" appeared in June. It had been condensed because Haggard spoke from notes and had not prepared a manuscript.

Another biography in Wallace McLeod's series on "Loyalist Masons" helped balance the overwhelming number of articles about the Freemasons who Americans term Patriots. Of John Walden Meyers, McLeod wrote: "If he had been on the other side, he would have been immortalized in song and story, on radio and television, as a hero, a sort of Scarlet Pimpernel. As it is, if he is remembered at all, it is in a more sinister light. Perhaps nothing else could be expected; as a great man once said, 'History is the propaganda of the victors.' "

To McLeod, the Canadian, Patriots on the Continental side are termed "rebels," and after Meyers had defected to the British. "He served as a courier and collector of intelligence, repeatedly traveling up and down the Hudson River from New York to the St. Lawrence Valley." McLeod believed: "The fact that he was able to move almost at will through hostile territory without being caught suggests, in the first place, that there were enough Loyalist sympathizers to help him along the way, and in the second place, that he was a pretty fair woodsman himself." It also adds credence to the statement that "Washington and a *handful* of Patriots won independence from the tyranny of Great Britain."

It was noted that two Fellows of The Philalethes Society had participated as speakers during the educational conference of The Phylaxis Society held in Washington, D.C., in March. "Both of us found a most receptive and intelligent audience," reported Allen E. Roberts. "We found men anxious and willing to learn more about all non-ritualistic facets of Freemasonry. We were highly impressed with the caliber of these Prince Hall Masons, several of whom were active Grand Masters." Both Roberts and Stewart M. L. Pollard said they would absolutely accept other invitations to address the group.

The column "Through Masonic Windows" mentioned solicitation, which had become a favorite topic in many Masonic circles. It was being called a "must" to prevent the drop in membership throughout the country. S. Brent Morris had presented a paper at the Northeast Conference on Masonic Education and Libraries in 1983. It was titled "The Siren Song of Solicitation." He had studied the subject scientifically and mathematically (this was his specialty). He pointed out that on the surface solicitation appeared a solution, but it wouldn't be. Ritualistic organizations similar to Freemasonry that permit solicitation have suffered greater declines than had Masonry. He said the Odd Fellows, for instance, has suffered an 82% decline since 1900; Freemasonry in the same period had increased by 390%.

"Free—For Philalethes Members, Only," read a heading in the August 1987 issue of *The Philalethes*. It went on to state that Iowa Research Lodge No. 2 had commissioned Allen E. Roberts to write a book on leadership for its members. This Lodge had graciously permitted The Philalethes Society to offer this book to its members. The Executive Board agreed. For the price of only the postage and handling any of the more than 3,000 members of the Society could receive a copy of *The Search For Leadership*. By the time the book was available in November, 700 members had taken advantage of the offer.

The August issue also carried memorials of two great Freemasons: Alphonse Cerza and Ronald E. Heaton. Each had been recognized by the Society when they were among the first to receive The Philalethes Society's Distinguished Service Medal. Throughout the pages of this book the name of Alphonse Cerza is mentioned frequently. Ronald Heaton was actually the leader behind the scenes for many years. Both are irreplaceable.

"On Masonic Research" was the topic S. Brent Morris covered in an article in August. He related some of his early experiences with would-be historical experts on Masonry. And he lived dangerously, as one always does when he is critical of those set up as Masonic deities. "Be leery of any research topic that takes you away from the United States during the nineteenth and twentieth centuries. Almost anything outside of this period will require your reliance on someone else's studies (and on their accuracy). Albert G. Mackey, for example was as prolific as he was inaccurate. He had his own pet theories on Freemasonry, and adjusted his view of history to fit his preconceived notions. His list of Landmarks is a classic example of a fabrication foisted upon the Craft, a fabrication which many Grand Lodges now wear as albatrosses around their necks.

"Papers of the general type 'Why Masonry is a Wonderful Organization' may be touching, moving, and interesting, but they are not good, solid research. They express, often eloquently, the deeply held affections of Masons for the Craft, but they don't qualify as research."

A semi-annual meeting of The Philalethes Society was held in Cleveland, Ohio, on September 26. It was well attended and well planned, and William H. Koeckart was given credit for his leadership. Each of the international officers of the Society participated in the talks and discussions. The ladies joined the men for the banquet in the evening to hear the newest Fellow of the Society, Royal C. Scofield, speak.

On the evening before the meeting, the Executive Board went into official session. It started plans for 1988 when The Philalethes Society will be sixty years old. It commissioned Allen Roberts to write its history, and it decided to give every member of the Society a copy. Additional copies are to be made available at a reasonable price to Research Lodges and individuals. Roberts suggested that much of the material for the book, tentatively entitled *Seekers of Truth*, should come from the excellent articles and items to be found in *The Philalethes* from 1946 to 1987. The Board agreed.

The Board also agreed to have every issue of *The Philalethes* copied on microfiche and made available at cost. It went further; *The Master Mason* formerly published by The Masonic Service Association, and *The Builder* of the International Masonic Research Society, would also be made available through microfiche.

Jerry Marsengill took his pen into his hand, instead of his blue pencil, and wrote a heartwarming article for December 1987 entitled "Des Moines, IA, Masons Host Annual Christmas Dinner." He told of a 96 year-old lady who was from one of the oldest and richest families in Iowa, but had outlived her friends. She attended the dinner for companionship. When she left, she wanted to pay for her dinner, but no one would take her money. When the driver left her at her home she pressed a hundred dollar bill in his hand.

A little three year-old girl was thrilled to find all the meat and potatoes she could eat. She was taken to Santa Claus and given a bear almost twice her size, plus candy and fruit, the only gifts she would receive. And the tales of love continued. Freemasonry was in action that Christmas day, as it had been for the Des Moines Freemasons for several years. Volunteers came from every segment of the population to help the Masons care for more than three thousand folks who otherwise would have had nothing to celebrate.

About two months after Leslie L. Walker, Jr., had been elected a Fellow of The Philalethes Society he suffered a severe stroke and died. His memorial was written by a fellow Texan, Dr. George H. T. French, FPS. Walker had been a remarkable historian and researcher. Many of the best articles appearing in *The Philalethes* over the years had come from his pen. And an unwritten rule was broken when he was awarded, for the second time, the Society's Certificate of Literature.

Another Masonic stalwart, James Royal Case, died on November 26, 1987. Case was one of the Masonic greats of any period. Rarely, indeed, does a man leave behind a legacy that will live forever. Rare is the man who becomes a legend in his life-time. Rare is the man whom his peers continually honor while he is living among them. James Royal Case was one of these unique individuals.

Jim was born in Connecticut, and in Connecticut he received the education that would take him to higher learning in New York City (where he earned his Master's degree), Chicago, back to New York, into World War I and World War II (and retirement as a Colonel), and back to his beloved Connecticut. Throughout his long and fruitful life he was a teacher, not only earning his livelihood as one, but using his knowledge to enrich the lives of countless other men and women.

Case could boast (which he never did) of being one of the few Mayflower descendants; that he belonged to Epsilon Sigma Phi and Phi Mu Delta; that he served in both World Wars; that he was a member of many civic and national associations; that he was one of the most highly decorated and honored Freemasons in the country. He loved deeply: his wife Bess, whom he married in 1918, his children, Grace, Maurice, Julie May, and J. Richard; his vocation; his research in genealogy; his Masonic research; his writing on numerous subjects; his fellowman; his Freemasonry.

In brief: In 1916 James Case became a Master Mason in Uriel Lodge No. 24, Connecticut, the beginning of a long and fruitful Masonic career. He was active in Virginia Freemasonry while stationed at Fort Eustis. He participated in all branches of the Craft and was Grand Historian in Connecticut of the Grand Lodge, Grand Chapter and Grand Commandery. He received the 33rd degree of the Scottish Rite, NMJ. He was awarded Masonic medals from several jurisdictions and appendant bodies. One of these, the Medal of Excellence of the Masonic Research Lodge of Connecticut became the James Royal Case Medal of Excellence. He was an Honorary Member of American Union Lodge No. 1 of Ohio, an honor granted him because of his writings about Freemasonry during the Revolutionary period.

He was a Fellow of The Philalethes Society and wrote extensively for its magazine. He had earned its first Certificate of Literature in 1958. He was a constant contributor to the **Knight Templar** magazine. Many items from this magazine were compiled by the Missouri Research Lodge into **The Case Collection: Biographies of Masonic Notables** in two volumes. He was Deputy Grand Abbot of the Society of Blue Friars, and a member of the Council of the Nine Muses of the Allied Masonic Degrees. He was a Past Grand Chancellor of Grand College of Rites. He was an original member of the Masonic Brotherhood of the Blue Forget-Me-Not. His work of almost 93 years will live as long as freedom survives.

The Philalethes Society and Freemasonry suffered a calamitous year in 1987. Two former Presidents of the Society had died, Robert H. Gollmar and Alphonse Cerza, both outstanding leaders. Three additional Fellows and prolific Masonic writers were also lost: Ronald E. Heaton, Leslie L. Walker, Jr., and James R. Case. Never before had the Craft lost so much in such a short period.

To try to replace them, new Fellows were elected: Royal C. Scofield of Ohio, a Masonic educator; Dr. Charles R. Glassmire of Maine, an outstanding Masonic editor; Richard H. Curtis of Massachusetts, editor of the excellent *The Northern Light*; C. Clark Julius of Pennsylvania, a Masonic writer; and John E. Jack Kelly of Texas, a Masonic educator. Certificates were presented to them during the Assembly, Feast and Workshop on February 12, 1988.

The February 1988 issue of *The Philalethes* continued its coverage of the anti-Masonic controversy created by certain religious factions. In the column "Through Masonic Windows" is a digest of several items:

> The *Church Times* of Great Britain has found many clergymen are courageous enough to continue their support of Freemasonry. It was noted that Freemasonry is condemned but polygamy is condoned. . . . Frank Grinsted of Colyton, Devon, wrote: "Let's be fair! Isn't the working group ungenerous in its harsh criticism of Freemasons? Jehova, Jahbulon, Father, Father-Mother God, if it is given with sincerity and respect, be it Jehova, Jahbulon, Father . . . Great Spirit, or whatever? Who among us knows the truth anyway? I am not a Mason . . . but I respect them for the good they do. Whether it is conceived in secrecy or not hardly matters; what counts is that it puts Christian principles into practice."
>
> Perhaps not too strangely, the *Times* reported: "Anglican clergymen predominated among people who wrote letters in support of Freemasonry to the working group which produced the report called 'Freemasonry and Christianity: Are They Compatible?' Canon Tydeman asked: "As for solemn oaths never to reveal Masonic secrets: 'Can you imagine any Government employee being asked to sign the Official Secrets Act demanding to know beforehand what the secrets are? So I am afraid that this particular accusation is one which should leave the working group somewhat redfaced.' "

"A Report from the Church of England" was the title of an article which contained a letter written by Reverend Eric E. Gaunt. It was published in the *Church Times* of Great Britain in the June 26, 1987 issue. It read:

> Sir,—it really is a piece of unmitigated humbug on the part of the Church of England to issue a report criticising Freemasonry. In the days when the Church could boast men of stature among its bishops, even archbishops found it not incompatible with their Christian convictions to belong to the Masonic Order.
>
> Today it is extremely difficult to know with any degree of certainty what the Church does, or does not subscribe to—even to the Creeds; to say nothing of acceptance of perversions which are clearly stated in Holy Scripture as being contrary to the law of God. Alas, the Church of England is in no position at

present to offer criticism of any order, Masonic or otherwise, but rather it should be employing its energies to sort out its own attitudes and doctrines.

Having been a member of the Church of England all my life and a Freemason for twenty-four years, I feel it is a great sadness that the Church is no longer able to set out its tenets as clearly, concisely and unambiguously as does Freemasonry, which promotes the highest ideals of morality, truth and justice. Indeed, whilst we have bishops casting doubts on the very fundamentals of Christian belief and others condoning such evils as homosexuality without there being so much as a whimper of official protest, can the Church maintain sufficient credibility to speak with authority?

Let me assure you: Freemasonry is not a religion, neither is it any form of religious substitute.

In writing about "Freemasonry and the Churches," The Reverend William H. Stemper, MPS, in a lengthy article wrote: ". . . it is crucial to note that nothing *programmatically* which the range of Masonic bodies do: e.g., in charitable and social activities, will ameliorate the present climate of religious, theological criticism. The attacks are not on what Freemasonry *does. They are rooted in what Freemasonry is perceived to be."*

He later adds that although Freemasonry correctly claims it isn't a religion, "Theological critics counter-claim that whether Freemasonry understands itself to be a religion or not it has several elements which are in fact religious. Among these are an implied doctrine of salvation by good works, non-Christian in character which claims in its rituals to have the power to resurrect the initiate to a new life, or awareness."

In an article entitled "Where Are We Now?", Frank A. Standring, MPS, strongly states "our own indifference" has caused a lack of attendance and a decline in membership. "Let me suggest to you as forcibly as I can," he adds, "that unless Freemasonry presents what it has to offer in a challenging manner, intelligent men will not be on the sidelines to witness and participate." Masonically educating the new Mason, he believes, is most important. The choice of efficient officers is also necessary.

The first "Computer Corner" article by John M. Taylor, MPS, appeared in the February issue. Taylor urges Freemasonry to enter the modern age, and describes several of the advantages computers have to offer the efficient leader.

The Executive Board met in the Hotel Washington on February 12, 1988. Jerry Marsengill was elected President, John Mauk Hilliard and Wallace E. McLeod First and Second Vice Presidents. Allen E. Roberts and Henry G. Law remained Executive Secretary and Treasurer. The Board agreed a new office, that of Librarian, should be established. Harold L. Davidson, a professional librarian, was named to this office. His duties were broadly outlined and will include collection and distribution of back issues of *The Philalethes*; providing photocopies of articles requested; and such other duties as may from time to time be considered appropriate. He was authorized to determine payments and charges for the services he renders.

It was reported that microfiche copies of the following magazines were now available: *The Philalethes*, *The Builder*, and *The Master Mason*. It was decided to see what interest would be shown in these before considering other publications to make available.

The Board decided that every member of The Philalethes Society will receive a free copy of *Seekers of Truth*, the 60 year history of the Society. At least 500 extra copies would be printed to offer to new members after the initial mailing. Multiple copies would be offered to Research Lodges, Macoy Publishing, and others at a pre-publication price.

It was also decided to establish a "History Fund" for the Society to which donations, including memorial gifts and gifts in honor of individuals, would be accepted and encouraged.

The Workshop remains a success and will be continued under a new name—THE FORUM. This will continue to follow the Assembly and Feast.

The registration for the Assembly and Feast was the largest ever; the number of tickets sold in the lobby was also greater.

During the Assembly and Feast it was noted that five Fellows had died during 1987, the most disastrous year suffered by the Society and Freemasonry. Certificates were presented to the new Fellows.

Forrest D. Haggard, D.D., FPS, for his courage in supporting the principles of Freemasonry under adverse conditions, and for his dedication to the Craft and the Society, was awarded the Distinguished Service Medal. Robin L. Carr was awarded the Certificate of Literature for 1987. Medallions were presented to Charles Snow Guthrie and J. Hampton Harley for their literary endeavors.

The Philalethes Society Lecturer was John E. Jack Kelly, FPS, of Texas, who spoke on "TANSTAAFL's Law" (There Ain't No Such Thing As A Free Lunch). His lecture would be published in full in *The Philalethes*.

The Workshop (Forum) was based on leadership. Questions were submitted on cards and answered by a panel of experienced Masons. For the Assembly and Feast 171 were registered; the Workshop brought in 92 others, most of them members of the Society. The comments on the registration cards ranged from "Good!" to "Excellent!!" Several claimed the affair improved with each passing year.

Such comments as these evoked mixed emotions among the members of the Executive Board. For sixty years they and their predecessors had set continuous improvement as one of the goals of the Society. They have never been content to rest on the laurels of the past.

The international Society that had been formed by a handful of Masonic writers in 1928 had grown to over 3,600 in sixty years. At first the growth had been slow because it was considered "exclusive." This notion had been removed to a large extent and the membership had more than doubled in the last decade. With this growth came a greater opportunity for the Society to improve its service for the Craft.

The sixtieth year found The Philalethes Society in an excellent financial condition. The investments in the Life Membership Fund ensured that the Society would always remain financially sound. The Grant Program had been designed to encourage new writers for *The Philalethes* and for Freemasonry in general.

In this, its sixtieth year, the Society continues to provide fresh examples in the way in which it can continue to serve the Craft in general and its members in particular. Every member gets six issues of that excellent publication, *The Philalethes* magazine, and almost seventy percent of the revenue is devoted to this purpose. But, in 1988 every member would receive a book that would more than repay him for his dues for the year. Beyond that, for a purely nominal cost, all who were interested had an opportunity to receive microform copies of every issue of three outstanding Masonic publications.

The Philalethes Society is **the International Research Society.** Its motto is "Let There Be Light." Its members are **"Lovers of Truth."** The foundation was firmly laid sixty years ago. Its founders saw that a few Freemasons needed something more for the mind. On their trestleboard they sketched out a rough design to meet this need. Their successors have improved on the blue-print, and have continued to toil in the quarries and at the building site.

The unfinished structure can never be complete. How could it ever be finished? Does research ever come to an end? Does truth have limits imposed on it? Can we ever say: "Now, at last, we know it all! Now our task is completed! Now the Society's work is done!?" Surely, the answer must be a resounding "NO!"

Cyrus Field Willard said in 1932: "We as a Society are needed. Let us then go forward, each and every one, and do our duty. Every one of our members can give, as he has done in the past, and even as he was asked in the past what he most desired. More light, was the answer. Each and every Fellow and Member should endeavor to secure new members for the Society, so they, too, may go forth to give light to their Masonic Brethren—a light which shall finally illumine the whole world."

In these days the necessity for the search for truth is greater than ever before. Our building, our Temple of Truth, must rise far above the mounds of ignorance, falsehood and despair. The light of Truth must shine as a beacon through the darkness to guide and encourage others.

Continued growth, continued activity, continued learning, continued

APPENDICES

Appendix A.

BYLAWS

THE PHILALETHES SOCIETY
THE Masonic Research Society

PREAMBLE

THE PHILALETHES SOCIETY was founded on October 1, 1928, by a group of Masonic students for Freemasons desirous of seeking and spreading Masonic light. In 1946, **The Philalethes** magazine was established to publish articles by its members.

The sole purpose of this Research Society is to act as a clearing house for Masonic knowledge. It exchanges ideas, researches problems confronting Freemasonry, and passes these along to the Masonic world.

Its membership consists of Members and Fellows who are Master Masons in good standing in a recognized Masonic Lodge anywhere in the world.

Chapters of the Society are encouraged to be formed and remain active. These are composed of Members and Fellows of the Society to assure fellowship among like-minded Freemasons. The papers presented during Chapter meetings should be sent to the Editor of **The Philalethes** for possible publication in the magazine.

Fellows are elected from Members of the Society who have shown a dedication to the knowledge of Freemasonry. The number is limited to 40 at any one time.

The Society is governed by an Executive Board which meets at the call of the President. An annual meeting of Members and Fellows of the Society is held at a time and place determined by the Executive Board.

The name of the Society is pronounced **fill a lay thees** with the accent on the third syllable—**lay**. It is derived from two Greek words, **phil-** and **alethes**. It means **lover of truth.**

ARTICLE I. NAME

The name of this organization shall be THE PHILALETHES SOCIETY.

ARTICLE II. PURPOSE

a. To provide a bond for Freemasons who desire to pursue the study of Freemasonry.
b. To provide a means of exchanging ideas and to mutually assist each other.
c. To encourage those Freemasons who have Masonic light to spread and those who so desire to receive it.

ARTICLE III. MEMBERSHIP

The membership shall consist of Freemasons who are members in good standing in a recognized Masonic Lodge. Members, not to exceed 40 at any one time, may be elected as Fellows. Non-Masons may become "subscribers" to receive **The Philalethes** magazine. Members and Fellows will be automatically suspended if their dues are not current. Members and Fellows will be automatically suspended if suspended by their Lodge.

ARTICLE IV. DUES AND FEES

The annual dues, payable on January 1, shall be $15. Life memberships may be obtained for a fee of $200. The joining fee shall be $5.00 and shall accompany the petition with the dues for the first year. *Amended 1985: A Fellow-elect must be, or become a Life Member, to be officially designated a Fellow of The Philalethes Society.

ARTICLE V. OFFICERS

The following officers shall be elected biennially by the Executive Board: President; First Vice President; Second Vice President; Executive Secretary; and Treasurer. The Editor of **The Philalethes** shall be elected by the Executive Board and serve until replaced by vote of the Executive Board. *Amended 1984: "Executive Board" replaced "Board of Directors." All officers must be Fellows of the Society with the exception of the Treasurer.

An elective officer may be removed for cause by four affirmative votes of the Executive Board.

ARTICLE VI. EXECUTIVE BOARD

The Executive Board shall consist of the President, First and Second Vice Presidents, Executive Secretary, Treasurer, Editor of **The Philalethes**, and all Past Presidents. The administrative affairs of the Society shall be managed by the Executive Board.

ARTICLE VII. DUTIES OF OFFICERS

The President shall be the presiding officer of the Society and the Executive Board. He shall appoint the committees he deems advisable.

The First Vice President shall assume the duties of the President in his absence or disability; he shall perform such other duties as may be assigned by the President.

The Second Vice President shall assume the duties of the First Vice President in case of his disability, and those of the President in case of the disability of both; he shall perform such other duties as may be assigned by the President.

The Executive Secretary shall attend to all correspondence of the Society; keep the records; receive all moneys due the Society and deposit them promptly in a bank designated by the Executive Board; keep the financial records; pay all bills when approved verbally or in writing by authorized officers; arrange to have his books audited after January 1 each year; and perform such other duties as may be assigned by the President.

The Treasurer shall collect the annual dues and pay them over to the Executive Secretary, or deposit them in the designated bank immediately, sending the deposit receipt to the Executive Secretary, and perform such other duties as may be assigned by the President.

The Editor of **The Philalethes** shall be responsible for its publication; he shall have the power to determine the contents of the magazine, and shall perform such other duties as may be assigned by the President.

ARTICLE VIII. PUBLICATIONS

The Society shall publish **The Philalethes** on a basis to be determined by the Executive Board; the Editor shall have full responsibility in determining what to publish; it shall be mailed to every Member and Fellow of the Society. Other publications may be approved by the Executive Board at its pleasure.

ARTICLE IX. ANNUAL MEETING

The Society shall meet annually at a time and place to be selected by the Executive Board and/or President. Other meetings may be held whenever and wherever the President and/or the Executive Board approve.

ARTICLE X. CHAPTERS

A dispensation to form a Chapter of The Philalethes Society may be obtained from the President, provided:

a. The formation of a Chapter does not conflict with the laws of the Grand Lodge in which the Chapter will reside. A dispensation will be considered by the President provided:

1. A letter of intent is signed by five Master Masons, one of whom must be a Member or Fellow of the Society, and returned to the Executive Secretary, or President, with a fee of $10.

2. The letter of intent must include the proposed name of the Chapter, the area of its jurisdiction, and the names of those who will serve as President, Vice President, Secretary/Treasurer.

3. All members of the proposed Chapter must become members of The Philalethes Society, if they are not at the time of signing. This may be accomplished by including an application from the Society along with the proper fees, and included with the request for a dispensation.

To obtain a charter, the Chapter must return the dispensation, along with a fee of $50, a copy of its bylaws which have previously been approved by the Executive Board, and the transactions of its meetings, all of which must be received by the Executive Secretary by January 1.

Charters will be presented at the annual meeting.

No Chapter may be named after a living person, or a city.

Each Chapter shall make an annual report by January 1 to the Executive Secretary. Failure to do so for two consecutive years shall result in the forfeiture of the charter, and all property of the suspended Chapter shall become the property of The Philalethes Society.

ARTICLE XI. AMENDMENTS

These Bylaws may be amended by a two-thirds vote of the Executive Board when the proposed amendment is submitted in writing and each member of the Board given sufficient notice of the action proposed; or by a two-thirds vote of the entire membership present, if at least five members, one of whom must be a Fellow, has submitted a proposed amendment in writing, which, if approved by the Executive Board, shall be printed in **The Philalethes**, along with a ballot, which shall be returned to the Executive Secretary; and the ballots counted by arrangements made by the Executive Board.

Adopted February 11, 1983

* * *

OFFICERS OF THE PHILALETHES SOCIETY
1988–1990

John Mauk Hilliard
First Vice President

Wallace E. McLeod
Second Vice President

Jerald D. Marsengill
President/Editor

Allen E. Roberts
Executive Secretary

Henry G. Law
Treasurer

Appendix B.

OFFICERS OF THE PHILALETHES SOCIETY
1928–1988

Date	President	Executive Secretary	Treasurer
1928	Cyrus Field Willard	George H. Imbrie	Louis Block
1931	Robert I. Clegg	Cyrus F. Willard	Emerson Esterling
1932	Alfred H. Moorhouse	"	Ernest E. Murray
1934	"	"	J. Hugo Tatsch
1938	Cyrus F. Willard *	Samuel H. Shepard	Samuel H. Shepard
1942	Henry F. Evans	"	"
1945	Walter A. Quincke	"	" *
1946	"	Allister J. McKowen	Allister J. McKowen
1952	Harold. H. Kinney *	"	"
1952	Lee E. Wells	Lawton E. Meyer	William M. Brown
1954	"	"	John B. Vrooman
1954	Alphonse Cerza	"	"
1956	Alphonse Cerza	John B. Vrooman	D. Johnson
1957	"	"	G. Andrew McComb
1958	William Moseley Brown	G. Andrew McComb	James R. Case
1959	"	"	Ronald E. Heaton
1959	"	John B. Vrooman	"
1959	"	Carl R. Greisen	"
1961	Elbert Bede	"	"
1964	Charles G. Reigner	"	"
1967	Robert H. Gollmar	"	"
1970	William R. Denslow	"	"
1970	"	Franklin J. Anderson	"
1973	William E. Yeager *	"	"
1974	Robert V. Osborne	"	"
1976	Eugene S. Hopp	"	"
1979	Dwight L. Smith	" *	"
1980	"	S. Brent Morris	John M. Hilliard
1981	Robert L. Dillard	"	"
1983	Bruce H. Hunt	"	"
1984	Allen E. Roberts	Allen E. Roberts	Henry G. Law
1986	John R. Nocas	"	"
1988	Jerry Marsengill	"	"

EDITORS OF *THE PHILALETHES*

Walter A. Quincke *	1946–1951
Harold H. Kinney *	1952
Alphonse Cerza	1954
John Black Vrooman	1955–1976
Jerry Marsengill	1977–

Officers 1988–90

President	Jerry Marsengill
First Vice President	John Mauk Hilliard
Second Vice President	Wallace E. McLeod
Executive Secretary	Allen E. Roberts
Treasurer	Henry G. Law

* Died in office

Appendix C.1

FELLOWS OF The Philalethes Society, 1928–1988
March 1, 1988

Harold V. B. Voorhis knew more about the Fellows of The Philalethes Society than any other person. He wrote to the Editor and Executive Secretary on September 15, 1967: "I was always afraid someone would ask me the dates when the Fellows were made. I am not going to try and give you all of them—a rather impossible task as no record has ever been made." The numerical order is correct. For this history an attempt has been made to establish the dates. From what records that could be unearthed, it appears the original 40 were selected in the same year. After this, until the 1940s, a date here and there was found. By inserting the known date where it belonged other dates fell into place. As far as can be determined, the dates that follow are close to being accurate.

Fellows are limited to 40 at any one time.

Imbrie, George H.	Missouri	0	1931
Clegg, Robert I.	Illinois	0	1931
Willard, Cyrus Field	California	1	1931
Moorhouse, Alfred H.	Massachusetts	2	1931
Evans, Henry F.	Colorado	3	1931
Rapp, William C.	Illinois	4	1931
Easterling, Emerson	Oregon	5	1931
Block, Louis	Iowa	6	1931
Crutcher, Ernest	California	7	1931
England, William	New Zealand	8	1931
Harris, Reginald V.	Nova Scotia	9	1931
Merz, Charles H.	Ohio	10	1931
Murray, Ernest E.	Montana	11	1931
Rear, Seneca A.	Missouri	12	1931
Saunders, Alfred H.	New York	13	1931
Tatsch, J. Hugo	New York	14	1931
Voorhis, Harold V. B.	New Jersey	15	1931
Beaman, A. Gaylord	California	16	1931
Hobbs, Alfred M.	South Africa	17	1931
Blight, Reynold E.	California	18	1931
Haydon, Nathaniel W. J.	Ontario	19	1931
Vibert, Lionel	England	20	1931
Plumb, Charles S.	Ohio	21	1931
Wirth, Oswald	France	22	1931
Mossaz, John	Switzerland	23	1931
Wright, Robert C.	Oregon	24	1931
Haywood, Harry LeRoy	New Mexico	25	1931

Bedarride, Armand	France	26	1931
Choumitsky, Nicolas-Andre	France	27	1931
Marchesi, Jose	Spain	28	1931
Fischer, Leo	Philippines	29	1931
Meekren, Robert J.	Quebec	30	1931
Hunt, Charles C.	Iowa	31	1931
Ward, John S. M.	England	32	1931
Schmidt, Hugo	Germany	33	1931
Cock, Maurice	Belgium	34	1931
Bey, Mehmet Rachid	Turkey	35	1931
Fischer, Julius	Belgium	36	1931
Pollock, Frederick	England	37	1931
Crossle, Phillip	Ireland	38	1931
Morgan, Alfred W.	England	39	1931
Kipling, Rudyard	England	40	1931
Espinoza, Carlos U.	Venezuela	41	1934
Shepherd, Silas H.	California	42	1934
Bingham, S. Clifton	New Zealand	43	1936
Claudy, Carl H.	Dist. of Col.	44	1936
Moister, William	South Africa	45	1936
Corneloup, J.	France	46	1936
Brown, William Moseley	North Carolina	47	1936
Vrooman, John Black	Missouri	48	1936
Calvert, Albert F.	England	49	1937
Waite, Arthur Edward	England	50	1937
Cantey, Sam B.	Texas	51	1938
Allen, J. Edward	North Carolina	52	1938
Braun, Walter H.	Wisconsin	53	1938
Johnson, Charles H.	New York	54	1938
Quincke, Walter A.	California	55	1939
Callon, Herbert I.	England	56	1939
Brain, Clarence	Oklahoma	57	1939
Leyns, Fred B.	Michigan	58	1939
Parker, Arthur C.	New York	59	1939
Clift, James M.	Virginia	60	1939
Zahn, John E.	California	61	1940
Lacey, Decatur N.	Washington	62	1940
Geffen, Hirsch	Georgia	63	1941
Brown, William Major	Oklahoma	64	1941
*Smith, James Fairbairn	Michigan	65	1944
McKowen, Allister	California	66	1945
Denslow, Ray V.	Missouri	67	1945
Gonzales, Antonio	Philippines	68	1946
Kramer, Suesskind	South Africa	69	1947
*Woody, Albert L.	Illinois	70	1947
Bede, Elbert	Oregon	71	1947
Harvey, George R.	California	72	1947
Lepage, Marius	France	73	1947
Wells, Lee E.	California	74	1947
Coad, Philip H.	Ohio	75	1948

Reigner, Charles Gottshall	Maryland	76	1948
Holmes, Charles E.	Quebec	77	1949
Hedblom, Edward E.	Colorado	78	1949
Malott, James R.	Arizona	79	1949
Hepburn, Ross E.	New Zealand	80	1950
Remick, James K.	California	81	1951
St. Clair, Ward K.	New York	82	1951
Knutz, William H.	Illinois	83	1951
Kinney, Harold H.	California	84	1951
Triggs, Arthur H.	California	85	1951
Meyer, Lawton E.	Missouri	86	1951
Cerza, Alphonse	Illinois	87	1953
Taylor, Laurence R.	Indiana	88	1955
Pound, Roscoe	Massachusetts	89	1955
Coil, Henry Wilson	California	90	1955
Oller, Jose	Panama	91	1955
Draffen, George S.	Scotland	92	1955
Franta, Edward J.	North Dakota	93	1955
Hubbard, John C.	Oklahoma	94	1955
Scully, Francis J.	Arizona	95	1955
Cullingford, Frederick W. E.	North Carolina	96	1955
Harris, R. Baker	Dist. of Col.	97	1956
Spaulding, William F.	England	98	1956
*Walker, Wendell K.	New York	99	1956
Johnson, Melvin M.	Massachusetts	100	1956
Case, James R.	Connecticut	101	1956
Lichliter, McIlyar	Massachusetts	102	1956
Bundy, Harry W.	Colorado	103	1956
McComb, G. Andrew	Ohio	104	1957
Cummings, William L.	New York	105	1958
Pugh, Charles H.	North Carolina	106	1958
*Greisen, Carl R.	Nebraska	107	1959
Heaton, Ronald E.	Pennsylvania	108	1961
Gollmar, Robert H.	Wisconsin	109	1961
Denslow, William R.	Missouri	110	1961
*Roberts, Allen E.	Virginia	111	1963
Curtis, Kenneth F.	Florida	112	1963
Erikson, Jerry R.	California	113	1963
*Dutt, Norman C.	California	114	1964
*Emmerson, Henry	New York	115	1964
Hahn, Conrad	Maryland	116	1964
*Hunt, Bruce H.	Missouri	117	1964
Yeager, William E.	Pennsylvania	118	1965
Wilson, Frank H.	Massachusetts	119	1966
Wendt, Wylie B.	Kentucky	120	1966
*Smith, Dwight L.	Indiana	121	1966
Adams, Charles F.	Nebraska	122	1966
White, Andrew J., Jr.	Ohio	123	1967
*Carter, James D.	Texas	124	1967
*McGaughey, Charles K. A.	Kentucky	125	1968

Ela, Benjamin W.	Maine	126	1968
*Peacher, William G.	New York	127	1968
Stowe, Bobby M.	Missouri	128	1968
*Bell, G. Wilbur	Illinois	129	1968
Anderson, Franklin J.	Iowa	130	1970
*Osborne, Robert V.	Wisconsin	131	1971
*Hopp, Eugene S.	California	132	1972
*Cook, Lewis C.	Missouri	133	1972
Horne, Alex	California	134	1973
*Marsengill, Jerald E.	Iowa	135	1974
Callaway, Walter M., Jr.	Georgia	136	1975
*Foss, Gerald D.	New Hampshire	137	1975
*Dillard, Robert L., Jr.	Texas	138	1978
*Haggard, Forrest D.	Kansas	139	1978
*Pollard, Stewart M. L.	Maryland	140	1978
*Williams, Louis L.	Illinois	141	1978
*Morris, S. Brent	Maryland	142	1980
*Hilliard, John Mauk	New York	143	1981
*Guthrie, Charles S., Jr.	Kentucky	144	1981
*Arrington, Keith	Iowa	145	1982
*French, George H. T.	Texas	146	1983
*Hogan, Mervin B.	Utah	147	1983
*Nocas, John R.	California	148	1983
*Sands, Richard H.	Michigan	149	1984
*McLeod, Wallace E.	Ontario	150	1986
*Law, Henry G.	Delaware	151	1987
*Haffner, Christopher	Hong Kong	152	1987
*Van Beusekom, Johannis	Guatemala	153	1987
*Glassmire, Charles R.	Maine	154	1988
*Scofield, Royal C.	Ohio	155	1988
Walker, Leslie L., Jr.	Texas	156	1988
*Curtis, Richard.	Massachusetts	157	1988
*Julius, C. Clark	Pennsylvania	158	1988
*Kelly, John E. Jack	Texas	160	1988
*Lewis J. Birt	New Jersey	161	1988

* Current Fellows of The Philalethes Society.

Appendix C.2

March 1, 1988

FELLOWS OF The Philalethes Society, 1928–1988

Adams, Charles F.	Nebraska	122	1966
Allen, J. Edward	North Carolina	52	1938
Anderson, Franklin J.	Iowa	130	1970
*Arrington, Keith	Iowa	145	1982
Beaman, A. Gaylord	California	16	1931
Bedarride, Armand	France	26	1931
Bede, Elbert	Oregon	71	1947
*Bell, G. Wilbur	Illinois	129	1968
Bey, Mehmet Rachid	Turkey	35	1931
Bingham, S. Clifton	New Zealand	43	1936
*Birt, Lewis J.	New Jersey	161	1988
Blight, Reynold E.	California	18	1931
Block, Louis	Iowa	6	1931
Brain, Clarence	Oklahoma	57	1939
Braun, Walter H.	Wisconsin	53	1938
Brown, William Major	Oklahoma	64	1941
Brown, William Moseley	North Carolina	47	1936
Bundy, Harry W.	Colorado	103	1956
Callaway, Walter M., Jr.	Georgia	136	1975
Callon, Herbert I.	England	56	1939
Calvert, Albert F.	England	49	1937
Cantey, Sam B.	Texas	51	1938
*Carter, James D.	Texas	124	1967
Case, James R.	Connecticut	101	1956
Cerza, Alphonse	Illinois	87	1953
Choumitsky, Nicolas-Andre	France	27	1931
Claudy, Carl H.	Dist. of Col.	44	1936
Clegg, Robert I.	Illinois	0	1931
Clift, James M.	Virginia	60	1939
Coad, Philip H.	Ohio	75	1948
Cock, Maurice	Belgium	34	1931
Coil, Henry Wilson	California	90	1955
*Cook, Lewis C.	Missouri	133	1972
Corneloup, J.	France	46	1936
Crossle, Phillip	Ireland	38	1931
Crutcher, Ernest	California	7	1931
Cullingford, Frederick W. E.	North Carolina	96	1955
Cummings, William L.	New York	105	1958
Curtis, Kenneth F.	Florida	112	1963
*Curtis, Richard.	Massachusetts	157	1988
Denslow, Ray V.	Missouri	67	1945

229

Denslow, William R.	Missouri	110	1961
*Dillard, Robert L., Jr.	Texas	138	1978
Draffen, George S.	Scotland	92	1955
*Dutt, Norman C.	California	114	1964
Easterling, Emerson	Oregon	5	1931
Ela, Benjamin W.	Maine	126	1968
*Emmerson, Henry	New York	115	1964
England, William	New Zealand	8	1931
Erikson, Jerry R.	California	113	1963
Espinoza, Carlos U.	Venezuela	41	1934
Evans, Henry F.	Colorado	3	1931
Fischer, Julius	Belgium	36	1931
Fischer, Leo	Philippines	29	1931
*Foss, Gerald D.	New Hampshire	137	1975
Franta, Edward J.	North Dakota	93	1955
*French, George H. T.	Texas	146	1983
Geffen, Hirsch	Georgia	63	1941
*Glassmire, Charles R.	Maine	154	1988
Gollmar, Robert H.	Wisconsin	109	1961
Gonzales, Antonio	Philippines	68	1946
*Greisen, Carl R.	Nebraska	107	1959
*Guthrie, Charles S., Jr.	Kentucky	144	1981
Haffner, Christopher	Hong Kong	152	1987
*Haggard, Forrest D.	Kansas	139	1978
Hahn, Conrad	Maryland	116	1964
Harris, R. Baker	Dist. of Col.	97	1956
Harris, Reginald V.	Nova Scotia	9	1931
Harvey, George R.	California	72	1947
Haydon, Nathaniel W.J.	Ontario	19	1931
Haywood, Harry LeRoy	New Mexico	25	1931
Heaton, Ronald E.	Pennsylvania	108	1961
Hedblom, Edward E.	Colorado	78	1949
Hepburn, Ross E.	New Zealand	80	1950
*Hilliard, John Mauk	New York	143	1981
Hobbs, Alfred M.	South Africa	17	1931
*Hogan, Mervin B.	Utah	147	1983
Holmes, Charles E.	Quebec	77	1949
*Hopp, Eugene S.	California	132	1972
Horne, Alex	California	134	1973
Hubbard, John C.	Oklahoma	94	1955
*Hunt, Bruce H.	Missouri	117	1964
Hunt, Charles C.	Iowa	31	1931
Imbrie, George H.	Missouri	0	1931
Johnson, Charles H.	New York	54	1938
Johnson, Melvin M.	Massachusetts	100	1956
*Julius, C. Clark	Pennsylvania	158	1988
*Kelly, John E. Jack	Texas	160	1988
Kinney, Harold H.	California	84	1951
Kipling, Rudyard	England	40	1931
Knutz, William H.	Illinois	83	1951

Kramer, Suesskind	South Africa	69	1947
Lacey, Decatur N.	Washington	62	1940
*Law, Henry G.	Delaware	151	1987
Lepage, Marius	France	73	1947
Leyns, Fred B.	Michigan	58	1939
Lichliter, McIlyar	Massachusetts	102	1956
Malott, James R.	Arizona	79	1949
Marchesi, Jose	Spain	28	1931
*Marsengill, Jerald E.	Iowa	135	1974
McComb, G. Andrew	Ohio	104	1957
*McGaughey, Charles K.A.	Kentucky	125	1968
McKowen, Allister	California	66	1945
*McLeod, Wallace E.	Ontario	150	1986
Meekren, Robert J.	Quebec	30	1931
Merz, Charles H.	Ohio	10	1931
Meyer, Lawton E.	Missouri	86	1951
Moister, William	South Africa	45	1936
Moorhouse, Alfred H.	Massachusetts	2	1931
Morgan, Alfred W.	England	39	1931
*Morris, S. Brent	Maryland	142	1980
Mossaz, John	Switzerland	23	1931
Murray, Ernest E.	Montana	11	1931
*Nocas, John R.	California	148	1983
Oller, Jose	Panama	91	1955
*Osborne, Robert V.	Wisconsin	131	1971
Parker, Arthur C.	New York	59	1939
*Peacher, William G.	New York	127	1968
Plumb, Charles S.	Ohio	21	1931
*Pollard, Stewart M.L.	Maryland	140	1978
Pollock, Frederick	England	37	1931
Pound, Roscoe	Massachusetts	89	1953
Pugh, Charles H.	North Carolina	106	1958
Quincke, Walter A.	California	55	1939
Rapp, William C.	Illinois	4	1931
Rear, Seneca A.	Missouri	12	1931
Reigner, Charles Gottshall	Maryland	76	1948
Remick, James K.	California	81	1951
*Roberts, Allen E.	Virginia	111	1963
St. Clair, Ward K.	New York	82	1951
*Sands, Richard H.	Michigan	149	1984
Saunders, Alfred H.	New York	13	1931
Schmidt, Hugo	Germany	33	1931
*Scofield, Royal C.	Ohio	155	1988
Scully, Francis J.	Arizona	95	1955
Shepherd, Silas H.	California	42	1934
*Smith, Dwight L.	Indiana	121	1966
*Smith, James Fairbairn	Michigan	65	1944
Spaulding, William F.	England	98	1956
Stowe, Bobby M.	Missouri	128	1968
Tatsch, J. Hugo	New York	14	1931

Taylor, Laurence R.	Indiana	88	1953
Triggs, Arthur H.	California	85	1951
*Van Beusekom, Johannis	Guatemala	153	1987
Vibert, Lionel	England	20	1931
Voorhis, Harold V.B.	New Jersey	15	1931
Vrooman, John Black	Missouri	48	1936
Waite, Arthur Edward	England	50	1937
Walker, Jr., Leslie L.	Texas	156	1988
*Walker, Wendell K.	New York	99	1956
Ward, John S.M.	England	32	1931
Wells, Lee E.	California	74	1947
Wendt, Wylie B.	Kentucky	120	1966
White, Andrew J., Jr.	Ohio	123	1967
Willard, Cyrus Field	California	1	1931
*Williams, Louis L.	Illinois	141	1978
Wilson, Frank H.	Massachusetts	119	1966
Wirth, Oswald	France	22	1931
*Woody, Albert L.	Illinois	70	1947
Wright, Robert C.	Oregon	24	1931
Yeager, William E.	Pennsylvania	118	1965
Zahn, John E.	California	61	1940

*Current Fellows of The Philalethes Society

FELLOWS OF THE PHILALETHES SOCIETY
March 12, 1988

*Arrington, Keith	Iowa	145	1982
*Bell, G. Wilbur	Illinois	129	1968
*Carter, James D.	Texas	124	1967
*Cook, Lewis C.	Missouri	133	1972
*Curtis, Richard.	Massachusetts	157	1988
*Dillard, Robert L., Jr.	Texas	138	1978
*Dutt, Norman C.	California	114	1964
*Emmerson, Henry	New York	115	1964
*Foss, Gerald D.	New Hampshire	137	1975
*Franta, Edward J.	North Dakota	93	1955
*French, George H.T.	Texas	146	1983
*Glassmire, Charles R.	Maine	154	1988
*Greisen, Carl R.	Nebraska	107	1959
*Guthrie, Charles S., Jr.	Kentucky	144	1981
*Haffner, Christopher	Hong Kong	152	1987
*Haggard, Forrest D.	Kansas	139	1978
*Hilliard, John Mauk	New York	143	1981
*Hogan, Mervin B.	Utah	147	1983
*Hopp, Eugene S.	California	132	1972

*Hunt, Bruce H.	Missouri	117	1964
*Julius, C. Clark	Pennsylvania	158	1988
*Kelly, John E. Jack	Texas	160	1988
*Law, Henry G.	Delaware	151	1987
*Marsengill, Jerald E.	Iowa	135	1974
*McGaughey, Charles K.A.	Kentucky	125	1968
*McLeod, Wallace E.	Ontario	150	1986
*Morris, S. Brent	Maryland	142	1980
*Nocas, John R.	California	148	1983
*Osborne, Robert V.	Wisconsin	131	1971
*Peacher, William G.	New York	127	1968
*Pollard, Stewart M.L.	Maryland	140	1978
*Roberts, Allen E.	Virginia	111	1963
*Sands, Richard H.	Michigan	149	1984
*Scofield, Royal C.	Ohio	155	1988
*Smith, Dwight L.	Indiana	121	1966
*Smith, James Fairbairn	Michigan	65	1944
*Van Beusekom, Johannis	Guatemala	153	1987
*Walker, Wendell K.	New York	99	1956
*Williams, Louis L.	Illinois	141	1978
*Woody, Albert L.	Illinois	70	1947

Appendix D.

THE PHILALETHES SOCIETY LECTURERS

Each year since 1981 an outstanding student of Freemasonry has been chosen to be "The Philalethes Society Lecturer at the Annual Assembly and Feast."

1981	Allen E. Roberts	"Leadership Often Sought; Seldom Attained"
1982	William P. Vaughan	"The Anti-Masonic Party"
1983	S. Brent Morris	"The Hidden Secrets of a Master Mason"
1984	Richard H. Sands	"The Northwest Ordinance"
1985	Donald H. Smith	"A Foundation for Century Twenty-one"
1986	Wallace E. McLeod	"The Effect of Victorian Obscenity Laws on Masonic Historians"
1987	Forrest D. Haggard	"Freemasonry in a Time of Crisis"
1988	John E. Jack Kelly	"Tanstaafl's Law" (There Ain't No Such Thing as a Free Lunch)

Appendix E.

PHILALETHES SOCIETY DISTINGUISHED SERVICE MEDALS

1986	Alphonse Cerza, FPS, Illinois
	Ronald E. Heaton, FPS, Pennsylvania
	Allen E. Roberts, FPS, Virginia
	Jerald E. "Jerry" Marsengill, FPS, Iowa
1987	S. Brent Morris, FPS, Maryland
	William F. Koeckert, MPS, Ohio
1988	Forrest D. Haggard, FPS, Kansas

Appendix F.

CERTIFICATE OF LITERATURE AWARDS

Year	Recipient	Article
1956	James R. Case	"The Hamilton Bi-Centennial"
1957	Allen Cabaniss	"Importance of the Fellowcraft Degree"
1958	Ronald E. Heaton	"Notes on a List of Some Conjectured American Freemasons"
1959	Roscoe Pound	"What Is Law?"
1960	Dr. William L. Cummings	"Masonic Background"
1961	Allen E. Roberts	"Masonry Under Two Flags" (series)
1962	Norman C. Dutt	"The Lewis Freemason"
1963	Andrew J. White, Jr.	"Let's Take a New Look at Masonic Funeral Service"
1964	*NO AWARD	
1965	Alphonse Cerza	"Recommended Masonic Reading"
1966	Ross Hepburn	"Freemasonry in New Zealand"
1967	*NO AWARD	
1968	Harold V.B. Voorhis	"Two Things to Think About"
1969	*NO AWARD	
1970	Franklin J. Anderson	"The Soul of Freemasonry"
1971	Dr. Eugene S. Hopp	"Defining Freemasonry: Traditional Becomes Practical"
1972	*NO AWARD	
1973	Dwight L. Smith	"Landmarks and Cuspidors"
1974	John R. Nocas	"Josephus, the Great Jewish Historian"
1975	Alex Horne	"Prince Edwin, 926 A.D.—Our First Speculative Mason"
1976	Mervin B. Hogan	"Confrontation of Grand Master Abraham Jones and John Bennett at Nauvoo"
1977	*NO AWARD	
1978	Louis C. King	"Building a Cathedral"
1979	Charles S. Guthrie	"Rob Morris and the Conservators in Kentucky"
1980	John Mauk Hilliard	"The Lodge as Primary Community"
1981	Richard H. Sands	"Physicists, The Royal Society and Freemasonry"
1982	Leslie L. Walker, Jr.	"Did Shakespeare Create Masonic Ritual?"
1983	Keith Arrington	"Iowa's Masonic Magazines"
1984	Wallace E. McLeod	"Why St. Alban?"
1985	Louis L. Williams	"Christopher Wren, Mason or No?"

| 1986 | Leslie L. Walker, Jr. | "Of Oaths, Vows & Obligations" |
| 1987 | Robin L. Carr | "Amadeus and Freemasonry" and "Goethe the Universal Man" |

Officers of The Philalethes Society are not eligible for this competition. An unwritten rule excludes prior winners of the Certificate of Literature; an exception was inadvertently made in 1986. This listing was not available at that time.

* No awards were made because the Committee selecting the recipients believed previous winners of the Certificate provided the outstanding articles during the years noted.

INDEX

INDEX

254

Whalen, William J. (anti-Mason), 72, 126, 197, 199
"What Are Our Rights", 155–156
"What Is Law?", 78
"What Is Truth?", 66
"What Was the Early Ritual?", 15
Wheeler, David R., 122
Whence Came You, 68
"Where Are We Now?", 211
Whipple, Capt. Abraham, 139, 140
Whipple, William, 140
White, Andrew J., Jr., 89, 106, 109, 114, 117, death of, 119
White Shrine of Jerusalem, 156
"Why Freemasons Lay Cornerstones", 110–111
"Why Masonry Must Teach By Symbols", 74–75
"Why is American Masonry Different?", 115
"Why St. Alban?", 185–186
Willard, Cyrus Field, xi, 2; quoted, 3, 4–5; Executive Secretary, 4; quoted, 5, 10, 11; 8, 9, 12, 50, 71, 112, 113, 213
Wm. M. Taylor Chapter, 188
Williams, Louis L., 118, 158, 190–191, 193
Williamsburg Lodge, VA, 74
Williamsburg, VA, 124
Wilson, Frank H., 87, 105
Wisconsin. 10

Wisconsin, Grand Lodge of, 84
Wood, Clement, 146
Wood, Grant, 175
Woody, Albert L., Frontispiece, 51, 118, 149, 193
Workshop, 64, 68, 70, 77, 83, 86, 89, 94, 103, 104, 105, 107, 111, 114, 116, 117, 118–119, 121, 125, 129, 135, 142, 149, 153, 158, 159, 161, 165, 167, 184, 194, 204, 210, 212 World War I, 22, 30, 58, 59, 65, 104, 209 World War II, ix, 4, 8, 13, 14, 17, 27, 91, 104, 122–124, 209
Worley, Dr. Lloyd, 199–200, 204
Wren, Christopher, Jr., 92
Wren, Sir Christopher, 47, 92, 190, 193
Wren, Stephen, 190
"Writer of History in the Future of Masonry, The", 87–88

Yeager, William E., 102, 103, 104–105, picture of, 105; 127, death of, 138
Yompkins, Daniel K., 119
York Manuscript No. 4, 32
York Rite Bodies, 77
York Rite Masonry, 163
"Young Man Who Lisped, The", 112
Young, Solomon, 149
Yugoslavia, 18

Zanuck, Darryl, 81
Zip code, 107